Ahmad Osman

Automated Evaluation of Three Dimensional Ultrasonic Datasets

Ahmad Osman

Automated Evaluation of Three Dimensional Ultrasonic Datasets

Steps towards automated in-line ultrasonic inspection systems: automated interpretation of the generated ultrasonic data

Südwestdeutscher Verlag für Hochschulschriften

Impressum / Imprint
Bibliografische Information der Deutschen Nationalbibliothek: Die Deutsche Nationalbibliothek verzeichnet diese Publikation in der Deutschen Nationalbibliografie; detaillierte bibliografische Daten sind im Internet über http://dnb.d-nb.de abrufbar.
Alle in diesem Buch genannten Marken und Produktnamen unterliegen warenzeichen-, marken- oder patentrechtlichem Schutz bzw. sind Warenzeichen oder eingetragene Warenzeichen der jeweiligen Inhaber. Die Wiedergabe von Marken, Produktnamen, Gebrauchsnamen, Handelsnamen, Warenbezeichnungen u.s.w. in diesem Werk berechtigt auch ohne besondere Kennzeichnung nicht zu der Annahme, dass solche Namen im Sinne der Warenzeichen- und Markenschutzgesetzgebung als frei zu betrachten wären und daher von jedermann benutzt werden dürften.

Bibliographic information published by the Deutsche Nationalbibliothek: The Deutsche Nationalbibliothek lists this publication in the Deutsche Nationalbibliografie; detailed bibliographic data are available in the Internet at http://dnb.d-nb.de.
Any brand names and product names mentioned in this book are subject to trademark, brand or patent protection and are trademarks or registered trademarks of their respective holders. The use of brand names, product names, common names, trade names, product descriptions etc. even without a particular marking in this works is in no way to be construed to mean that such names may be regarded as unrestricted in respect of trademark and brand protection legislation and could thus be used by anyone.

Coverbild / Cover image: www.ingimage.com

Verlag / Publisher:
Südwestdeutscher Verlag für Hochschulschriften
ist ein Imprint der / is a trademark of
OmniScriptum GmbH & Co. KG
Heinrich-Böcking-Str. 6-8, 66121 Saarbrücken, Deutschland / Germany
Email: info@svh-verlag.de

Herstellung: siehe letzte Seite /
Printed at: see last page
ISBN: 978-3-8381-3759-9

Zugl. / Approved by: Erlangen, Friedrich-Alexander-Universität Erlangen-Nürnberg, Diss., 2013

Copyright © 2014 OmniScriptum GmbH & Co. KG
Alle Rechte vorbehalten. / All rights reserved. Saarbrücken 2014

Abstract

Non-destructive testing has become necessary to ensure the quality of materials and components either in-service or at the production stage. This requires the use of a rapid, robust and reliable testing technique. As a main testing technique, the ultrasound technology has unique abilities to assess the discontinuity location, size and shape. Such information play a vital role in the acceptance criteria which are based on safety and quality requirements of manufactured components. Consequently, an extensive usage of the ultrasound technique is perceived especially in the inspection of large scale composites manufactured in the aerospace industry.

Significant technical advances have contributed into optimizing the ultrasound acquisition techniques such as the sampling phased array technique. However, acquisition systems need to be complemented with an automated data analysis procedure to avoid the time consuming manual interpretation of all produced data. Such a complement would accelerate the inspection process and improve its reliability.

The objective of this thesis is to propose an analysis chain dedicated to automatically process the 3D ultrasound volumes obtained using the sampling phased array technique. First, a detailed study of the speckle noise affecting the ultrasound data was conducted, as speckle reduces the quality of ultrasound data. Afterward, an analysis chain was developed, composed of a segmentation procedure followed by a classification procedure. The proposed segmentation methodology is adapted for ultrasound 3D data and has the objective to detect all potential defects inside the input volume. While the detection of defects is vital, one main difficulty is the high amount of false alarms which are detected by the segmentation procedure. The correct distinction of false alarms is necessary to reduce the rejection ratio of safe parts. This has to be done without risking missing true defects. Therefore, there is a need for a powerful classifier which can efficiently distinguish true defects from false alarms. This is achieved using a specific classification approach based on data fusion theory.

The chain was tested on several ultrasound volumetric measures of Carbon Fiber Reinforced Polymers components. Experimental results of the chain revealed high accuracy, reliability in detecting, characterizing and classifying defects.

Acknowledgment

Back in March 2008, i came to Fraunhofer EZRT to write my master thesis. Those were my first days in Franconia when i heard for the first time the word "Servus" which means at your service. I heard this word from Dr. Ulf Hassler to whom i am deeply thankful for giving me the opportunity to seek my Phd degree in his Image Processing group. His trust, encouragement, valuable advices and support made this work possible.

I am very grateful for my supervisors Assoc. Prof. Valérie Kaftandjian and Prof. Dr.-Ing. Joachim Hornegger. Dr. Valérie guidance, expertise and full support greatly helped me, and I am truly thankful for the fruitful discussions and valuable contributions from her. Having Prof. Hornegger as a supervisor was a great chance for me. His remarks and advices were of great importance and helped me to develop myself.

I thank Prof. Christian Grosse and Prof. Thierry Denoeux for accepting to review my dissertation.

My thanks go to my colleagues at EZRT and especially to my colleagues at the Image Processing group. I am grateful to Markus Rehak for his continuous support and encouragement. I also like to thank Steven Oeckl for his valuable advices.

Finally, I would like to express my deepest gratitude to my parents Fadia and Mohammad Osman, to my wife Diana, to my daughter Lujane, to my sisters and to my brothers for their never ending support. This work is dedicated to them.

Ahmad Osman

Contents

1. **Context of the thesis**   1
   1.1. Introduction 1
   1.2. Scientific focus and contributions 3
   1.3. Outline 4

2. **Ultrasound NDT technique: acquisition and image analysis**   5
   2.1. Introduction 5
   2.2. Phased array technique 6
      2.2.1. Principle 7
      2.2.2. Applications of phased array techniques in non-destructive testing   9
      2.2.3. Advantages and limitations of the phased array technique . . . 11
      2.2.4. Reconstruction algorithms 13
   2.3. Sampling phased array technique 15
      2.3.1. Principle 15
      2.3.2. Sampling phased array advantages 18
      2.3.3. Acquisition system 20
   2.4. Inspection of composite components 22
   2.5. Ultrasound image analysis 24
      2.5.1. Artifacts of ultrasound images 25
      2.5.2. Segmentation of ultrasound images 27
   2.6. Conclusion 31

3. **Speckle characterization in SPA data**   33
   3.1. Introduction 33
   3.2. Modeling the speckle 34
      3.2.1. Theoretical parametric models of speckle 35
      3.2.2. Empirical models of speckle 39
   3.3. Speckle distribution in SPA data 40
      3.3.1. Proposed model 41
      3.3.2. Experimental results 42
   3.4. Speckle noise reduction 48
      3.4.1. Spatial domain filtering techniques 50
      3.4.2. Transform-domain filtering techniques 52
   3.5. Conclusion 52

4. **Proposed method for automated segmentation and classification of SPA data**   53
   4.1. Analysis chain 53

	4.2.	Segmentation procedure	54
		4.2.1. Overview	54
		4.2.2. Definitions	55
		4.2.3. Data correction	57
		4.2.4. Data enhancement	59
		4.2.5. Detection of entrance and backwall layers	65
		4.2.6. Thresholding	68
		4.2.7. Features extraction	72
	4.3.	Classification procedure	75
		4.3.1. Basic concept and definitions	76
		4.3.2. Information combination	78
		4.3.3. Data fusion classification	79
	4.4.	Conclusion	89

5. Experimental evaluation of the proposed segmentation and classification method   **91**

	5.1.	Experimental environment	91
		5.1.1. 3D ultrasound datasets of CFRP specimens	92
		5.1.2. Ultrasound data segmentation tool	93
		5.1.3. Data fusion classification tool	93
	5.2.	Experimental results of the segmentation procedure	95
		5.2.1. Data correction results	95
		5.2.2. Data enhancement results	98
		5.2.3. Entrance and backwall layers detection results	107
		5.2.4. Thresholding results	109
		5.2.5. Features extraction results	118
	5.3.	Experimental results of the classification procedure	119
		5.3.1. Results for CFRP-14	119
		5.3.2. Results for CFRP-8	124
	5.4.	Discussion	126

6. Summary and outlook   **129**

	6.1.	Summary	129
	6.2.	Outlook	131

A. Definitions   **133**

	A.1.	Ultrasonic imaging concepts	133
		A.1.1. Reflection and transmission coefficients	133
		A.1.2. Ultrasound display formats	136
		A.1.3. A-scan displays	136
		A.1.4. B-scan displays	136
		A.1.5. C-scan display	137

B. List of features   **139**

	B.1.	Input data format for the DFC method	139
	B.2.	Features characterizing suspicious regions	139

C. Experimental results: Entrance and Backwall layers detection   141
    C.1. Results for the CFRP-14 volumes 141
    C.2. V8-21 and V8-24 143
    C.3. V8-22 144

D. Experimental results: hysteresis thresholding   147
    D.1. V14-15 147
    D.2. V14-100 149
    D.3. V8-21 151
    D.4. V8-24 152

List of abbreviations and symbols   152

Bibliography   161

1. Context of the thesis

Contents
    1.1. Introduction 1
    1.2. Scientific focus and contributions 3
    1.3. Outline 4

1.1. Introduction

Non-destructive testing (NDT) techniques are quality control methods which allow the examination of the quality of manufactured components. Such control is necessary in order to track defects that can appear in the components either in-service or at the production process. NDT techniques, integrated in inspection systems, represent an essential part of the production chain. These techniques are permanently subjects of research and development in order to meet the demands of increasingly higher quality materials and components from industrial sectors. Primary imaging modalities are ultrasound and X-ray based.

Despite the advantages procured by X-ray technology especially with the appearance of in-line Computed Tomography (CT) inspection systems in the market, ultrasound technology continues to be the preferred technique to be applied. This is due to several advantages that this technique provides. Unlike X-ray tubes which need expensive radiation protection, ultrasound instruments are safe and do not require any protection. Ultrasound technology provides a high sensitivity for most defects, accuracy in locating defects and possibility to use single sided access to the test part. This property is very important for the inspection of large components, where the application of other NDT techniques, for example X-ray CT, is relatively complicated and may require the dismantling of the component.

Ultrasound imaging modality has benefited from major technological advances in the last two decades. Indeed, advances in computer technology and visualization techniques have made 3D ultrasound imaging viable [1]. Nowadays, the range of clinical and industrial applications of 3D ultrasound scanners keeps growing and it is anticipated that some clinical and industrial applications offered by 3D ultrasound will replace X-ray CT [2, 3]. Common approaches for acquiring 3D ultrasound volumes are based on [4]: 2D transducer array [5, 6], mechanically swept transducers (mechanical scanners) [7] and free-hand techniques with/without position sensing [8, 9].

Moreover, the ultrasound technology is largely used to inspect, at manufacture, the quality of Fiber Reinforced Polymer (FRP) composites. These materials are considered as excellent alternatives of traditionally used metals (such as steel, aluminum, etc.). Main advantages of FRP composites are their high strength to weight ratio, their resistance against environmental conditions and the possibility to melt them into various shapes. Manufacturing of FRP components is done by bonding fiber filaments, i.e. carbon, glass, to a polymer matrix. The fibers give the composite the strength and stiffness while the matrix provides rigidity and protection against environmental factors. Thus the durability of the manufactured FRP component is directly dependent on the manufacturing process and is subjected to various types of defects which can appear in the composite like delamination, debonds, fiber breakage and classical discontinuities like voids, porosity and cracks. The quality control of these anisotropic materials is an essential procedure to enable their secured appliance in manufactured parts.

Manual ultrasonic testing has often provided a solution for conventional small scale inspection tasks. However, manual testing requires highly trained operators. Besides, large FRP structures are produced especially for aeronautical, naval and construction applications. For such large components, the application of manual testing is no longer possible. With the development of ultrasound phased array technology, it became possible to replace the conventional manual testing technique by an automatic inspection procedure. Nowadays, a rapid acquisition of ultrasound data over large structures is possible by using automated acquisition systems which often use the phased array technique. Moreover, the development of the sampling phased array (SPA) technique [10] further reduced the inspection time compared to phased array technology. It also allowed fast representation of defects at their original positions in the inspected component in 3D space, in addition to an improved quality of ultrasound images.

However, the manufacturers are realizing that a rapid acquisition is only a part of the solution for NDT testing of large composites. The second factor which has to be solved is the analysis of the measured data. Indeed, an enormous amount of data must be processed by highly trained NDT operators. For instance, this amount can go up to Terabytes of data per composite in an aircraft of the size of a B787 or A350, each aircraft can require several man-months to analyze the NDT data manually [11]. Moreover, boredom and fatigue of operators can lead to unreliable and inconsistent results, where significant defects are not reported [12]. Therefore, there is an imminent need to replace the manual analysis of the data by an automated analysis chain.

The presented research activity tackles the automated analysis of industrial volumetric ultrasound data. It is realized in the Development Center for X-Ray Technology EZRT of the IIS Fraunhofer Institute, in Fuerth, Germany. The center is focusing on the following areas of research: X-ray sensors, computed tomography, image processing and applications. As for ultrasound technique, EZRT employs an acquisition system developed by the Fraunhofer Institute for Non Destructive Testing IZFP, in Saarbruecken, Germany. The acquisition system is a mechanical scanner built by QNET Engineering [13]. In EZRT, the system is mainly used to inspect planar Carbon Fiber Reinforced Polymers (CFRP) specimens and to produce real time volumes via SPA technique.

The PhD thesis is a joint work between Fraunhofer EZRT, the Vibration and Acoustic laboratory of the National Institute of Applied Sciences INSA de Lyon in France and the Pattern Recognition laboratory of the Friedrich-Alexander University Erlangen-Nuremberg in Germany.

1.2. Scientific focus and contributions

The scientific focus of this thesis is to complete the ultrasound acquisition system with an automated robust method for the analysis of 3D reconstructed volumes. The work consists of two packages:

- Evaluation and segmentation of the 3D ultrasound data. Here, the study of the initial image quality is important for improving the detection of defective or suspicious regions.

- Classification of the detected regions. Here, the separation of true defects and false alarms (i.e., false defects) is the main aspect and furthermore the assignment of properties to each defect.

To reach these objectives, an analysis chain is proposed, which is composed of: a) a segmentation procedure which has the role to detect all potential defects inside the 3D volume and b) a classification methodology based on data fusion theory. The classification method has the aim to successfully classify all defects with the minimal false alarms rate. The list below summarizes the scientific contributions of this thesis:

Evaluation:

- An intensive study of speckle noise is presented in this work. The origin of this noise and the modeling methods applied until now are discussed. The appropriate model for the SPA data is found, which is an extension of an existing model to fit speckle noise distribution in our data.

- The use of the Contrast to Noise ratio (CNR) metric of a given defect to assess the filtering quality is proposed. The interest of this metric is to define a criterion to choose the best filter in the sense of defects detectability and not only noise reduction.

- After evaluating the quality of acquired data (characterization of speckle noise), an analysis chain is proposed. The chain's input is a 3D ultrasound volume, the output of the chain is the list of defects and false alarms inside the volume with their corresponding characteristics.

Classification:

As for the classification procedure, the following points resume the contribution:

- New features (shadow and damage index) are proposed to describe the suspicious regions.

- Features measured on the detected suspicious regions are considered as sources of information for the data fusion classification method. The main part of this method relies on the translation of features values into confidence levels (socalled mass values) to a set of hypotheses dedicated to our application „true defect", „false defect" or „ignorance".

- A selection methodology of pertinent features is proposed. It is based on the usage of Receiver Operating Characteristics (ROC) and aims to improve the classifier performance.

- A study of data fusion classifier for 3D datasets: usage of conjunctive and cautious information combination rules.

Application:

- Application of the proposed method on planar CFRP specimens.

1.3. Outline

The thesis is organized in six chapters: chapter 2 gives a review of the ultrasound technique with main focus on phased array and sampling phased array technique. It will describe the acquisition system that is used to collect the data and gives an overview on the inspection of composite pieces. In addition, a review of the existing ultrasound data analysis techniques is presented in this chapter.

Chapter 3 is dedicated to the noise study, where the noise origin, modeling methods and bibliography about speckle reduction are investigated.

Chapter 4 will introduce the proposed analysis chain. It will describe each step of this chain in detail.

The experimental evaluation of the analysis chain is presented in chapter 5. In this chapter, experimental results are reported on several volumes of two planar CFRP specimens.

The conclusion and outlook are finally presented in chapter 6.

2. Ultrasound NDT technique: acquisition and image analysis

Contents

2.1.	Introduction	5
2.2.	Phased array technique	6
	2.2.1. Principle	7
	2.2.2. Applications of phased array techniques in non-destructive testing	9
	2.2.3. Advantages and limitations of the phased array technique .	11
	2.2.4. Reconstruction algorithms	13
2.3.	Sampling phased array technique	15
	2.3.1. Principle	15
	2.3.2. Sampling phased array advantages	18
	2.3.3. Acquisition system	20
2.4.	Inspection of composite components	22
2.5.	Ultrasound image analysis	24
	2.5.1. Artifacts of ultrasound images	25
	2.5.2. Segmentation of ultrasound images	27
2.6.	Conclusion	31

2.1. Introduction

Ultrasonic waves are mechanical vibrations which propagate through a medium (solid, liquid or gas) at a wave speed characteristic of the elastic and inertial properties of the propagation medium. They are generated by a piezoelectric probe excited by an electrical voltage. The piezoelectric effect is reversible allowing the usage of the same probe to detect the reflected waves in form of electrical signals. By analyzing these signals, conclusions are drawn about the existence of discontinuities inside the medium. Typical ultrasonic frequencies are in the range of 20 kHz to 50 MHz. In industrial applications, used frequencies are between 0.5 MHz and 15 MHz. Another aspect of ultrasound imaging is the Scanning Acoustic Microscopy (SAM) where the applied frequencies are above 100 MHz and can reach 2 GHz [14]. The high frequency provides the possibility to obtain accurate measurement results for crack and void distributions with a resolution of up to 1 μm at a depth of 10 μm.

In the first built ultrasonic non destructive testing systems, ultrasound signals were converted into electrical signals and immediately displayed on a screen. Interpretation required highly skilled operators to examine the signals (called A-scans, see appendix A.1.2) and to give an immediate decision on the quality of the test. Such interpretation can be a complex task. Especially when large structures are inspected, the amount of produced data can be enormous. The modern test equipments are digital and facilitate the work of the operators with special features such as automatic calibration, depth compensation, storage and revoke of the recorded ultrasonic signals etc.

However, conventional manual scanning has many limitations: operators need to be highly trained which naturally comes from expensive long training procedures and the repeatability and consistency of test results are not guaranteed. Moreover one single probe cannot be used to detect all types of defects. For instance, it is not possible to detect transverse cracks using a straight transducer, an angular transducer is used to detect such defects. Limitations in speed, in accuracy of detection, sizing, location and orientation of such critical defects pushed toward the search for new technologies. Phased array technology was developed to overcome these limitations.

Referred to as Conventional Phased Array (CPA), this technique procured higher inspection speed, better flexibility (the same probe can be used to detect defects in all orientations), electronic setup instead of manual setup, possibility to inspect geometrically complex components with higher reliability and new imaging modes such as sector scan which permits easier interpretation and analysis of ultrasound indications.

Moreover the development of the new Sampling Phased Array technique (SPA) by the Fraunhofer IZFP Institute [10] provides a faster reconstruction of ultrasonic images in 3D space. This new inspection technique, registered as patent [15], opens the doors towards a fully or semi-automated analysis of ultrasonic images, which provide a maximum support to the operator by evaluating inspection results. This task has to be solved by means of modern 3D image processing methods, adapted to the needs and requirements of the automatic ultrasonic testing. This is the main purpose of the doctoral thesis.

2.2. Phased array technique

Originally developed for medical applications [16], phased array technology found its first applications in the industrial field in the beginning of the 1980s [17, 18]. Advances in piezocomposite technology, microelectronics and computing power allowed the development and application of ultrasonic phased arrays to reach a mature status

2.2.1. Principle

Consider a straight array consisting of $N = 2Q + 1$ elementary rectangular shaped transducers from $i = -Q$ to $i = Q$, where $i = 0$ refers to the central element and $N, Q \in \mathbb{N}$.

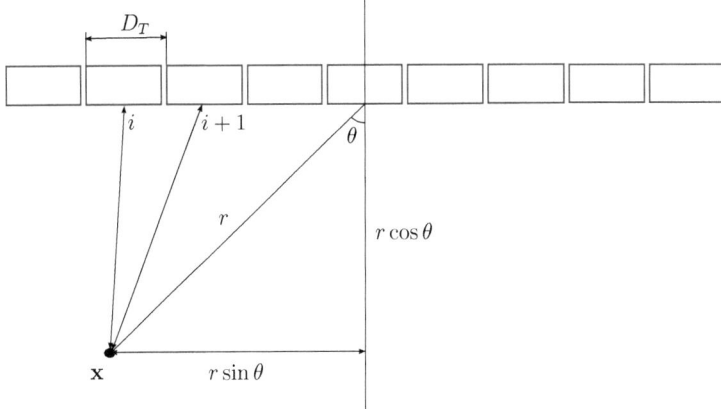

Figure 2.1.: Schematic view of a phased array transducer: the blue boxes represent the elementary transducers $i = -Q \cdots 0 \cdots Q$, and r denotes the focal distance between a point $\mathbf{x}$ and the central element ($i = 0$) of the array. The angle θ is the incidence angle.

Let $\mathbf{x}$ be a point in the focal region of the array. The focal length $r \geqslant 0$ is defined as the distance from $\mathbf{x}$ to the central element of the array. Note that the distance separating $\mathbf{x}$ from element i is less than the distance separating the point $\mathbf{x}$ of the element $i+1$. Accordingly, if one desires that the ultrasonic waves generated by each of these elements can be added constructively at the interference point $\mathbf{x}$, the multiple wave fronts must have the same global time-of-flight arrival at $\mathbf{x}$. This effect can only be achieved if the various active probe elements are pulsed at slightly different and coordinated times with proper time-delays, ensuring that all these waves arrive in phase at point $\mathbf{x}$ producing maximum ultrasonic energy in this area (constructive interference). Thus, the ultrasonic beam is focused and steerable. The time delays series applied to the array elements is called „focal law".

The emitted waves from individual elements construct a propagating wave front whose propagation direction is a function of the time delay $\Delta \tau$ between adjacent elements, the wave speed c in the medium and the distance D_T between adjacent elements of the array. For an incidence angle $\theta \in [-\pi/2, \pi/2]$ (also called steering angle), the time delay between adjacent elements $\Delta\tau \geq 0$ can be written as [19]:

$$\Delta\tau = \frac{D_T}{c}\sin\theta + \tau_0 \qquad (2.1)$$

where τ_0 is a constant ensuring that $\Delta\tau$ is positive.

For a focal length r at a required incidence angle θ, the time delays t_i to trigger element i of the array can be computed by the following formula [18, 20]:

$$t_i = \frac{r}{c}\left(1 - [1 + \left(\frac{iD_T}{r}\right)^2 - 2\frac{iD_T}{r}\sin\theta]^{1/2}\right) + t_0 \qquad (2.2)$$

where $i = -Q \cdots 0 \cdots Q$ is the number of array elements, c (m/s) is the speed of sound in the medium considered to be homogeneous and $t_0 \geq 0$ is the travel time from the central element of the array to the focal point **x**.

The basic design of the phased array electronics is presented in figure 2.2. The transmission and reception modes are regulated independently. When sending with appropriate time delays, a beam with a specific angle and focused at specific depth is generated. This beam hits the defect and is back reflected. Each of the phased array elements measures a certain proportion of the reflected ultrasonic energy. After amplification and filtering, the signals which are arriving with different time of flight values are time shifted for each element according to the receiving focal law. Then, the received signals of all the elements are summed to form a single ultrasonic signal. The signal summing can be either analog or digital. In modern test equipment, digital signal processing is preferred for many reasons, one of them is the low cost of modern digital microelectronics [10, 21, 22, 23].

The analog electronic used for time shifting (delay) and amplification, is implemented in a separate block in the immediate vicinity of the phased array probe to reduce interference and to simplify cable connections (see figure 2.2). Nowadays, the computing power and programming flexibility of FPGAs allow all functions for signal processing to be implemented in hardware independently of the PC environment. The phased array system is connected to a PC which plays the role of interfacing and mediation between the phased array system and the user. The users can control the test system and receive results in a form they understand. A variety of options are possible to display the results: A-scan, B-scan, C-scan, S-scan etc. (see appendix A.1.2). The PC options include storage, reuse and archiving of test parameters and test results. The communication between the PC and the data processing front end can be realized using fast hardware-network protocols such as the Serial Attachment (SATA). Among the advantages of SATA is the fast data transfer (up to 6 Gbits/second) from the data processing front to the PC.

2.2.2 Applications of phased array techniques in non-destructive testing

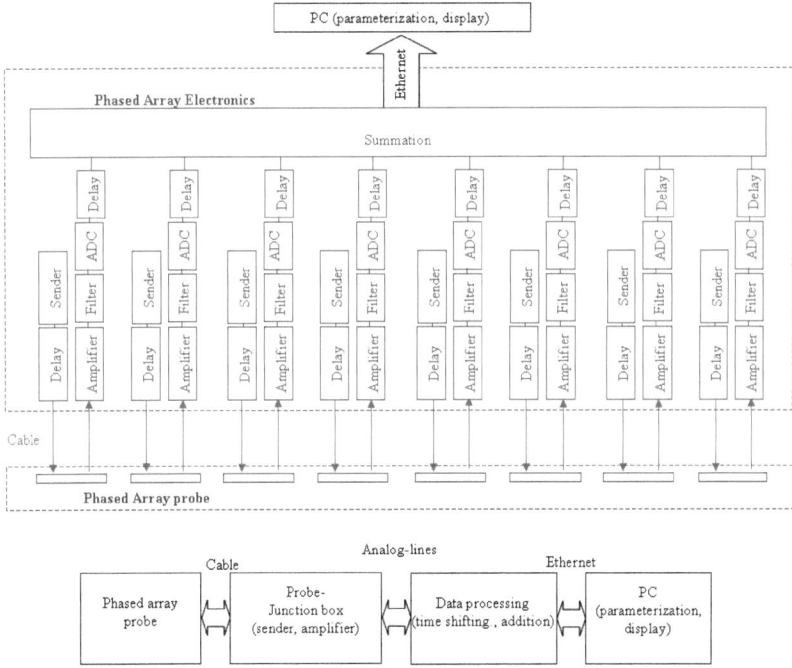

Figure 2.2.: Basic design of the phased array system and its connectivity (according to [10]).

2.2.2. Applications of phased array techniques in non-destructive testing

The phased array technique offers great application potentials in materials testing tasks. Several special inspection techniques have been developed to put the advantages of this method into specific testing procedures. The main scanning modalities procured by this technique are cited in the following paragraphs.

Sector scanning

One major advantage of the phased array transducers is their capability to sweep the ultrasound beam through an angular range for a specific focal depth. This procedure is known as sector scanning. Different incidence angles can be achieved by changing the time delays in transmission and reception. Let us examine figure 2.3: ultrasound beam with incidence angles θ_1 and θ_2 can be generated when triggering the array elements using focal laws 1 and 2 respectively. Consider that the incidence angle θ

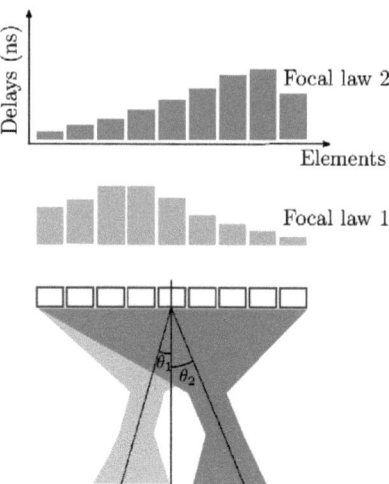

Figure 2.3.: Beam steering at angles θ_1 and θ_2 with the phased array technique.

is changing between θ_1 and θ_2 with a 1° step. At each incidence angle, the received signal can be recorded. The signal (A-scan) can then be back projected into the test specimen using an image reconstruction algorithm such as synthetic aperture focusing technique (see paragraph 2.2.4). The amplitudes of the pixels corresponding to each A-scan can be encoded as color or gray scale. The result is a 2D representation of the inspected specimen, the so-called sector scan (S-scan) between angles θ_1 and θ_2 (see as example figure 2.11).

Sector scan is rarely used for inspection tasks due to different reasons. Among them is the time consumption due to the necessity for numerous sending/receiving at each test position. Nevertheless, sector scan can be used to test the functionality of the phased array inspection system and its testing parameters, such as the resolution with different angles of incidence.

Dynamic depth focusing

Many inspection tasks require a high lateral resolution. One way to improve the lateral resolution is the focus. In conventional probes, focus is achieved by a focusing lens where the focus distance is determined by the curvature of the lens and cannot be changed. With phased array transducers, different focus distances can be set, for which the corresponding time delays of the array elements can be programmed. In practice, a single transmitted focused pulse is used and refocusing is performed on reception for all programmed depths. Figure 2.4 illustrates the dynamic focusing at depths r_1 and r_2, for a steering angle $\theta = 0$, using focal law 1 and focal law 2 respectively.

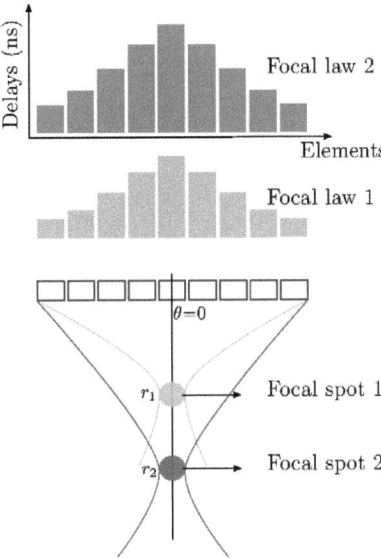

Figure 2.4.: Beam focusing at depths r_1 and r_2 with the phased array technique.

Electronic scanning

In electronic scanning (E-scan), the same focal law and delay is multiplexed across a group of active elements. Scanning is performed at a constant angle and along the phased array probe length by a group of active elements, called a virtual probe aperture (see figure 2.5). This is equivalent to a conventional ultrasonic transducer performing a step by step mechanical scanning. Electronic scanning is useful for typical testing applications like corrosion mapping and shear-wave inspection of welds (detecting sidewall lack of fusion or inner-surface breaking cracks).

2.2.3. Advantages and limitations of the phased array technique

The phased array technique has several benefits which include:

- A single phased array probe can cover a wide range of applications, unlike conventional ultrasonic probes.
- The usage of focused beams allows to achieve better a lateral resolution and to improve the signal to noise ratio. Moreover, an increased sensitivity can

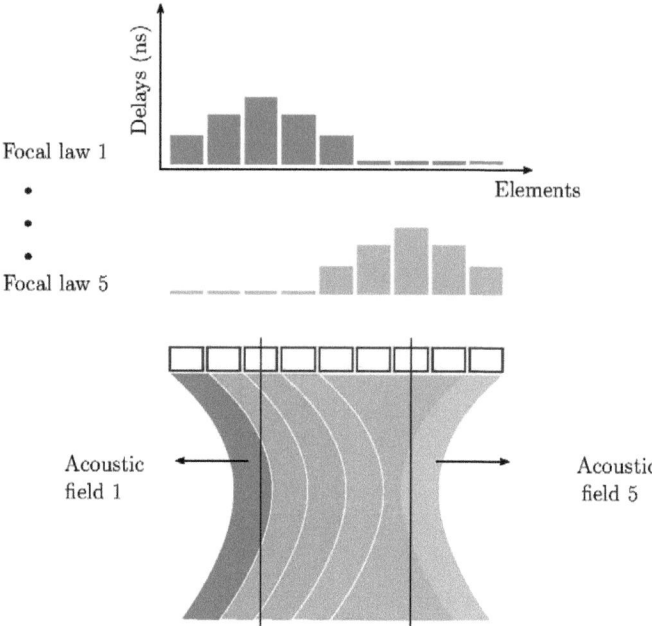

Figure 2.5.: Electronic scanning principle for zero-degree scanning: the virtual probe aperture consists of five elements. Focal law 1 is active for elements 1-5, while focal law 5 is active for elements 5-9.

be achieved through the optimization of the beam propagation angle to ensure that it is perpendicular to the surface of an expected discontinuity.

- Electronic scanning reduces the inspection time by reducing the need to move the probe. This also helps into maintaining uniform scanning conditions by less degrading the coupling between the transducer and the specimen each time the transducer is moved. Thus, the reliability of inspections is improved.

- Defects visualization in multiple views using the redundancy of information in S-scan, E-scans and other displays offers a powerful imaging tool. This visualization can be done during the scanning process with storage and reuse possibilities. With real-time imaging, inspections are easier to perform and the reliability of the measurements is also improved.

- Acquired data can be reconstructed into a 3D volume (see paragraph 2.2.4). With 3D representation, a better location and sizing of defects can be achieved.

- Replacing physical movement with electronic control, phased arrays can be programmed to inspect geometrically complex components such as automated welds.

- The phase array technique can be integrated into automated or semi-automated inspection system allowing fast inspection and repeatability of testing tasks.

- Electronic setups are obtained by simply loading a file and calibrating. Different parameter sets (such as inspection angle or focal distance) are easily accommodated by pre-prepared files.

Despite the advantages of ultrasonic phased arrays, there are many limitations hindering their employment for NDT tasks. A useful reference for many practical limitations of phased array is [24]. Following are resumed some of these limitations:

- The main obstacle is that the method is still not standardized. Phased array techniques are difficult to integrate into existing standards due to the complexity of this technology.

- Phased array equipments are much more expensive than conventional systems.

- The first time setup is time consuming, complex and requires very skilled operators. Indeed, phased-array equipments are more complex and thus more difficult to operate than conventional instruments.

Nowadays, a high probability of detection is expected from ultrasound equipments. High resolution B, C and S-scans imaging are therefore required. This imposes the increase of the number of sweeping angles and focusing depths. Phased array transducers can indeed be electronically re-focused and steered, nevertheless the overall inspection time may become impractical. In this context and instead of real time focusing, focusing can be performed after acquiring the data by synthetic aperture imaging explained in the next paragraph.

2.2.4. Reconstruction algorithms

Accurate detection and sizing of defects are essential tasks for a safe operation of the inspected specimen. This requires a high lateral resolution which is largely determined by the aperture of the transducer array. Thus, the use of a highly divergent beam is needed to keep the discontinuity in view over as large an aperture as possible. The main reconstruction algorithm which proved to be very efficient is the well known Synthetic Aperture Focusing Technique (SAFT). This method was developed by the University of Michigan, Southwest Research Institute and Battelle Pacific Northwest Laboratory [25].

SAFT was originally developed to improve the resolution of radar systems. The first synthetic aperture radar (SAR) appeared in 1950s [26, 27]. Later on the method was applied in ultrasound systems in medical imaging and industrial testings [28]. To illustrate the SAFT principle in time domain (SAFT can be implemented also

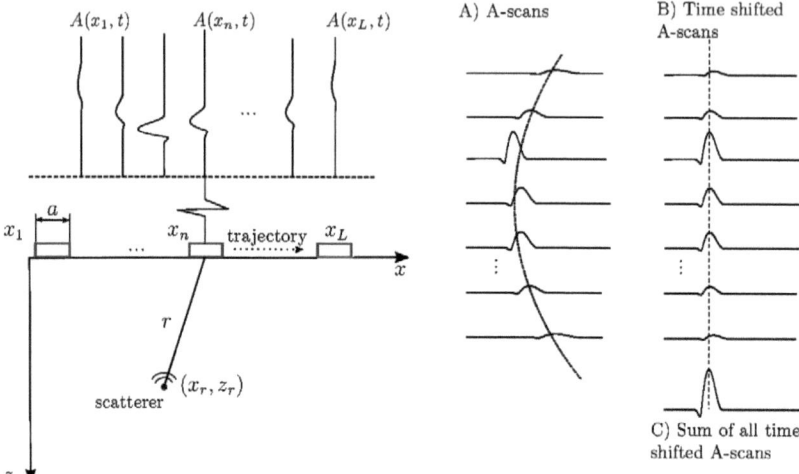

Figure 2.6.: Illustration of SAFT principle. The transducer is mechanically scanned along the x-axis and at each position x_n, $n = 1 \cdots L$, an A-scan $A(x_n, t)$ is acquired. At the end of the scanning, all A-scans are time shifted and signal summation or correlation takes place.

in frequency domain [29]), let us consider a simple case where a single transducer is mechanically scanned along the x-axis as seen in figure 2.6 and let us suppose that the propagation medium is homogeneous (i.e., the speed of sound c is constant).

The basic idea of SAFT is to collect A-scans from different scanning positions x_n, as to simulate a larger transducer. Then, with adequate computation, the A-scans are time shifted and correlated to give a much better resolution. In fact, different insonification angles give a more accurate information about the location and the size of the scatterer. In SAFT technique, the focus of the ultrasound transducer is assumed to be an observation point (x_r, z_r) of constant phase through which all the sound waves pass before diverging in a cone whose angle is determined by the width of the transducer a and the focal length r [30] (see figure 2.6).

When the transducer is directly above the observation point (scatterer), the time to receive the back scattered wave front is minimum. This time increases non-linearly when the transducer moves away from this position. SAFT consists of signal averaging, where at first all the A-scans have to be processed to introduce a time shift to each one of them. Afterward, the summation of these individual signals takes place. Reflections coming from defects will be constructively added and signals forming the noise will be destructively added (due to phase change). As a result, defects are enhanced and the noise is reduced.

More precisely, consider that the observation point is at spatial coordinates (x_r, z_r) in

xz plane. The wave front generated by the transducer at position $(x_n, 0)$ propagates through the medium and reaches the point (x_r, z_r) where it is scattered back to the transducer. The back scattered wave front reaches the transducer at time:

$$t_r = \frac{2r}{c} = \frac{2\sqrt{z_r^2 + (x_n - x_r)^2}}{c} \tag{2.3}$$

where t_r is measured from the beginning of the sending, remind that c is the speed of sound in the homogeneous medium. Consequently, the time shifts necessary to compensate the differences in the traveling time can be calculated using this equation. After introducing the necessary time shifts, the summation of the A-scans can be done. Finally, focusing at the observation point (x_r, z_r) can be expressed in continuous time form as follows [31]:

$$f(x_r, z_r) = \sum_{n=1}^{L} A(x_n, \frac{2\sqrt{z_r^2 + (x_n - x_r)^2}}{c}) \tag{2.4}$$

where $f(x_r, z_r)$ is the back projected signal amplitude function (also known as target function) at focusing point (x_r, z_r) and A is the ultrasonic signal (A-scan) acquired at position x_n of the transducer.

Normally measured A-scan signals are digitized with a ceratin sampling period. Therefore, the time shift t_r must be rounded towards the nearest sampling instance which introduces some errors. A common way to reduce the rounding error is to perform interpolation or to over-sample the signal [32, 31].

2.3. Sampling phased array technique

The SPA technique is developed to bring further the ultrasonic inspection speed without loss in image quality. In this section, a summary of this technique and for further information is presented, readers have the possibility to see references [10] and [33] for more details.

2.3.1. Principle

The main characteristic of the SPA technique is that it does not require electronic phase shifting for steering and focusing. These two functionalities are done via adapted reconstruction procedures. Let us consider an array formed of N transducer elements. In SPA technique, one transducer element i sends an ultrasound wave into the inspected specimen and all the other elements, including i, receive the reflected echo signals (see figure 2.7). This is the basic principle of SPA technique. The received signals are saved in the SPA information matrix (see figure 2.8).

At each sending pulse, one line of the matrix will be filled with the received echoes by different transducer elements. Thus, N sendings lead to the filling up of the complete matrix with $[N, N]$ elements (see figure 2.8). This operating mode is referred to as $1 \times N$ SPA mode. Two other modes are also applicable to fill the information matrix: $N \times 1$ SPA mode where all elements of the transducer send and only the ith received signal is considered and $N \times N$ mode where all elements of the transducer send and all receive. The SPA information matrix contains all necessary data for a reconstruction process. In fact, from the saved signals, all respective angles of incidence can be synthesized.

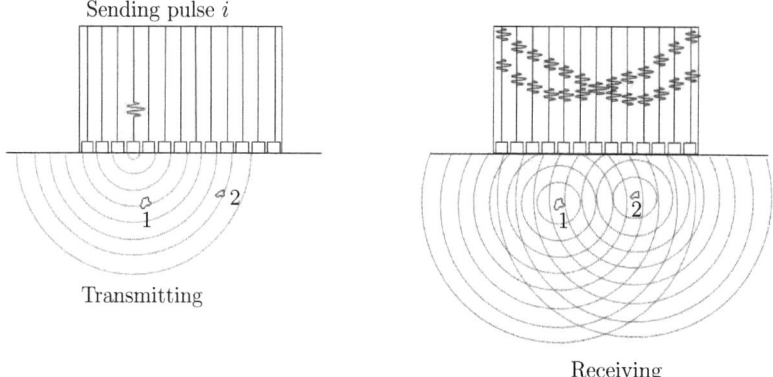

Figure 2.7.: Data acquisition in SPA mode: one transducer sends, all others receive (Image source: [10]). In this figure, the propagation medium is considered homogeneous thus the speed of sound is constant. Note that in the right image, the reflected signals from defects 1 and 2 are represented as if they were simultaneous, although they are not because the defects did not receive the incoming signals at the same time.

Synthetic focusing-sampling phased array

So far, the SAFT reconstruction method for a single transducer was discussed. For the case of a sampling phased array transducer, it comprises elements arranged at equal distances. Since these elements are sequentially triggered and operate independently, they can be considered as different probe positions in the SAFT-data recording. The difference is that the receivers are located in multiple locations, not just at the position of the transmitter, as in the classical SAFT reconstruction. More information is thus available.

Indeed, SAFT A-scans are simply the diagonal elements of the information matrix. The remaining matrix elements contain considerably more data than necessary for the reconstruction. Nevertheless, these additional information about the defects can be used in the SAFT reconstruction for each pixel. The reconstruction method is referred to as Synthetic Focusing-Sampling Phased Array (SynFo-SPA) [10]. The

2.3.1 Principle

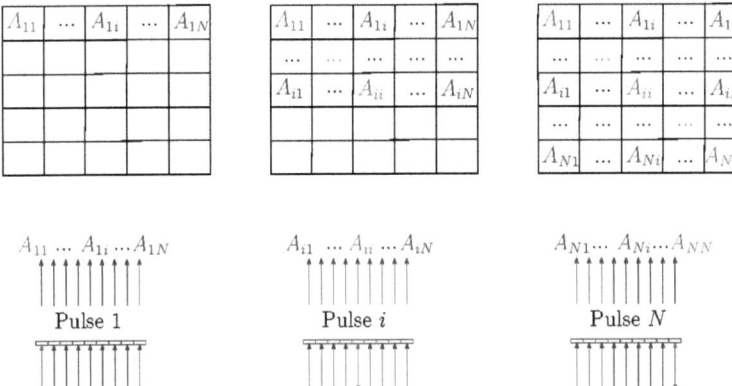

Figure 2.8.: Illustration of the filling of the Information matrix in the operating mode $1 \times N$: A_{ij} corresponds to the detected reflection of the signal emitted by i and received by j. For Pulse 1, only element 1 sends and all elements receive: the first row of the matrix is filled. For Pulse i, only element i sends and all elements receive: filling of the row i of the matrix. For Pulse N, only element N sends and all elements receive: filling of the last row N of the matrix.

advantage of this technique, utilizing all time-domain signals $A_{ij}(t)$, lies in the automatic focusing of every image point. Actually, by means of the SynFo-SPA algorithm 1, received signals can be synthesized for any required incidence angle θ and focusing point at discrete focal length r_k from the central element (see figure 2.9): each digitized signal generated by receiver j and transmitter i can be projected on the central axis of the phased array and added to the other information matrix components A_{ij}.

Algorithm 1 Reconstruction algorithm for any required incidence angle θ (according to [10]).

$$\text{ForwardPath[Samples]} = \left[\left(D_i + \frac{r_k}{2} \cdot \sin\theta\right)^2 + \left(\frac{r_k}{2} \cdot \cos\theta\right)^2\right]^{1/2}$$

$$\text{BackwardPath[Samples]} = \left[\left(D_j - \frac{r_k}{2} \cdot \sin\theta\right)^2 + \left(\frac{r_k}{2} \cdot \cos\theta\right)^2\right]^{1/2}$$

$$\text{Sum}[r_k] = \sum_{i=1}^{N}\sum_{j=1}^{N} A_{ij}(\text{ForwardPath} + \text{BackwardPath})$$

▷ Samples stands for discrete values
▷ D_i: distance from sender i to the central axis
▷ D_j: distance from receiver j to the central axis
▷ r_k: discrete focal distance on the central axis
▷ θ: incidence angle
▷ i: sender and j: receiver

As a result, the aperture of the transducer array can be increased up to the complete information matrix which permits focusing at different depths without any increase in complexities of transducer arrays and ultrasonic channels.

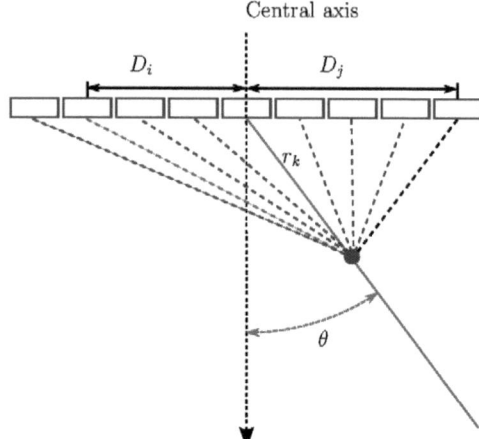

Figure 2.9.: Illustration of the different distances involved in the SynFo-SPA reconstruction algorithm for an incidence angle θ and focus point at distance r_k from the central element of the array. The distances D_i and D_j are the distances from the sender i and the receiver j to the central axis. The green dotted line correspond to the forward path of the emitted wave. The black dotted line correspond to the backward path of the reflected wave received by receiver j.

The end result of the SynFo-SPA algorithm is a high image quality: B-scan, C-scan or S-scan. Three dimensional volumes (using mechanical scanners) can also be generated by stacking the 2D B-scans according to the geometry of the scanned specimen and the actual index value (see figure 2.10). Actually, at each index position (y-axis) the transducer is moved in scan direction (x-axis) over the complete scan trajectory. The generated B-scan fills the voxels of its corresponding xz plane.

Figure 2.11 compares resulting sector scans obtained via CPA and SynFo-SPA. Note that the reflectors located near the surface are much better identified in the second technique.

2.3.2. Sampling phased array advantages

Important advantages of SPA using the SynFo reconstruction algorithm are resumed as follows:

With SPA the image quality is vastly improved. Moreover, high inspection speeds are made possible at reduced system expenditures primarily caused by omitting electronic phase shifting components [33].

2.3.2 Sampling phased array advantages

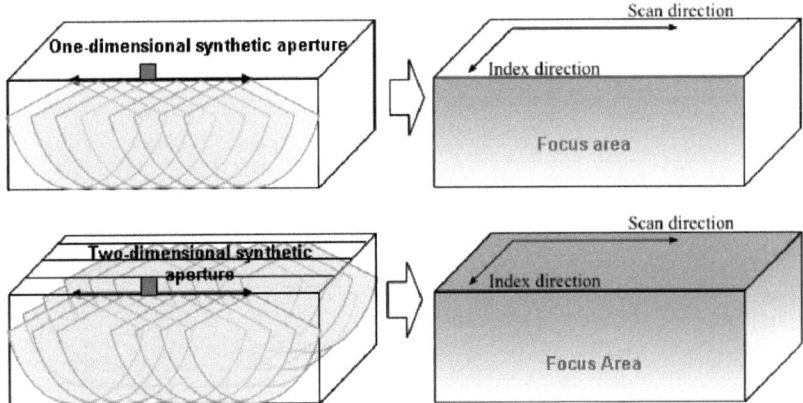

Figure 2.10.: Illustration of a volume reconstruction with SynFo-SPA (Image source: Fraunhofer IZFP). The scan direction is x direction. The index direction is y direction. Upper image: the green focus area is the reconstructed B-scan obtained by scanning the transducer array over the complete scan trajectory. Lower image: the 3D volume obtained after scanning the transducer over the complete scan trajectory at each index y.

Another advantage of SPA is that the directional characteristics of the array are the same as the single element transducer directional characteristics because the transmission of the ultrasound waves is done in all directions. This means that the received ultrasonic signals contain information about reflectors, which are located in all scanning directions. Thus, with the correct assignment of the phase, the received signal can be synthesized in any required irradiation direction [33].

Moreover, by giving access to the elementary wave phase conditions, the SPA technique improves the ability of ultrasound systems to inspect anisotropic materials such as carbon fibers. In fact, in homogeneous materials, the wave fronts of elementary waves are spherical and propagate in perpendicular direction to the wave front. This is different in anisotropic materials, where the wave fronts are not spherical and the sound field is rather distorted [35]. In other words, in anisotropic materials, the speed of sound is not the same throughout the complete volume and the traveling path is not always straight. This leads to many difficulties, among them is the estimation of the depth of discontinuities. SPA technique gives access to the elementary wave phase conditions and relations allowing them to be adjusted to a quasi-normal test condition of anisotropic materials. This technique is referred to as *Reverse Phase Matching* [36] and is currently an active research theme at Fraunhofer IZFP labs in Saarbruecken. Further explanation about Reverse Phase Matching application can be found in [37]. Figure 2.12 shows a sector scan of a CFRP specimen via conventional phased array and SPA with Reverse Phase Matching.

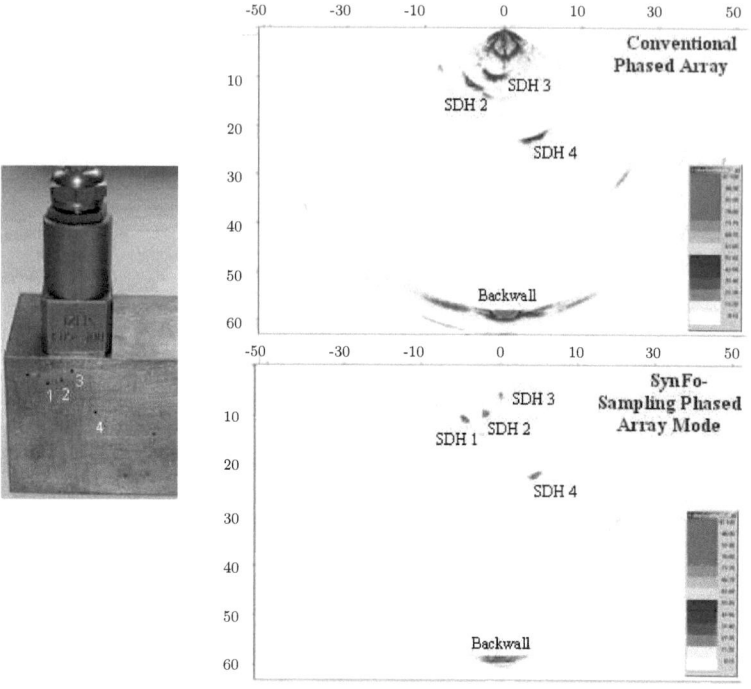

Figure 2.11.: Sector scan of a test specimen: near surface side drilled holes (SDH) artificial defects 1, 2 and 3 are more clear with SynFo-SPA compared to CPA (Image source: [34]).

Yet another important advantage of the technique is the almost total elimination of near-surface dead zones resulting in a much better identification of surface reflectors, as visible in figures 2.11 and 2.12. Indeed, in CPA technique, all elements send and receive. Thus, dead zones of the elements of the transducer yield a bad image quality near the surface. In $1 \times N$ mode of SPA technique, only one element sends but all the others receive. Therefore, the near surface defects are not in the dead zone of all of the elements of the transducer, the image quality near the surface is thus better.

2.3.3. Acquisition system

The SPA technique is integrated in a platform, built by QNET Engineering [13], based on cutting edge microelectronic components. Data processing and image reconstruction are done based on parallel computer architecture which allows very fast in-line visualization of the measured data.

2.3.3 Acquisition system   21

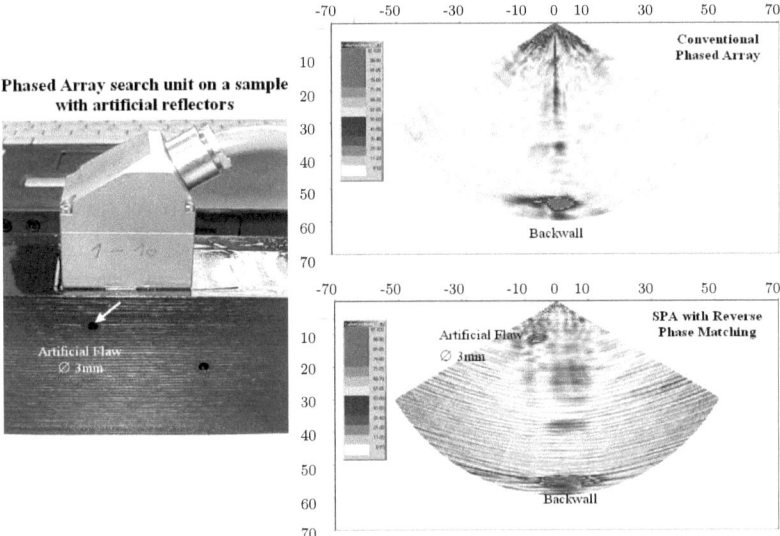

Figure 2.12.: Sector scan ultrasound inspection of a CFRP specimen: the defect near the surface is obviously seen by SPA with Reverse Phase Matching (Image source: [34]).

The measuring station consists of an immersion tank, 3-axes manipulator and a 64-channel phased array system capable of multichannel inspection as well as CPA and SPA inspection in contact or immersion technique (see figure 2.13).

An acquisition software (called sampling software) for automated ultrasonic testing is also available for experimental settings, data visualization and manual analysis (view figure 2.14). Figure 2.15 shows the inspection of a CFRP specimen with the corresponding results where defects appear in the inner structure of the specimen. The settings required for each specific ultrasound inspection procedure can be defined using the sampling software. It is important to use the proper settings in order to have a satisfactory quality of reconstructed ultrasound data. Important parameters that can be set by the sampling software are as follows:

- Sound velocity: each material is characterized by a specific sound velocity which depends on the elastic and inertial properties of the material. Thus, it is primordial to use the adequate sound velocity corresponding to the component being tested. For CFRP, sound velocity is around 2880 m/s and is determined using a specimen of known thickness.

- Water wedge: in this work, measurements were done in immersion testing technique, where the transducer is coupled to the test component by water. This means that sound propagates through the water to reach the component. Thus, the depth of the water wedge has to be measured in the inspection procedure.

This can be done by setting the sound speed at the velocity of sound in water (1480 m/s), then by measuring the signal peak which corresponds to the end of the water path. Errors in detecting the end of the water will lead to a total distortion of the reconstructed data.

- Gain: offset amplification can be applied to the amplitude of the reconstructed signals. Adequate amplification gives an improved data quality.

- Time gain compensation: ultrasound waves are considered to be exponentially attenuated while propagating in the medium, thus they need to be amplified in order to allow the visualization of near surface regions simultaneously with deep regions. This corresponds to the application of a time compensation gain TGC(z) at each depth z. TGC can be interpolated using a step wedge of the same type as the inspected component.

- Dimensions: the [x, y, z] dimensions of the reconstructed volume need to be specified. The scanned surface is specified by x and y. The maximal depth of the scan is specified by z.

- Resolution: the voxel size in the 3D reconstructed volume can be specified in the sampling software (see figure 2.14). On one hand, the image resolution depends on the specified voxel size. On the other hand, the spatial resolution is defined by the wavelength of the ultrasound wave which is equal to the ratio of the sound velocity in the medium over the frequency. Thus, better spatial resolutions are obtained with higher frequencies. In practice, the voxel size is chosen smaller than the wavelength in order to preserve the spatial resolution. For instance, when scanning a CFRP specimen with a 5 MHz transducer, the wavelength is 0.576 mm: planar CFRP are primarily tested with an incidence angle $\theta = 0°$ for delaminations and porosity that are usually detected best perpendicular to the accessible surface of the specimen [38]. Therefore in this case, the voxel size in depth (z) direction should be less than 0.576 mm.

- Scanning speed: this parameter can be set by an additional software which controls the scanning speed (the motion control unit) of the 3-axes manipulator. It specifies at which scan speed the transducer moves in x direction and the step for each index move y.

2.4. Inspection of composite components

Fibers Reinforced Polymers (FRP) are composite materials formed of bonded fibers with polymer matrix (or resin). Fibers are long filament materials with diameters ranging from 0.8 μm up to 12 μm [39]. Their role is to provide strength and stiffness for the FRP component. Examples of fibers used for industrial application are glass and carbon fibers. Matrix material is a polymer which binds the fibers together. Primary functions of the matrix are to transfer stress between fibers, to provide

2.4 Inspection of composite components

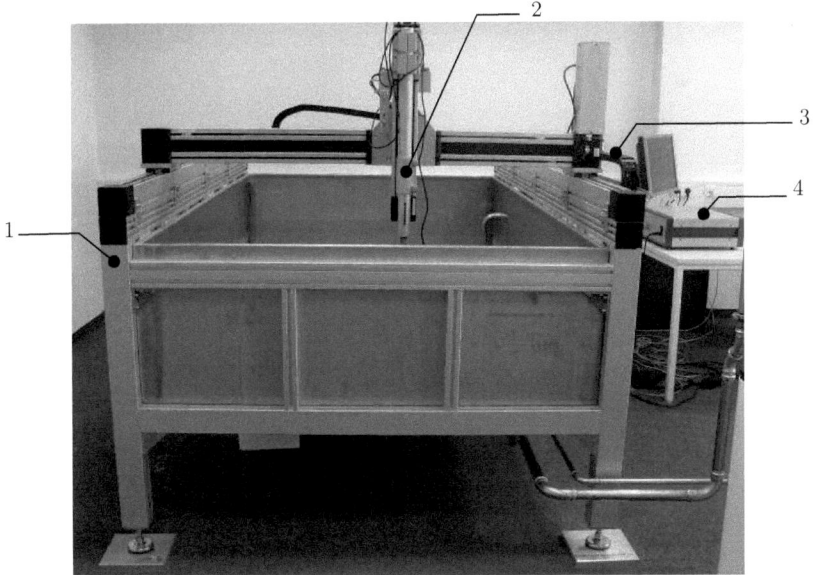

Figure 2.13.: Measurement station with corresponding: immersion tank (1), probe holder (2), 3-axes manipulator (3) and manipulator control unit (4).

protection against the environment and to protect the surface of the fibers from mechanical abrasion [39]. Typical resin materials are thermoplastic and thermosetting polymers. The bond between the fibers and the matrix material needs to be perfect so that no discontinuity appears across the interface fiber-matrix. The output composite components have low weight, high strength and stiffness and resistance to environmental conditions, which result in low maintenance costs.

Indeed, the usage of FRP composites has significantly incremented in wide range of aerospace, naval, aeronautical, civil infrastructure and automotive industrial applications. Quality of complex FRP structures is subjected to very high requirements in order to ensure that the composite performs satisfactorily. Moreover, the high production rate of FRP production in industry requires efficient and reliable non-destructive in-line testing modality in order to guarantee the highest quality and reliability of the produced structures.

The most applied NDT technique to inspect the quality of FRP components is the ultrasound technology. The use of this technique is strongly correlated with the types of defects that potentially appear in FRP composite structures. Particularly, ultrasound waves are sensitive to delamination defects. These are inter-laminar cracks which appear in the composite element and are caused by loss of adequate adhesion between adjacent plies due to poor quality in lying plies, shrinkage in the matrix etc. They can appear both at near surface or deep locations in the composite and can

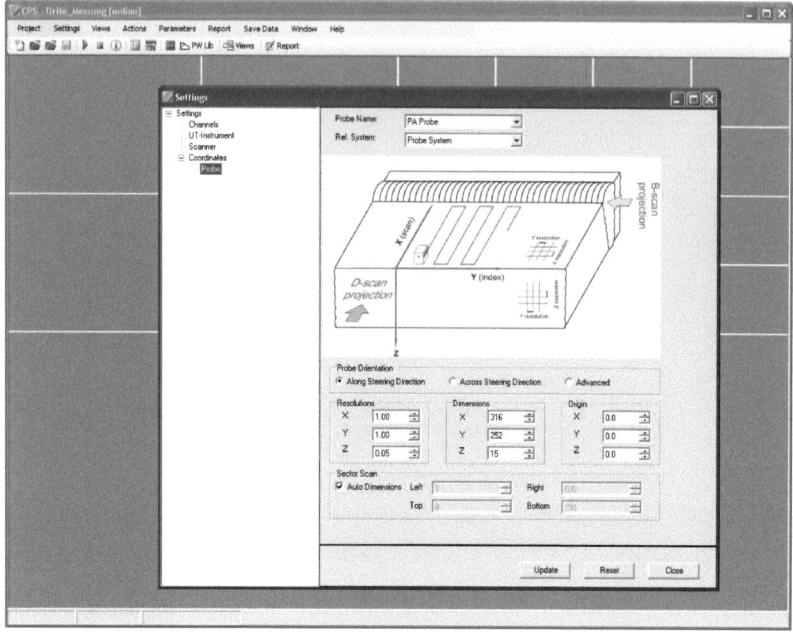

Figure 2.14.: Software environment including all settings, among others are the resolution settings of the reconstructed volume.

grow and propagate in the structure leading to complete malfunctioning of the FRP element. Debonding of the fibers from the matrix in addition to other common types of defects like porosity, voids and inclusions can also appear in the FRP elements. Readers interested in knowing more about potential defects in FRP structures, their criticality and NDT testing modalities are referred to document [40].

Our objective is to find a method for the automatic interpretation of measured data dedicated to in-line inspection via SPA technology which represents the latest advancement in the phased array technology. The proposed interpretation requires an adequate ultrasound image analysis technique. Section 2.5 is dedicated to introduce the main artifacts that are characteristic of ultrasound images and to review the state of the art on ultrasound image analysis approaches.

2.5. Ultrasound image analysis

The quality of ultrasound images has relatively improved over the recent years. This has led to a rising interest in segmenting ultrasound images both for medical and in-

2.5.1 Artifacts of ultrasound images

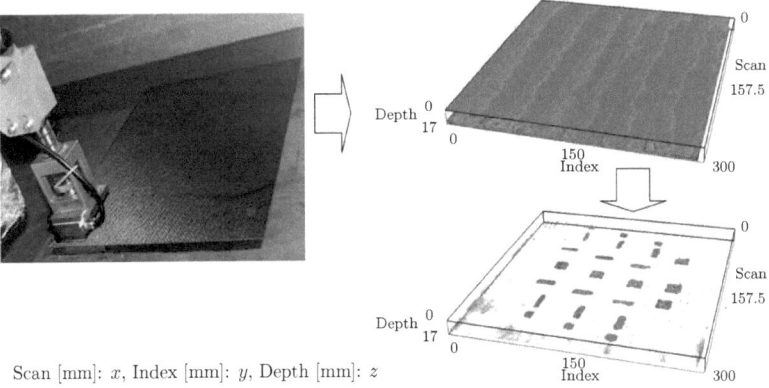

Scan [mm]: x, Index [mm]: y, Depth [mm]: z

Figure 2.15.: Inspection of a CFRP specimen using SPA 1 × 16 mode and the obtained 3D reconstruction (upper right image) revealing the presence of defects inside the structure (lower right image).

dustrial applications. However, ultrasound images are still considered hard to segment and conventional image analysis techniques often do poorly on ultrasound images as they assume good boundary definition (defect-material) and acceptable contrast to noise ratio. In fact, the appearance of geometric boundaries is dependent on the acoustic impedance difference between medium and defect, on the assumption of usage of the true speed of sound in the medium, which can significantly influence the obtained signal and on the characteristics of the inspected medium. Certainly, anisotropic materials such as CFRP are a true challenge for any segmentation process. The next section will discuss the main artifacts that affect the quality of the ultrasound images.

2.5.1. Artifacts of ultrasound images

Diverse phenomena provoke the appearance of artifacts in ultrasound data. Arising artifacts can be due to the physical interaction between the sound waves and the propagation medium, the propagation of sound in matter [41], the formation of the ultrasound pulse (i.e. ultrasound beam characteristics) and reflected echoes acquisition, processing and reconstruction techniques. Artifacts can also be caused by improper scanning techniques, although these artifacts can be avoidable [41]. Many of these artifacts can be wrongly interpreted as real discontinuities in the reconstructed data, thus it is important to reduce them either during the acquisition time (pre-processing enhancement techniques, see for instance [42]) or after acquisition by means of signal and image processing methods (post-processing enhancement techniques). The ulterior techniques aim at reducing noise and enhancing edges and contrasts in the reconstructed data.

As will be elaborated in chapter 3, a first major difficulty encountered in ultrasound imaging is the speckle noise. Speckle severely degrades the quality of ultrasonic images, it especially blurs edges and details in the image. Additionally, it causes a sort of granular texture appearing in the image.

Secondly, the speed of sound is considered to be constant inside the medium. Nevertheless, changes in the speed of sound may occur depending on the characteristics of the medium. The change in the speed of sound will provoke a distortion in the appearance, shape and size of the structures being inspected [43, 44].

Thirdly, attenuation artifacts occur when a strong absorber (high reflector) is encountered (for instance a void), because it reflects the majority of the incoming waves. Thus, the waves passing through the strong absorber are weakened. This has an effect of shadowing appearing after the strong absorber (see figure 2.16).
Similarly, when a weak absorber is encountered within the imaging field, the amplitude of the beam passing through it will be higher than the amplitude of the nearby beam passing through the medium. Thus, the returning echo from the structures under the weak absorber will be higher. This effect causes an increase in the intensity of the received signal and is identified as a bright band extending from an object of low attenuation [41].

Fourthly, reverberation artifacts can appear in the reconstructed data when one or more highly reflective structures are encountered in the path of the sound beam including the probe itself (in case of a reflected wave). High reflectors produce a series of closely spaced reflections [44]. The first reflection has the highest amplitude appearing as the largest width, while the later received reflections uniformly decrease in amplitude (this artifact is known as *comet tail*) [41]. In case of multiple reflections between the reflective structure and the probe, ghost images of the structure appear at a distance multiple to the real distance between the structure and the probe (see figure 2.16). This type of artifacts appears when the depth of the inspected medium is a multiple of 2 of the reflective structure depth [42].

Other type of artifacts may also appear: diffraction artifacts [45], guided wave artifacts [42], ring down [43], mirror images [41] and refraction. For instance, refraction may occur when there is a change in direction of the ultrasound beam as it crosses a boundary of two regions with different speed of sound. This causes errors in the lateral position of structures [43, 44].

All these characteristic artifacts make the segmentation of ultrasound images a complicated task. However, the quality of information from the ultrasound devices has significantly improved over the last years. This has led to an increased use of ultrasound in NDT applications. Thus, there is currently an augmented interest in the image segmentation task.

2.5.2 Segmentation of ultrasound images

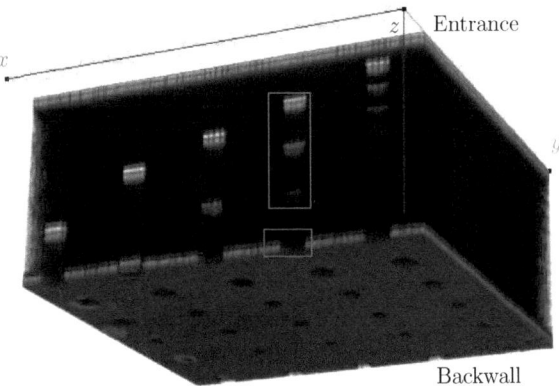

Figure 2.16.: 3D view of a CFRP volume: the red upper box corresponds to the reverberation (ghost) artifact where the reflector appears at integer multiple of the distance between reflector and the phased array. The lower green box corresponds to shadowing. Notice the reverberations of reflectors and that the boundaries of the reflectors are not clear due to speckle noise influence.

2.5.2. Segmentation of ultrasound images

Diverse methods have been proposed to segment ultrasound images. Most techniques are 2D techniques developed for B or C scans mainly because these modes are usually available on commercial systems [46]. Comparatively little work is done on the segmentation of 3D ultrasonic volumes reflecting the lately rising use of 3D imaging systems in practice.

Before starting to distinguish and categorize different techniques, it is useful to keep in mind that most proposed segmentation approaches serve to address a specific task. Moreover, a successful segmentation is strongly depending on the quality of the available data. As proposed by Noble et al. [47], a good way to characterize segmentation methods is to categorize them in terms of the prior knowledge that they use in order to solve the segmentation task. Prior knowledge includes [47]:

- Intensity level distribution: where the intensity level distribution models including Nakagami [48], Gamma [49, 50], Fisher-Tippett [51], Rayleigh [52, 53] etc. are used in order to distinguish between different regions of interest.

- Image gradient: where the idea is to use the intensity gradient to localize boundaries of objects. To reduce the noise effect before gradient estimation, a filtering is sometimes applied to the initial image. Due to the anisotropy of ultrasound image acquisition, boundaries of real objects often have missing edges [46]. Thus, some authors propose to use local image phase [54, 55]. The argument is that local image phase is more robust than intensity gradient in detection of acoustic boundaries.

- Image texture: in ultrasound imaging image texture is dependent on different factors. In fact, the wavelength, the structure of the medium and the distribution of scatterers and their sizes relative to the wavelength produce different texture patterns. Texture features can be statistical, structural, model based, spectral based etc. Texture based segmentation algorithms were used, for instance, in various clinical applications such as liver [56], prostate [57] and breast [58] etc.

- Shape: knowledge here is based on model shapes which are built on sets of training samples. It is embedded in the segmentation approaches (mainly active contour approaches) in order to accurately detect boundaries yielding more reliable results. The accurate detection of organs or objects from ultrasound images plays a key role in many applications, especially in ultrasound medical images segmentation and tracking (dynamic shape priors). This information was largely and successfully used, for instance, in [59, 60, 61, 62, 63].

Next is presented a survey of some approaches to segment ultrasound images coming from the medical community and industrial applications of ultrasound.

Review of ultrasound image segmentation approaches in the medical community

Clinical ultrasound application is well established in medicine field since it is safe, produces dynamic images and is economic. It helps into viewing the actual function of organs (echocardiography, liver etc.) and to determine diseases (breast cancer, prostate etc.). Nevertheless, the interpretation of ultrasound data is not an easy task, especially when the quality of the measured data is poor. For more than two decades efforts have been made to improve image quality and advanced segmentation approaches were proposed to help in the evaluation of measured data.

Proposed segmentation approaches are driven by the corresponding clinical application which can for example be the location and tracking of organs or detection and sizing of diseases. I consider the papers written by Noble [46] et al. [47] as good references covering the main segmentation techniques applied to ultrasound images in medical applications. Readers are also referred to [64] for a more recent review of the special case of carotid plaque image segmentation.

Segmentation approaches can include one or more of the previously cited prior knowledge. The mostly used techniques are to be cited here. Primary approaches to cite are those based on active contours models. Their general idea is to find the contour that minimizes the segmentation criterion which is in general a cost function also called energy function. The initial contour is defined with a prior knowledge in terms of shape, continuity, smoothness and it is then deformed according to the

2.5.2 Segmentation of ultrasound images

image characteristics [65]. Two kinds of active contour models can be distinguished: edge based and region based active contour models. Edge based segmentation models typically use the information of an image gradient to locate the boundaries. Region based segmentation models separate regions with different statistics [51] rather than a local image gradient. Those methods are considered to be very well suited to process noisy ultrasound images since object boundaries are not necessarily complete in ultrasound images. Both edge based and region based active contour models can be solved using level set introduced by [66]. This method has been used to segment ultrasound data. Recent applications of level set based active contour can be found in [51, 67, 68]. A major disadvantage of active contours models is the requirement of a good initialization in order not to fall on local minima of the energy function. Hence the segmentation result is sensitive to the initialization.

The second approach is a machine learning approach. The machine-learning segmentation technique is more or less a classification approach. These techniques are based on learning, done on a large dataset, where measured features (contrast, autocorrelation, wavelet coefficients etc.) on each region of interest are used as input to the classifier in order to distinguish the class of the region. Advanced machine learning techniques are used; Kotropoulos et al. [50] applied Support Vector Machine (SVM) on medical B-scans to distinguish between lesion and background. Artificial Neural Networks (ANN) are as well used in region segmentation [59, 69, 70]. Pujol et al. [71] used AdaBoost in Vascular diseases characterization. Yaqub et al. [72] applied Random Forests [73] to segment 3D ultrasound volumes. The machine learning approaches are able to solve problems that cannot be explicitly modeled like in case of ultrasound image formation [47]. Their main drawback is the need of a large learning database, and an adequate choice of input features.

Review of ultrasound image segmentation approaches in the industrial community

In the industrial application of ultrasound, different techniques are used in order to analyze the received signal (A-scans) and to segment the images (B or C scans). Some methods applied on A-scans are considered because this mode is still widely used in industrial inspection, especially in welds inspection. In the following the main ideas being applied are resumed.

For A-scans of welds, Discrete Wavelet Transform (DWT) was used by Matz et al. [74] to filter the A-scans while Short Time Fourier Transform (STFT) was used by Otero et al. [75]. After features extraction, Matz et al. [74] applied SVM to distinguish between the backwall echo, the signal with fault echo and the signal measured on weld. Otero et al. [75] applied Clustering analysis to differentiate volume defects from planar defects.

For B-scans of welds, texture measures and fuzzy-neural based classifiers were used by Shitole et al. [76]. The authors did not give further details about the segmentation and classification methods or the amount of data they used in their study, however, they conclude that the developed neural-fuzzy classifier has given a promising performance [76]. Zahran et al. [77] worked on backwall echo removal, texture analysis and intelligent background removal to segment and classify defects in B-scans of welds. Obtained results were shown for one example and the authors concluded that the results were quite promising in terms of accuracy. Correia et al. [78] proposed an interesting approach, where DWT is used to de-noise and compress the B-scan of steel samples, then to build the Covariance matrix of level 2 decomposition DWT. The authors showed that the diagonal elements of the covariance matrix could be used as a reference pattern associated with the nature of the flaws spatial amplitude distribution. Four types of reflectors were investigated: lack of fusion, crack, pores cluster and non metallic inclusion. The experimental results obtained for lack of fusion, non-metallic inclusion and crack were limited. However, pores cluster were positively identified.

For C-scans of welds, Polikar et al. [79] and Spanner et al. [80] applied DWT to extract coefficients used to train a Multilayer Perceptron (MLP) which automatically segments and generates classification images. In [79], training was done on 106 C-scans of welds with different defect types: cracks, lack of fusion, porosity and slags. MLP gave a good classification performance with 99% defects classification. Nevertheless, results of validation, done on 50 C-scans, were reduced to 84%. As for [80], the initial results obtained also on C-scans of welds (with cracks, counter bound and weld root defects) were promising, nevertheless no validation was reported. Mandal et al. [81] used a similar technique for Glass Epoxy Composite containing delamination caused by impact damages. The authors used time and frequency domain features to generate C-scan images where the damage could be clearly visible. Peak amplitude, Rise time and Fall time of the waveform were computed as time domain features. Frequency domain features considered by the authors were the amplitudes at different frequencies. Time domain features were used as inputs for Least Mean Square (LMS) classifier to generate C-scans. Time domain and frequency domain features were used separately by a Minimum Difference classifier to generate the C-scans. The MD classifier performed better than the LMS classifier. In their work on C-scans, Kieckhoefer et al. [82] proposed to work on the difference image obtained by subtraction of a reference image from the original image. The reference image was generated by filtering the original image. The method was tested on a limited set of C-scan images of glass-fiber reinforced aluminum with known defects and was able to detect all defects. Nevertheless, the obtained number of false detections was considerable.

Cornwell et al. [83] proposed an automatic 3D inspection system for 3D ultrasound images of welds. 3D images were reconstructed from A-Scans using CAD models of test specimen. Concerning the evaluation process, a simple threshold on the amplitude of voxels was applied to data containing low noise levels.

2.6. Conclusion

In this chapter, phased array and sampling phased array techniques were briefly described. Afterward, the acquisition system and the inspection of CFRP components were discussed. The last section was dedicated to present a review of ultrasound data analysis techniques. Here the techniques were distinguished between image segmentation methods applied in medical and methods used in industrial applications of ultrasound. Main analysis approaches in the industrial applications are in 2D, although 3D segmentation methods of ultrasound data were done in the medical field (for specific applications, see references [84, 85, 86]). It can be globally said that each proposed segmentation approach is dedicated each to a particular application. However, classification methods (SVM, neural networks etc.) are extensively used. In this work, a similar methodology will be followed.

In a matter of fact, a crucial point for the success of any segmentation method is the quality of acquired data. The speckle noise heavily affects the quality of ultrasound measures. Thus, next chapter has been specifically devoted to study the speckle noise in SPA data.

3. Speckle characterization in SPA data

Contents

3.1.	Introduction	33
3.2.	Modeling the speckle	34
	3.2.1. Theoretical parametric models of speckle	35
	3.2.2. Empirical models of speckle	39
3.3.	Speckle distribution in SPA data	40
	3.3.1. Proposed model	41
	3.3.2. Experimental results	42
3.4.	Speckle noise reduction	48
	3.4.1. Spatial domain filtering techniques	50
	3.4.2. Transform-domain filtering techniques	52
3.5.	Conclusion	52

3.1. Introduction

Behind the formation of an ultrasound image are complicated physical phenomena. When propagating inside a medium, ultrasound waves are subjected to non linear attenuation and scattering by the medium's micro-structures. In fact, scattering is caused by small inhomogeneities in the acoustic impedance, which are randomly distributed in the three dimensional space of the medium. As a consequence, emitted waves which were traveling in phase on their way to the scatterers are no longer in phase after being back scattered. Due to the phase-sensitive detection of back scattered waves interfering in the resolution cell of the transducer, an ultrasound image is characterized by a granular pattern of white and dark spots. This phenomenon is denoted speckle and is considered as a process which tends to degrade the resolution and contrast of ultrasound images [87].

The speckle noise is assumed to have a multiplicative model and in most applications it needs to be effectively reduced in order to have a successful automatic image segmentation which is our case. Note, however, that it is not always desired to remove speckle as its presence is critical to the success of some techniques such as speckle

 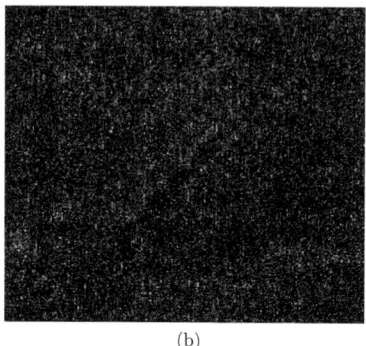

(a) (b)

Figure 3.1.: (a) SAR image of an agricultural region of Feltwell (U.K.) by a fully polarimetric PLC-band NASA/JPL airborne sensor (Image source: [94]). (b) Ultrasound image using SPA technique of a CFRP component without internal structure.

tracking [88, 89] and for many methods of ultrasound tissue characterization [46, 90]. Objectives of this chapter are to understand the origin of the speckle, to review the models for intensity levels distribution (commonly referred to as speckle pattern) in ultrasound images, to propose and investigate an empirical model for speckle in data measured using the SPA technique. The last part of this chapter presents a review on the main techniques used in speckle reduction.

3.2. Modeling the speckle

The modeling of the statistical properties of the speckle was a main query for many scientific works. From a methodological point of view, either parametric or non-parametric estimation strategies can be employed for this purpose [91]. Specifically, our focus will be on the parametric modeling approach. Here, the principle idea is to postulate a given mathematical distribution for the statistical modeling of ultrasound images. Afterward, parameter estimation for the distribution is performed in order to determine the statistical properties of speckle in images. The modeling process forms a crucial task for specific image analysis purposes, for instance characterization [92, 93] or classification [67, 49] of image regions. Parametric models can be organized into two classes: theoretical and empirical models.

The theoretical parametric models are derived using a scattering model of waves. On the opposite, empirical models are obtained by directly fitting a model to the experimental values, without any assumption of physical concepts.

Moreover, it is useful to note that similarities exist between the images obtained by Synthetic Aperture Radar (SAR) and ultrasound techniques where their main characteristic is the appearance of speckle grains giving them a noisy appearance. This explains the reason why established speckle models in SAR are as well applied for speckle modeling in ultrasound images (see figure 3.1).

On another hand, the speckle problem is well investigated in the medical field (on radio frequency signal and image levels). However, much less work has been done to characterize the speckle in industrial data. Indeed, the micro-structures are completely different between a CFRP, a fiber glass and a human carotid arteries or liver for example. A question poses itself: are speckle models proposed for medical ultrasound data valid for industrial data as well?

Thus, and independently of the application's type, the next section is devoted to present a review of theoretical parametric models of speckle.

3.2.1. Theoretical parametric models of speckle

Let a resolution cell (also called range cell) of a transducer correspond to the smallest resolvable detail [95]. Moreover, consider a scatterer i which is randomly located inside the waves propagation medium. The back scattered echo Λ_i from the scatterer i is characterized by an amplitude $\alpha_i \geq 0$ and a phase ϕ_i. It can be expressed as:

$$\Lambda_i = \alpha_i \cdot \exp(j(\omega_0(t) + \phi_i(t))) \tag{3.1}$$

where $\omega_0 \geq 0$ is the angular frequency of excitation and $j = \sqrt{-1}$ is the imaginary number.

In the case when N_s scatterers, $N_s \in \mathbb{N}$, interfere in the same resolution cell, the back scattered echoes in the cell can be expressed as [96, 97]:

$$\Lambda = \sum_{i=1}^{N_s} \alpha_i \cdot \exp(j(\omega_0(t) + \phi_i(t))) = \Re(\Lambda) + j \cdot \Im(\Lambda) \tag{3.2}$$

where $\Re(\Lambda)$ is the real part and $\Im(\Lambda)$ is the imaginary part of the complex back scattered echo Λ.

Consequently, the interference of the back scattered echoes can be constructive or destructive according to each particular repartition of scatterers. If interference is mainly constructive then the intensity in the resolution cell will be high. In case of mainly destructive interference, the intensity will be low. The envelope of the back scattered echo $E\Lambda$ is given by:

$$E\Lambda = \sqrt{\Re(\Lambda)^2 + \Im(\Lambda)^2} \tag{3.3}$$

Speckle is explained as an interference phenomenon between all the back scattered echoes interfering in the same resolution cell. Therefore the size of speckle granules is about the same as the resolution of the transducer both in longitudinal and lateral direction [95]. Additionally, note that the speckle size is not only dependent on the transducer's characteristics, but varies with the scatterers density as well [98].

In the modeling process, the following hypotheses are usually considered to be fulfilled [99, 100, 101]:

- The amplitude of the back scattered echo from each scatterer is considered to be deterministic and the phase is considered to be uniformly distributed in $[0, 2\pi[$.

- The number of scatterers is large enough so that each resolution cell contains sufficient scatterers ($N_s \geq 10$ [102]).

- The scatterers are independent and there is no single scatterer dominating inside the resolution cell.

Under the above cited hypotheses and according to the central limit theorem [103], in case of a large number of randomly located scatterers (figure 3.2a), the scatter is fully developed. In this case, the real and imaginary parts of Λ are Gaussian, thus, $E\Lambda$ follows a Rayleigh distribution [95, 104, 105]. The probability density function (pdf) of Rayleigh distribution is given by:

$$P_R(s, \beta) = \frac{s}{\beta^2} \cdot \exp\left(-\frac{s^2}{2\beta^2}\right) \quad (3.4)$$

where $s \geq 0$ is the intensity value in the range cell of the transducer (also called local brightness in [47]) and $\beta > 0$ is the scale parameter.

Nowadays, with the advent transducers emitting high frequency waves, it is possible to obtain high resolution ultrasound images. Due to the increased resolution, the number of reflectors per cell is reduced. Note that the back scattering characteristics of a scatterer are depending on its dimensions relatively to the wavelength of the ultrasound [106, 107]. Hence, the fundamental assumption of fully developed speckle is no longer valid. Consequently, the Rayleigh distribution tends to fail in modeling the speckle distribution in ultrasound data.

As alternative, in case of non-fully developed scatter[1], Shankar [96] proved that the envelope $E\Lambda$ will be Rician distributed. This model is considered to be appropriate in case of regular repartition of scatterers that might, for instance, account for regular structures or quasi periodic scatterers in the medium (figure 3.2b). The pdf of Rician distribution is given by:

$$P_{Rician}(s, \beta, \nu) = \frac{s}{\beta^2} \cdot \exp\left(-\frac{s^2 + \nu^2}{2\beta^2}\right) \cdot I_0\left(\frac{s\nu}{\beta^2}\right) \quad (3.5)$$

$I_0(\cdot)$ is the modified Bessel function of the first kind of order zero defined as:

$$I_0\left(\frac{s\nu}{\beta^2}\right) = \frac{1}{\pi} \int_0^\pi \exp\left(\frac{s\nu}{\beta^2} \cos \alpha\right) d\alpha \quad (3.6)$$

---

[1]Case of few scatterers.

3.2.1 Theoretical parametric models of speckle

where $s \geqslant 0$, $\beta > 0$ and $\alpha \in [0, \pi]$.

The parameter $\nu \geqslant 0$ is considered as specular component which is added to the Rayleigh pdf. Thus, when ν is null, the Rician distribution is reduced to a Rayleigh distribution.

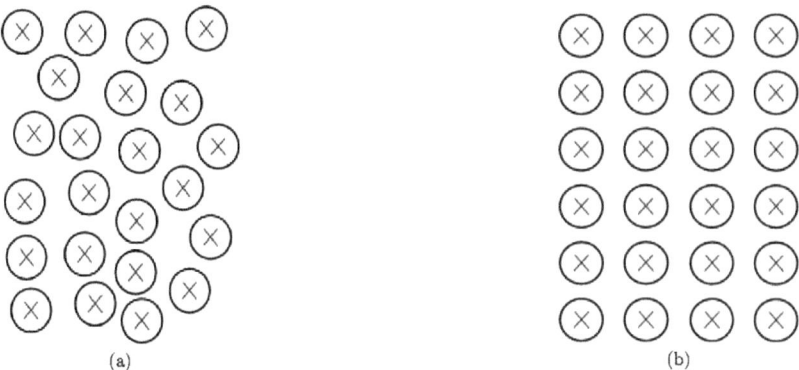

Figure 3.2.: (a) Array of randomly located scatterers. (b) Regular array (similar to CFRP structures).

Jakeman et al. [108] proposed to use K-distribution as a model for a weak scattering condition which corresponds to a small number of scatterers. The pdf of the K-distribution is given by:

$$P_K(s, \beta, N_s) = \frac{2\beta}{\Gamma(N_s + 1)} \cdot \left(\frac{\beta s}{2}\right)^{N_s+1} \cdot K_{N_s}(\beta s) \qquad (3.7)$$

In this equation, $\beta > 0$ is a scaling factor, $N_s > -1$ is the number of scatterers in the resolution cell and $K_{N_s}(\cdot)$ represents the modified Bessel function of second kind and order N_s:

$$K_{N_s}(\beta s) = \int_0^\infty \cosh(N_s t) \exp(-\beta s \cosh t) dt \qquad (3.8)$$

where $t \in [0, \infty)$ and $s \geq 0$.

The function $\Gamma(.)$, known as gamma function, is a generalization of factorial function to non integer values n and defined by:

$$\Gamma(n+1) = \int_0^\infty t^n e^{-t} dt \qquad (3.9)$$

where $t \in [0, \infty)$. In case of integer values, $\Gamma(n)$ is reduced to be $n!$.

In [96], the author proposed a simpler model called the Nakagami distribution in order to model the speckle in ultrasound data. This distribution is derived from the basic assumption of a Gaussian model for the back scattering phenomena. According to the study done by Shankar et al. [96], Nakagami distribution is claimed to be suitable for modeling almost all scattering conditions. The pdf of the Nakagami distribution is defined as:

$$P_N(s, \nu, \Omega) = \frac{2\nu^\nu s^{2\nu-1}}{\Gamma(\nu)\Omega^\nu} \cdot \exp\left(-\frac{\nu s^2}{\Omega}\right) \quad (3.10)$$

where $\nu \geq \frac{1}{2}$ is the Nakagami shape parameter and $\Omega > 0$ is a scaling factor. When $\nu = 1$, the Nakagami pdf is equivalent to a Rayleigh pdf: $P_N(s, \Omega) = \frac{s}{\Omega} \cdot \exp\left(-\frac{s^2}{\Omega}\right)$ where $\Omega = 2\beta^2$. Nakagami pdf becomes Rician for $\nu > 1$.

Further investigations on modeling the statistical properties of the received echo signal and more complex models have been proposed to take into account different scatterer conditions. Among these models are the generalized K-distribution [109], the homodyned K-distribution [110] and the Rician inverse of Gaussian distribution [111]. Anastassopoulos et al. [112] proposed the generalized Gamma distribution ($G\Gamma D$) [113, 114] to model the characteristics of radar clutter. In their study [112], the authors proved and validated that the pdf of $G\Gamma D$ distribution performs better than K-pdf and can model the speckle and the modulation component of the radar clutter (speckle) in case of a high resolution radar. The $G\Gamma D$ pdf is given by:

$$P_{G\Gamma D}(s, \beta, \xi, \nu) = \frac{\xi}{\beta \Gamma(\nu)} \cdot \left(\frac{s}{\beta}\right)^{\xi\nu-1} \cdot \exp\left(-\left(\frac{s}{\beta}\right)^\xi\right) \quad (3.11)$$

In this equation $\beta > 0$ is the scale parameter, $\nu > 0$ is the shape parameter and $\xi > 0$ is the power of $G\Gamma D$ [112]. $G\Gamma D$ forms a general model. Standard models commonly used in modeling SAR data, like exponential ($\xi = 1, \nu = 1$), Rayleigh ($\xi = 2, \nu = 1$), Nakagami ($\xi = 2$), Weibull ($\nu = 1$), and gamma pdf ($\xi = 1$) are special cases of the $G\Gamma D$.

Assuming that the real and imaginary parts of the back scattered signal are independent zero-mean generalized Gaussian, Moser et al. [97] introduced the Generalized Gaussian Rayleigh distribution (GGR) with a pdf given by:

$$P_{GGR}(s, \beta, \nu, \alpha) = \frac{\beta^2 \nu^2 s}{\Gamma\left(\frac{1}{\nu}\right)^2} \cdot \int_0^{\frac{\pi}{2}} \exp\left[-(\beta s)^\nu \cdot (|\cos\alpha|^\nu + |\sin\alpha|^\nu)\right] d\alpha \quad (3.12)$$

where $\beta > 0$ is a scaling factor, $\nu > 0$ is a shape factor dealing with the sharpness of the pdf and $\alpha \in [0, \pi/2[$.

The effectiveness of the proposed GGR model was validated on SAR images [97]. The pdf of GGR gave a higher correlation value with the histogram of the SAR images compared to other probability density functions (pdfs) of: the Nakagami, Skewed α Stable ($S\alpha S$) generalized Rayleigh [115, 116, 117] and K-distributions. Note that $S\alpha S$ statistical model was applied by Kappor [118] to describe woodland regions in ultra-wideband synthetic aperture radar images, where it was shown that it provides a better fit to the tails of the clutter amplitude distribution than the Gaussian or K distribution. Similar work was done by Banerhee [119] where the authors proved that $S\alpha S$ statistical model provides better segmentation and detection results when compared to Gaussian models.

To summarize, theoretical models are usually derived from the analysis of the acoustic physics and the information available of the ultrasound transducer [120]. However, as stated by Tao et al. [49], these models only give the speckle probability density at the transducer. The density has to be transformed into speckle density in the image. This task is complicated for two reasons. First, the transducer signal passes through different signal processing stages such as amplification and interpolation etc. before its presentation as an image. Propagating the density through the complex signal processing chain is difficult [49]. A second reason is that the complete information during the acquisition process is not always available. A common method to avoid these difficulties is to use empirical pdfs which can be accurately fitted to the speckle in the image.

3.2.2. Empirical models of speckle

For $P, S, T \in \mathbb{N}$, let $\Omega^{P,S,T} \subset \mathbb{N}^3$ be a set of coordinates defined as:

$$\Omega^{P,S,T} = \{(x,y,z) \in \mathbb{N}^3 : 1 \leqslant x \leqslant P;\ 1 \leqslant y \leqslant S;\ 1 \leqslant z \leqslant T\}$$

where P, S and T are respectively the dimension of the volume's grid.

Let u denote a ultrasound noisy volume[2] defined as a mapping from $\Omega^{P,S,T}$ to $\mathbb{R}_+$:

$$\begin{aligned} u: \quad \Omega^{P,S,T} &\longrightarrow \mathbb{R}_+ \\ (x,y,z) &\longmapsto u(x,y,z) \end{aligned}$$

where $u(x,y,z) \in \mathbb{R}_+$ is the noisy intensity observed at coordinates (x,y,z). For simplicity reasons, $u(x,y,z)$ will be only written as u in the pdfs of table 3.1.

Several empirical models have been reported for modeling the speckle in ultrasound images. These models are validated on the actual ultrasound images by measuring the goodness of fit of the model to the actual data distribution. Thus, results are completely data-dependent and cannot be considered as general models valid for other types of data.

In general, many applied models in ultrasound speckle characterization are taken from SAR speckle studies. These models include Gamma [99, 121], Weibull [99, 122, 123] and Lognormal [124, 125] distributions (see table 3.1).

Vegas-Sanchez-Ferrero et al. [120] studied the distribution of fully developed speckle noise by comparing the goodness of fit of ten families proposed in the literature.

---
[2]An array or an image are special cases of a volume.

The work was done on 120 clinical cardiac ultrasound images. The compared pdfs were for: Gamma, Lognormal, Rayleigh, Normal, Nakagami, Beta, Rician Inverse Gaussian [111], Rice, Exponential and K-distribution. The authors used χ^2 goodness of fit test and concluded that the pdf of Gamma distribution fits at best the speckle noise.

Tao et al. [49] compared the validity of four families of distribution of the speckle noise on clinical cardiac ultrasound images: Gamma, Weibull, Normal and Lognormal [126, 127]. The pdf of the Gamma distribution was found to have the best fit to the data and classified blood and tissue at a low misclassification rate. The authors used Rao-Robson [128] statistic to measure the goodness of fit and the generalized likelihood ratio test to classify regions into tissue and blood.

The pdf of Fisher-Tippett distribution was proposed by [102, 129] as a model for fully formed speckle in log-compressed ultrasound images. In fact, in ultrasound imaging log-compression is often applied to the amplitude of the received echoes in order to adjust their values to fit in the 8 bits digitization dynamic range [106].

In their recent contribution, Li et al. [130] proposed to use the pdf of the Generalized Gamma distribution $G\Gamma D$ to empirically model SAR images data distribution. The authors compared the pdf of $G\Gamma D$ distribution with Weibull, Nakagami, K, Fisher [131], GGR [97] and Generalized Gamma Rayleigh $G\Gamma R$ [94] pdfs. The obtained qualitative (visual comparison) and quantitative results proved that, in most cases, the pdf of $G\Gamma D$ provided better performance in fitting SAR image data histograms than the majority of the previously developed parametric models.

Although empirical models are used in many segmentation approaches, c.f. [47, 46] for extensive surveys, authors often assume that speckle is Rayleigh, Gamma [121, 132, 133, 134] or Fisher-Tippett [135] etc. distributed, without proving the validity of this assumption.

In the next section, the focus will be on finding the model which fits the speckle in SPA volumetric data.

3.3. Speckle distribution in SPA data

The speckle degrades the quality of the reconstructed SPA volumes and it is important to study it in order to have more knowledge about its statistics. The aim is to find the model that fits at best the speckle affecting the data measured with the SPA technique.

3.3.1 Proposed model   41

Model	Probability density function	Parameters
Weibull	$p(u) = \dfrac{\nu}{\beta} u^{\nu-1} \exp\left(-\dfrac{u^\nu}{\beta}\right)$ $\alpha, \beta > 0$	ν: shape β: scale
Normal	$p(u) = \dfrac{1}{\beta\sqrt{2\pi}} \exp\left(-\dfrac{(u-\mu)^2}{2\beta^2}\right)$ $\mu \in \mathbb{R},\ \beta > 0$	μ: location β: scale
Lognormal	$p(u) = \dfrac{1}{u\beta\sqrt{2\pi}} \exp\left(-\dfrac{(\ln(u)-\mu)^2}{2\beta^2}\right)$ $\mu \in \mathbb{R},\ \beta > 0$	μ: location β: scale
Gamma	$p(u) = \dfrac{1}{\Gamma(\nu)\beta^\nu} u^{\nu-1} \cdot \exp\left(-\dfrac{u}{\beta}\right)$ $\nu, \beta > 0$	ν: shape β: scale
Fisher-Tippett X: magnitude image, Y: log of X	$Y = \ln(X),\ P_X(u) = \dfrac{u}{\beta^2} \exp\left(-\dfrac{u^2}{2\beta^2}\right)$ $P_Y(\rho) = 2\exp\left([2\rho - \ln(2\beta^2)] - \exp\left([2\rho - \ln(2\beta^2)]\right)\right)$ $\rho \in \mathbb{R},\ \beta > 0$	β: scale

Table 3.1.: Probability density functions used in modeling speckle in SAR and ultrasound images. Note that u is used as abbreviation (to simplify the pdf formulas) for the intensity at voxel (x, y, z) in the volume u and $u(x, y, z) \geq 0$.

3.3.1. Proposed model

From a methodological point of view, the parametric approach for noise distribution statistical analysis will be followed. Here, the Four-Parameters Generalized Gamma (4P-$G\Gamma D$) distribution is proposed to model speckle in SPA data. Its pdf is defined as:

$$P_{G\Gamma D}(u(x,y,z), \beta, \xi, \nu, \gamma) = \frac{\xi}{\beta \Gamma(\nu)} \cdot \left(\frac{u(x,y,z) - \gamma}{\beta}\right)^{\xi\nu - 1} \cdot \exp\left(-\left(\frac{u(x,y,z) - \gamma}{\beta}\right)^\xi\right) \quad (3.13)$$

where $u(x,y,z) \in [\gamma, +\infty[$ is the intensity value, $\beta > 0$ is the scale parameter, ν is non null and represents the shape parameter, $\xi > 0$ is the power of $G\Gamma D$ and the new parameter $\gamma \in \mathbb{R}$ is the translation parameter. Note that for $\gamma = 0$ the model is reduced to the original model of the $G\Gamma D$ [113, 114].

The proposed 4P-$G\Gamma D$ model is compared with the following commonly used pdfs to model speckle in ultrasound images: Gamma, Lognormal, Inverse Gaussian, Weibull, Rayleigh, Rice, Nakagami and Normal. In addition, the translation parameter γ was introduced into each of the previously cited pdfs. For instance when introducing a translation parameter to the original Gamma distribution, the newly obtained distribution will be:

$$p(u(x,y,z)) = \frac{(u(x,y,z) - \gamma)^{\nu-1}}{\Gamma(\nu)\beta^\nu} \cdot \exp\left(-\frac{u(x,y,z) - \gamma}{\beta}\right) \quad (3.14)$$

Type	Original volume dimensions $[x,y,z]$	Extracted volume dimensions $[x,y,z]$	Voxel size $[mm^3]$
CFRP	[316, 301, 341]	[100, 113, 92]	[1, 1, 0.05]
Aluminum	[841, 171, 951]	[761, 133, 101]	[1, 1, 0.05]
Ceramic	[379, 95, 301]	[291, 81, 41]	[1, 1, 0.05]

Table 3.2.: Speckle noise study conducted on three different materials: CFRP, aluminum and ceramic.

In order to apply the 4P-$G\Gamma D$ (also applies for the other pdfs) as a model for SPA data, it is mandatory to estimate the pdf parameters β, ξ, ν and γ from the experimental data. In fact, in parametric modeling, the pdf estimation problem can be formulated as a pdf parameters estimation problem [97]. Several strategies have been presented in the literature to solve parameters estimation. The standard methods include the maximum likelihood (ML) [99, 91] and the method of moments (MoM) [136]. More explanation about different parameters estimation methods of pdfs can be found in [137]. As for the estimation of pdfs used in this study, robust parameter estimation using ML estimate is obtained by using EasyFit tool provided by MathWave [138].

Quantitative measure of the goodness of fit is obtained using the Kolmogorov-Smirnov (K-S) statistic. The K-S statistic is a well known distance measure commonly adopted for the study of goodness of fit [112, 139, 140]. It is a simple measure based on the largest vertical difference D between the empirical (i.e., experimental) cumulative distribution function (ecdf) $S_Q(s)$ of a dataset and the known cumulative distribution function (cdf) $F(s)$.

$$D = \max_{-\infty < s < +\infty} |S_Q(s) - F(s)| \qquad (3.15)$$

Remind that the cdf of a real random variable λ, with a given pdf p_λ, is the probability that λ takes a value less than or equal to s: $F(s) = p_\lambda(\lambda \leqslant s)$. Moreover, the ecdf can be defined as follows: let $\lambda_1, \cdots, \lambda_Q$ be Q data points from a common distribution with cdf $S(s)$, the ecdf is defined as: $S_Q(s) = \frac{1}{Q}\sum_{i=1}^{Q} \mathbf{I}(\lambda_i \leqslant s)$ where $\mathbf{I}$ is the indicator function ($\mathbf{I}$=1 if $\lambda_i \leqslant s$ and $\mathbf{I}$=0 if $\lambda_i > s$). Small K-S distance D indicates a better fit of the particular pdf to the experimental data.

3.3.2. Experimental results

Experiments are reported on three reference volumes, without defects, extracted from original volumes which contain defects. The considered original volumes are: a CFRP volume, an aluminum volume and a ceramic volume (see table 3.2). Intensity values in the three volumes are encoded on unsigned 16 bits.

Figure 3.3a illustrates (on a layer) the selection of the reference volume (without defects) from the original volume. The obtained reference volume is presented in figure 3.3b and its dimensions are reported in table 3.2.

3.3.2 Experimental results   43

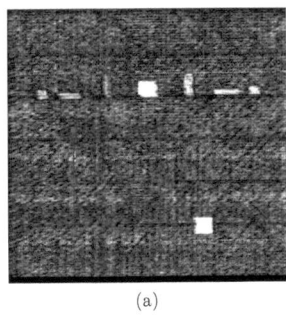   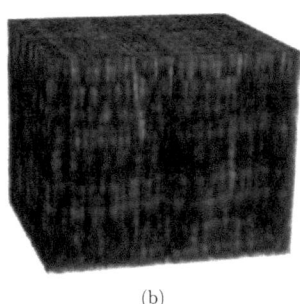

         (a)   (b)

Figure 3.3.: (a) xy view of a layer in the CFRP original volume, the red rectangle represents the zone which is selected as a reference in this layer. (b) Reference volume extracted from the original 3D volume.

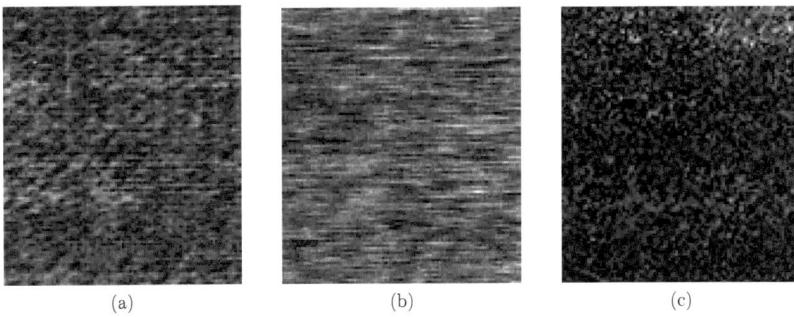

     (a)   (b)   (c)

Figure 3.4.: One example layer extracted from the reference volume of a) CFRP, b) aluminum and c) ceramic.

For visual comparison of speckle in the considered materials, one layer of respectively, CFRP, aluminum and ceramic reference volumes is presented in figure 3.4.

In order to assess the effectiveness of the proposed parametric pdf, the different pdfs for each reference volumes are estimated. Evaluation of the estimation results are presented both: qualitatively by means of a visual comparison between the top ranked estimated pdfs and the data distributions (reference volume intensity levels histograms) and quantitatively by the K-S goodness of fit values between fitted distributions and the experimental data.

Speckle in CFRP material: in case of CFRP material, the quantitative measure K-S suggests that the best fit for the intensity values distribution in the reference volume is given by the pdf of the 4P-$G\Gamma D$ distribution with a K-S value of 0.003

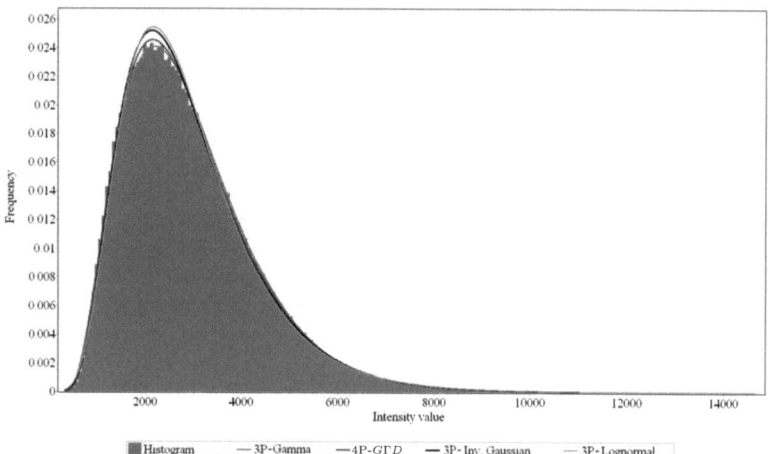

Figure 3.5.: Plot of the volume's normalized histogram and of the best four estimated pdfs: for the CFRP reference volume. Note that the number of bins is equal to the number of intensity values in the reference volume.

(see table 3.3). Moreover, a visual comparison in figure 3.5 between the normalized histogram and the plots of the top four best estimated pdfs illustrates the result obtained based on the quantitative measure.

Speckle in aluminum material: the analysis of the speckle in the aluminum reference volume reveals that the pdf of 3P-Lognormal fits at best the intensity values distribution in the volume. In the second rank comes the 4P-$G\Gamma D$. Table 3.4 resumes the complete quantitative results obtained for all the considered pdfs. For a visual comparison see figure 3.6.

Speckle in ceramic material: lastly, the speckle in the ceramic reference volume is investigated. Table 3.5 reports the K-S distances measured between the experimental data and the pdfs. As it can be noticed, the K-S distance obtained for the fitted pdf of the 4P-$G\Gamma D$ distribution is the smallest. In the second rank comes the pdf of the 3P-Lognormal distribution. This is also visible in figure 3.7, it can be seen that the pdf of the 4P-$G\Gamma D$ distribution tracks the evolution of the intensity values histogram better than other pdfs. However, it can be noticed that the histogram is not very well fitted by none of the pdfs.

Different conclusions can be drawn from the obtained results. Based on the qualitative and quantitative measures, there is a clear evidence that the speckle in high resolution SPA data exhibit a non-Rayleigh behavior. The reason is that, with the

3.3.2 Experimental results

Parametric model	K-S distance	Rank
4P-$G\Gamma D$	0.003	1
3P-Gamma	0.006	2
3P-Inv.Gaussian	0.008	3
3P-Lognormal	0.01	4
Gamma	0.0138	5
$G\Gamma D$	0.0157	6
Lognormal	0.0188	7
Inv.Gaussian	0.022	8
2P-Rayleigh	0.0313	9
3P-Weibull	0.032	10
Weibull	0.042	11
Rice	0.065	12
Rayleigh	0.066	13
Normal	0.073	14
Nakagami	0.079	15

Table 3.3.: Values of the K-S distance obtained using the different pdfs to model speckle in the CFRP reference volume.

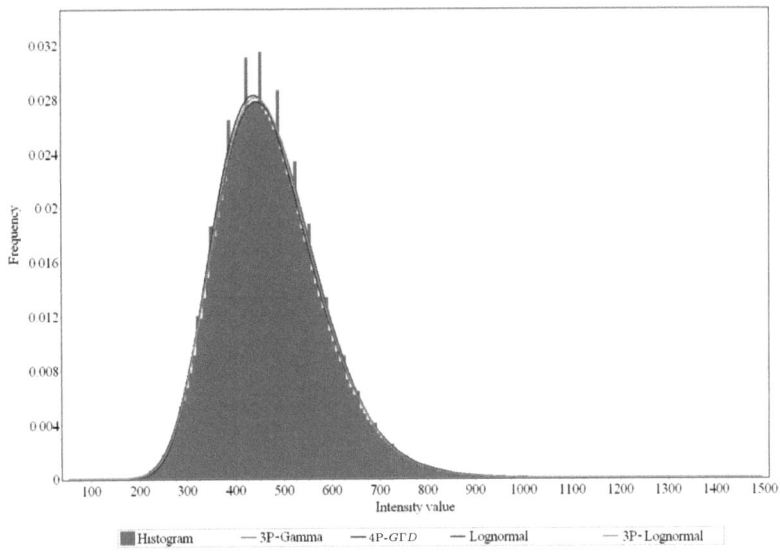

Figure 3.6.: Plot of the volume's normalized histogram and of the best four estimated pdfs: for the aluminum reference volume.

3.3 Speckle distribution in SPA data

Parametric model	K-S distance	Rank
3P-Lognormal	0.005	1
4P-$G\Gamma D$	0.007	2
Lognormal	0.008	3
3P-Gamma	0.01	4
$G\Gamma D$	0.0137	5
Gamma	0.0141	6
Nakagami	0.0305	7
Normal	0.0434	8
3P-Inv.Gaussian	0.0436	9
Inv.Gaussian	0.0439	10
Rice	0.0505	11
3P-Weibull	0.055	12
Weibull	0.06	13
Rayleigh	0.248	14
2P-Rayleigh	0.267	15

Table 3.4.: Values of the K-S distance obtained using the different pdfs to model speckle in the aluminum reference volume.

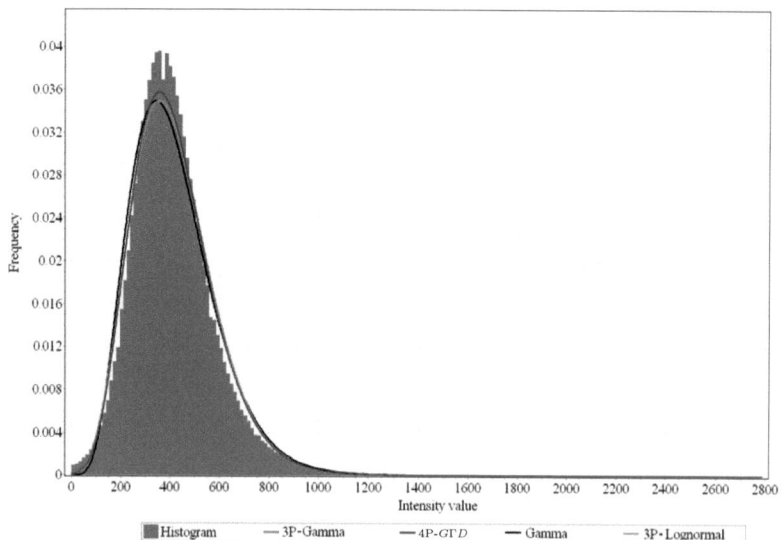

Figure 3.7.: Plot of the volume's normalized histogram and of the best four estimated pdfs: for the ceramic reference volume.

3.3.2 Experimental results

Parametric model	K-S distance	Rank
4P-$G\Gamma D$	0.0214	1
3P-Lognormal	0.0264	2
3P-Gamma	0.0273	3
Gamma	0.0317	4
$G\Gamma D$	0.034	5
Inv.Gaussian	0.036	6
3P-Weibull	0.055	7
Weibull	0.055	8
Lognormal	0.0623	9
Normal	0.066	10
Rice	0.068	11
3P-Inv.Gaussian	0.101	12
Nakagami	0.109	13
Rayleigh	0.111	14
2P-Rayleigh	0.128	15

Table 3.5.: Values of the K-S distance obtained using the different pdfs to model speckle in the ceramic reference volume.

increase of resolution, the hypothesis that each resolution cell contains a sufficient number of scatterers is not satisfied, therefore the central limit theorem cannot be invoked. The same remark applies for the Nakagami models which could not be the best fit to the SPA data. It was noticed that the pdf of the Rician distribution gave a better performance than the original Rayleigh's pdf (without the translation parameter). A possible explanation is that the Rician model was initially proposed for the case of non-fully developed scatterers. Nevertheless, it was not top ranked. Other models including Weibull/3P-Weibull, Inv.Gaussian and Normal models could not successfully provide the best fit to the speckle in SPA data. On the contrary, the proposed 4P-$G\Gamma D$ performed best for the CFRP and ceramic volumes, although it was slightly inferior to the 3P-Lognormal model for the aluminum volume. Thus, it can be seen that the speckle distribution depends on the material type, since the obtained best fitting model for CFRP and aluminum are not the same. Indeed, the visual appearance of the speckle in the layers at figure 3.4 is different from one material to another. The reason is because each material has a specific internal micro-structure.

To sum up, the 4P-$G\Gamma D$ could, in all cases, successfully track the statistical properties of the SPA volumetric data. Visual and quantitative results proved that, in case of CFRP and ceramic volumes, the 4P-$G\Gamma D$ provided better performance than all other parametric models. Although, in case of the aluminum SPA volume, it was not the best, it had still achieved the second rank after the 3P-Lognormal.

N_L	Fitting parametric model	ξ	ν	β	γ
1	4P-$G\Gamma D$	1.522	2.311	2408	501.38
2	4P-$G\Gamma D$	1.568	2.067	2695	467
3	4P-$G\Gamma D$	1.685	1.767	3107	481.8
4	4P-$G\Gamma D$	1.739	1.643	3237	486.16
5	4P-$G\Gamma D$	1.637	1.81	2978	430.8
6	4P-$G\Gamma D$	1.535	1.912	2691	432.6
7	4P-$G\Gamma D$	1.378	2.241	2204	433
8	4P-$G\Gamma D$	1.241	2.674	1727	432.6
9	4P-$G\Gamma D$	1.151	3.108	1385	431.8
10	4P-$G\Gamma D$	1.096	3.415	1185	431.7
92	4P-$G\Gamma D$	0.823	5.32	334.7	289.35

Table 3.6.: Variation of the fitting parametric model and its estimated parameters with the increase of the amount of considered layers.

Influence of the number of layers on the noise distribution

The above mentioned speckle modeling results were conducted on volumetric 3D SPA data. The aim now is to investigate how the estimated pdf varies with the variation of the number of layers inside the reference volume. The investigation is carried out on the CFRP reference volume. Let N_L be the number of layers inside a volume. By increasing N_L, the number of voxels inside the volume will be incremented. N_L was varied between 1 and 10, and the estimated best ranked pdf was found for each value of N_L.

When $N_L = 1$, the first layer of the reference volume is considered, the pdf of the 4P-$G\Gamma D$ distribution remained the best fit to the data. Then the number of layers N_L in depth z direction was increased to 2 until 10. The obtained results are shown in table 3.6. As it can be noticed, all parameters ξ, ν, γ and β vary with the number of layers considered due to the change in the intensity values statistics reflecting a change in the speckle noise (see figure 3.8). Nevertheless, the pdf of the 4P-$G\Gamma D$ stayed ranked first. Therefore, it represents a stable and accurate model for the speckle in our CFRP SPA data.

After the study of speckle modeling and the investigation of speckle noise in SPA data, the next section is devoted to present a survey of applied methods for speckle noise reduction which represents a key step in many segmentation approaches.

3.4. Speckle noise reduction

The estimation of the speckle noise allows to find a mathematical model that fits intensity levels in the image. Another kind of modeling is necessary to relate the

3.4 Speckle noise reduction

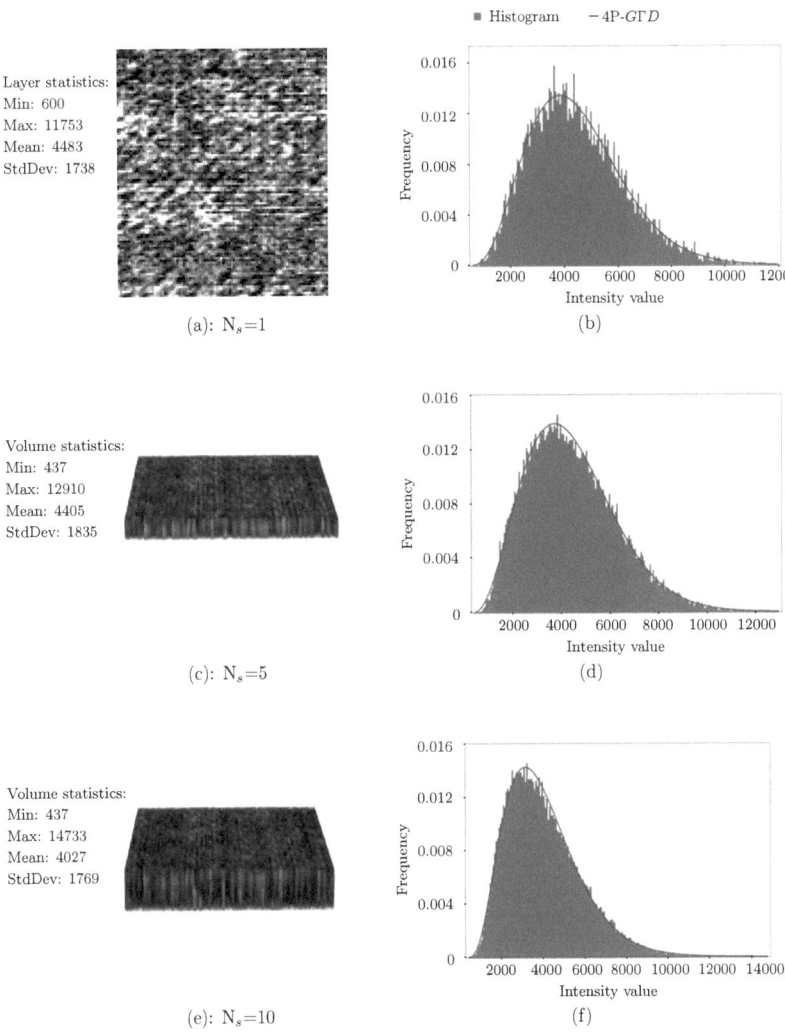

Figure 3.8.: Influence of the number of layers N_L on the fitting model to speckle in the CFRP SPA data: volumes are shown for $N_L = 1$ (a), $N_L = 5$ (c) and $N_L = 10$ (e). The corresponding plots, respectively (b), (d) and (f), of the normalized histogram and the best estimated pdf reveal that the pdf of the 4P-$G\Gamma D$ distribution still provides the best fit for the data. This is despite the variation in intensity values statistics and thus histogram shapes between $N_L = 1$, 5 and 10.

noisy image to the ideal free noise image. If available, this model should theoretically allow to restore the noise free intensities from the experimental ones.

In the literature, two models were proposed to take into account the characteristics of speckle noise which is considered to be a multiplicative noise. The first model presented by Jain [141] is:

$$u(x,y,z) = v(x_i) \cdot \varepsilon_m(x,y,z) + \varepsilon_a(x,y,z) \qquad (3.16)$$

where v is the noise free image, ε_m is the multiplicative noise (i.e., the speckle noise) and ε_a is the additive noise. Note that the effect of additive noise (such as sensor noise) is considerably small compared with that of multiplicative noise [142, 143].

The second model is more recent and used by [144, 145, 146, 147, 148] in which the general speckle model is given by:

$$u(x,y,z) = v(x,y,z) + v^\psi(x,y,z) \cdot \eta(x,y,z) \qquad (3.17)$$

where η is a zero-mean Gaussian noise and $\psi \in \mathbb{R}$ is a factor depending on the ultrasound devices and additional processing related to image formation. This model is more flexible and less restrictive than the first model and is able to capture reliably image statistics [148].

Now, returning to the speckle noise reduction, filtering techniques are used to reduce the noise level while preserving details in the ultrasound image. This process is called image enhancement. Filtering techniques can be generally separated into two different categories: spatial domain- and transform-domain-based filtering techniques.

3.4.1. Spatial domain filtering techniques

The spatial domain techniques are based on the image statistics. They attempt to balance between speckle reduction and details preservation via filtering. Spatial domain filtering can be expressed as:

$$\widetilde{v}(x,y,z) = g(u(x,y,z)) \qquad (3.18)$$

where $\widetilde{v}$ is the filtered image, $\widetilde{v}(x,y,z)$ is the new value of $u(x,y,z)$ and $g(\cdot)$ is an operator on the noisy image u defined over some neighborhood of voxel at coordinates (x,y,z). In fixed filtering, a mask $B(x,y,z)$ of a specific size (defining the neighborhood of voxel at (x,y,z)) is moved over the complete image. At each iteration, the central value of the mask will be replaced by the result of the function g applied (i.e. convolution for linear filters, partial sorting for median filter etc.) on the intensity values of the pixels in the mask B.

In adapted filtering, largely used in ultrasound image enhancement, the weights and size of filters are determined according to the image local statistics and position inside the image. Early works included classical filters: Lee filter [149], Kuan filter [150] and

3.4.1 Spatial domain filtering techniques

Frost filter [151]. These filters consider the multiplicative noise model and include the use of linear minimum mean square error. Their main advantage is that, they are easy to implement and could to a certain degree reduce the speckle noise. Nevertheless, many details in the image are lost, especially weak and diffuse edges.

An adaptive Median filter was also used for speckle reduction by Loupas et al. [152] and Karaman et al. [153]. This non linear filter can effectively reduce the speckle but many useful details are lost. Wiener filter is as well used to reduce the speckle noise [154], nevertheless, this filter is developed mainly for reducing additive random noise. To address this issue, Jain [141] proposed to convert the multiplicative into an additive noise by taking the logarithm of the image, and consequently apply the Wiener filter.

Yu and Acton [155] proposed an anisotropic diffusion filtering method based on Lee filter called Speckle Reducing Anisotropic Diffusion (SRAD). Aja-Fernandez and Alberola-Lopez [156] modified the SRAD filter to rely on the Kuan filter rather than the Lee filter. They call this modified approach the Detail Preserving Anisotropic Diffusion (DPAD).

Krissian et al. [145], [157] extended the SRAD filter to a matrix anisotropic diffusion, allowing different levels of filtering across the image contours and in the principal curvature directions. In their contribution, the authors showed a relation between the local directional variance of the image intensity and the local geometry of the image. Thus, this filter takes into account the local image geometry.

Sheng et al. [143] proposed an approach based on Total Variation (TV) minimization for speckle suppression. Tay et al. [158] proposed a stochastically driven filtering method called Squeeze Box Filter (SBF) method to despeckle B-scans. This method iteratively removes outliers and reduces local variance at each pixel. The main drawback of this method is that it smooths the edges. Nevertheless, it effectively reduces the speckle noise in the image. Thangavel et al. [159] compared 16 different noise removing algorithms applied to medical ultrasonic images of prostate. Results showed that a hybrid filter of the mean and the median filters (M3 filter) performed better than others filters.

Buades el al. [160] introduced a new filtering method based on the redundancy properties inside images: the Non Local Means filter (NL-means). This method is based on the idea that in any image, pixels (or voxels) with similar values exist which are not necessarily direct neighbors (like in conventional filtering approaches). The NL-means filter was extensively studied, updated and successfully used in many contributions (see [161, 162, 163, 164, 165]). This filter was updated by Coupé et al. [166] to the Optimized Bayesian NL-means and applied to Magnetic Resonance Imaging (MRI) [166] and ultrasound data [148]. Compared to other well established filtering methods [148], the NL-means and Optimized Bayesian NL-means filters proved quantitatively to be much more efficient at speckle noise reduction and are qualitatively considered to relatively preserve edges.

3.4.2. Transform-domain filtering techniques

Transform domain techniques are based on the transformation of the original image into another domain in order to take advantages of certain image characteristics which are not seen in the original domain. In fact filtering in transform domain, namely in frequency domain, can be more effective than in the original domain. For example, when transformed into frequency domain, via Fourier transform, smooth regions of the image will correspond to low frequency components while image details, edges and noise will appear as high frequency components. Frequency based transform filtering techniques are well reputable and demonstrated remarkable performance improvements [167]. Other commonly applied techniques are wavelet based speckle reduction methods [168, 169]. Wavelet transform based methods saw extensive usage in ultrasound image despeckling; Some applications of Wavelets on medical ultrasound images can be found in [170, 171, 142].

Hence different approaches have been used to reduce the speckle noise but none of these methods includes an explicit usage of the noise distribution model in the filtering process. It seems that the most successful filtering approaches are the data-dependent approaches, which aim at reducing the influence of the neighboring voxels dissimilar to the voxel under study by exploiting the redundancy that appears in the image (such as the NL-means filter approach which will be detailed in paragraph 4.2.4 of chapter 4).

3.5. Conclusion

In this chapter, a review concerning the speckle noise in ultrasound data was presented. First, an examination of different theoretical and empirical techniques for speckle modeling in SAR and ultrasound images was conducted. Then, the speckle noise in SPA data was investigated. An extension of the original pdf of the $G\Gamma D$ distribution was proposed to model speckle in SPA data. Experimental results were reported for three different materials: CFRP, ceramic and aluminum.

Although the 4P-$G\Gamma D$ model is in most cases the best fit to the experimental data, nevertheless it was shown (for the aluminum specimen) that the fitting model is not the same for all materials types. Thus, the model is dependent of the material micro-structure. Since the ultrasound technique can be used to inspect a wide range of materials, the preference in this work is not to further use the speckle model because an analysis chain with minimal prior knowledge about the inspected material is required.

The last part of this chapter was devoted to review the main approaches followed to reduce speckle noise in ultrasound images. The most promising results seem to be given by filters which explore the redundancy in images.

4. Proposed method for automated segmentation and classification of SPA data

Contents

4.1.	Analysis chain	53
4.2.	Segmentation procedure	54
	4.2.1. Overview	54
	4.2.2. Definitions	55
	4.2.3. Data correction	57
	4.2.4. Data enhancement	59
	4.2.5. Detection of entrance and backwall layers	65
	4.2.6. Thresholding	68
	4.2.7. Features extraction	72
4.3.	Classification procedure	75
	4.3.1. Basic concept and definitions	76
	4.3.2. Information combination	78
	4.3.3. Data fusion classification	79
4.4.	Conclusion	89

This chapter introduces the analysis chain proposed to evaluate the information contained in the 3D ultrasound volumes. The next section will give an overview on the analysis chain. In section 4.2, detailed explanations of each step of the segmentation procedure are presented. The classification procedure is then detailed in section 4.3.

4.1. Analysis chain

As presented in figure 4.1, the proposed analysis chain is composed of two procedures: segmentation and classification. The input of the chain is a 3D ultrasound volume produced by the acquisition system. The output of the chain is a list of defects where each defect is described by geometrical and intensity based features.

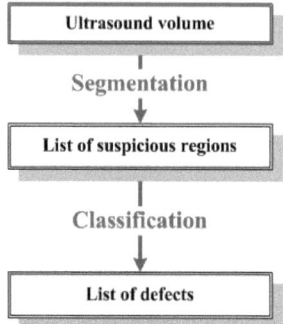

Figure 4.1.: Flow chart of the proposed analysis chain.

The objective of the segmentation procedure is to locate and characterize suspicious regions by a list of features. A major difficulty in ultrasound image segmentation is the presence of speckle noise distributed all over the volume. The compromise is to detect fine defects without noise detection. Another difficulty is the detection of defects located near the entrance and backwall (or end) layers. Strong echoes reflected from the surface and the backwall of the inspected specimen can hide information obtained from reflections by nearby discontinuities.

Thus, the number of suspicious regions after segmentation can be high. Therefore, a classification procedure is necessary to distinguish the appropriate type (true or false defect) of each region.

4.2. Segmentation procedure

4.2.1. Overview

The proposed segmentation procedure is resumed in figure 4.2. Besides the thickness estimation by the detection of entrance and backwall layers, the main characteristic of the segmentation procedure is a reference-less inspection, i.e. there is no need for any a priori knowledge of the geometry of the specimen. However, the segmentation is restricted to planar geometries. First step of the segmentation is the data correction in the input ultrasound volume where voxels with invalid values are corrected. Then, noise reduction takes place by filtering the corrected volume layer by layer in depth direction. Afterward, the entrance and/or backwall layers are detected and then, the internal volume is extracted from the pre-processed volume.

The segmentation is later carried out on the internal volume by applying a thresholding method on voxel intensities and then connecting similar voxels to form labeled suspicious regions. Each region is characterized by a list of features.

4.2.2 Definitions

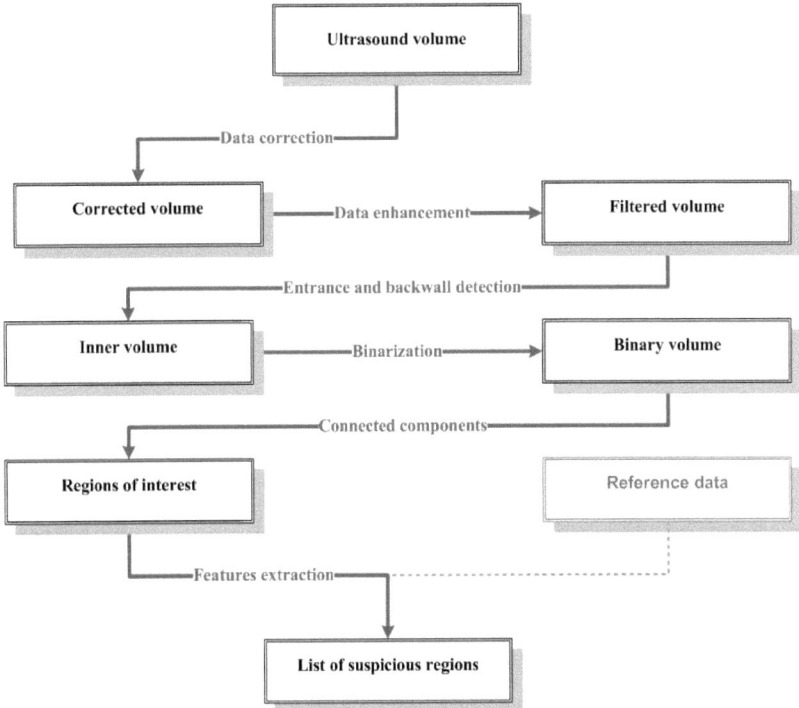

Figure 4.2.: Flow chart showing the different stages of the segmentation procedure.

4.2.2. Definitions

Before further explanations, let us first remind of the definitions of the volume mapping introduced in chapter 3.2.2 and consider some further notations (see figure 4.3) defined in a 3D Cartesian coordinates system:

- For $P, S, T \in \mathbb{N}$, $\Omega^{P,S,T} \subset \mathbb{N}^3$ is a set of coordinates defined as:

$$\Omega^{P,S,T} = \{(x,y,z) \in \mathbb{N}^3 : 1 \leqslant x \leqslant P;\ 1 \leqslant y \leqslant S;\ 1 \leqslant z \leqslant T\}$$

  where P, S and T are respectively the dimension of the volume's grid.

- The volume u denote the original noisy volume defined over the domain $\Omega^{P,S,T}$ as:

$$u : \begin{array}{rcl} \Omega^{P,S,T} & \longrightarrow & \mathbb{R}_+ \\ (x,y,z) & \longmapsto & u(x,y,z) \end{array}$$

$u(x,y,z) \in \mathbb{R}_+$ is the noisy intensity observed at coordinates (x,y,z).

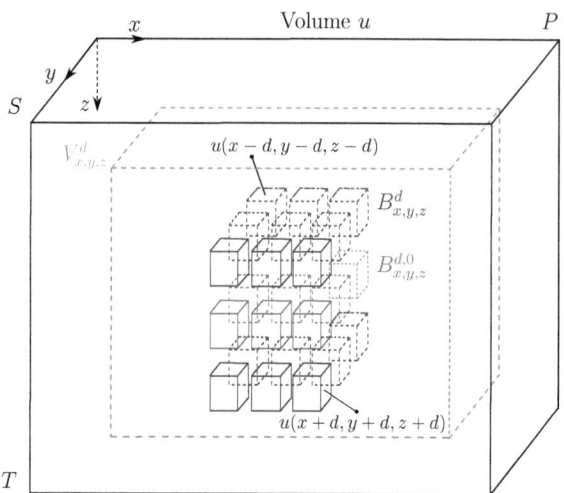

Figure 4.3.: Illustration of the coordinates system and the notations for $d = 1$. The searching window $V_{x,y,z}^M$ is illustrated by the dashed green box. The local 3D block $B_{x,y,z}^d$ is illustrated by the set of blue and red boxes. The 2D local block $B_{x,y,z}^{d,0}$ is illustrated by the set of red boxes. In this example, the 3D block $B_{x,y,z}^d$ and the 2D block $B_{x,y,z}^{d,0}$ are centered at the same coordinates (x, y, z).

- The volume v denotes the noise free volume which has the same dimensions as volume u.

- For $M \in \mathbb{N}$ with $2M < \min\{P, S, T\}$ (3D operators), $\Omega_M^{P,S,T} \subset \Omega^{P,S,T}$ is defined as:

$$\Omega_M^{P,S,T} = \{(x, y, z) \in \Omega^{P,S,T} : M < x \leq P{-}M;\ M < y \leq S{-}M;\ M < z \leq T{-}M\}$$

- For $M \in \mathbb{N}$ with $2M < \min\{P, S\}$ (2D operators), $\Omega_{M,0}^{P,S,T} \subset \Omega^{P,S,T}$ is defined as:

$$\Omega_{M,0}^{P,S,T} = \{(x, y, z) \in \Omega^{P,S,T} : M < x \leq P - M;\ M < y \leq S - M\}$$

- $V_{x,y,z}^M$ is a 3D window (called searching window) centered at the voxel of coordinates $(x, y, z) \in \Omega_M^{P,S,T}$ and of size $[2M+1, 2M+1, 2M+1]$:

$$V_{x,y,z}^M = \{(i, j, k) \in \Omega^{P,S,T} : x - M \leq i \leq x + M; y - M \leq j \leq y + M;\\ z - M \leq k \leq z + M\}$$

- $V_{x,y,z}^{M,0}$ denotes the 2D searching window centered at the voxel of coordinates

4.2.3 Data correction

$(x, y, z) \in \Omega_{M,0}^{P,S,T}$ of size $[2M+1, 2M+1, 1]$:

$$V_{x,y,z}^{M,0} = \{(i,j,k) \in \Omega^{P,S,T} : x - M \leq i \leq x+M; \ y - M \leq j \leq y+M; \ k = z\}$$

- For $d \in \mathbb{N}$ and $d \leq M$, $B_{x,y,z}^{d} \subset \Omega^{P,S,T}$ denotes the local 3D neighborhood (block) centered at the voxel of coordinates $(x,y,z) \in \Omega_M^{P,S,T}$ and of size $[2d+1, 2d+1, 2d+1]$:

$$B_{x,y,z}^{d} = \{(i,j,k) \in \Omega^{P,S,T} : x-d \leq i \leq x+d; \ y-d \leq j \leq y+d; \ z-d \leq k \leq z+d\}$$

- For $d \in \mathbb{N}$ and $d \leq M$, $B_{x,y,z}^{d,0} \subset \Omega^{P,S,T}$ denotes the 2D local block, centered at the voxel of coordinates $(x,y,z) \in \Omega_{M,0}^{P,S,T}$ and of size $[2d+1, 2d+1, 1]$:

$$B_{x,y,z}^{d,0} = \{(i,j,k) \in \Omega^{P,S,T} : x-d \leq i \leq x+d; \ y-d \leq j \leq y+d; \ k = z\}$$

- $\mathbf{u}(B_{x,y,z}^{d}) = [u(x-d, y-d, z-d), \cdots, u(x,y,z), \cdots, (x+d, y+d, z+d)]$: is a vector of size $(2d+1)^3$ gathering the intensities of voxels inside the 3D block $B_{x,y,z}^{d}$.

  Vector elements are accessible via $\mathbf{u}^{(p)}(B_{x,y,z}^{d})$ where the index $p \in [1, (2d+1)^3]$.

- $\mathbf{u}(B_{x,y,z}^{d,0}) = [u(x-d, y-d, z), \cdots, u(x,y,z), \cdots, (x+d, y+d, z)]$: is a vector of size $(2d+1)^2$ gathering the intensities of voxels inside the 2D block $B_{x,y,z}^{d,0}$. The same index $p \in [1, (2p+1)^2]$ allows to access the elements of this vector.

4.2.3. Data correction

During the inspection, the transducer moves with a specified speed over the surface of the specimen (typically 70 mm/s). The inspection speed needs to be complemented with adequate hardware architecture and efficient software implementation of reconstruction algorithms able to track and use all the received data. It was noticed that when a 3D inspection is conducted, points with no valid values are obtained. This causes the appearance of black voxels in the reconstructed volume (see figure 4.4). The higher the inspection speed, the more black voxels appear in the volume. Invalid (or defect) voxels interpolation is necessary to correct the received data.

To interpolate the invalid voxels, a method based on a modified median filter is proposed where a block $B_{x,y,z}^{d}$ is applied over the volume. If the central voxel in the block is null then, it is replaced by the median value of all non null voxels inside the block (see algorithm 2). The position of the corrected voxel in the layer is saved into a map, which can serve in the classification step afterward. If the central voxel is not null then it will not be modified.

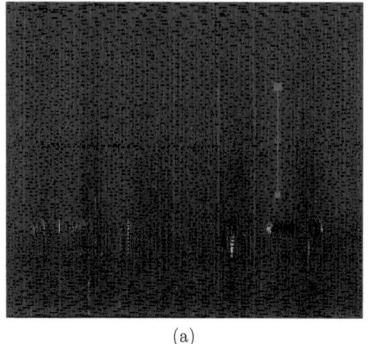 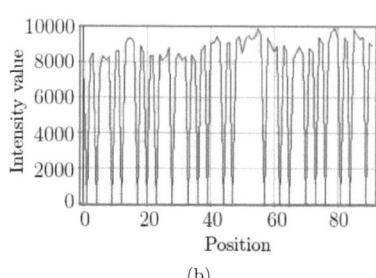

Figure 4.4.: (a) xy view of a layer of a CFRP plate where invalid voxels texture appears. (b) Intensity profile corresponding to the red line tracker where the sudden drops of intensity values to zero can be noticed.

The interpolation can be either applied in 2D[1] or 3D. However, it is important to remind that the 3D interpolation does not allow to interpolate all layers in the volume due to boundaries issues.

When using a 3D block $B_{x,y,z}^d$, at least the first and the last layer (for $d = 1$) will not be processed. Since these particular layers could be part of the entrance and backwall of the sample, it is important for the ulterior stages to correct these two layers. While by using a 2D block, all layers will be processed. However, the 2D interpolation may be less efficient in correcting the voxels. Thus, both interpolations need to be quantitatively compared in order to decide whether interpolating in 2D give similar results to the 3D interpolation.

Algorithm 2 Defect voxel interpolation algorithm

Map=Zeros$[P, S, T]$ ▷ the volume Map is filled with 0
for $z \leftarrow d + 1 : T - d$ **do**
  for $x \leftarrow d + 1 : P - d$ **do**
    for $y \leftarrow d + 1 : T - d$ **do**
      if $u(x, y, z) == 0$ **then**
        $u(x, y, z) =$ median $\left\{ \mathbf{u}^{(p)}(B_{x,y,z}^d) \neq 0;\ p = 1 : (2d+1)^3 \right\}$ ▷ voxel interpolated
        Map$(x, y, z) = 1$ ▷ position of the interpolated voxel is registered
      else
        continue
      end if
    end for
  end for
end for

The interpolation algorithm is quantitatively evaluated on a volume without invalid

---
[1] To apply the interpolation algorithm 2 in 2D, two modifications are to do: z should loop from $1 : T$ and $\mathbf{u}^{(p)}(B_{x,y,z}^d)$ should be replaced by $\mathbf{u}^{(p)}(B_{x,y,z}^{d,0})$ with index $p : (2d+1)^2$

4.2.4 Data enhancement

voxels by means of two measures: the first measure is the difference measure (substitution) between the original voxel's intensity and the obtained interpolated values. The second measure is a similarity measure and is defined as the mean value of Pearson distance[2]. The difference measure simply indicates how much the interpolated value is close to the original value. However, a high difference measure does not necessarily represent a poor correction. In fact, the applied modified median filter can remove the impulse noise which corresponds to the case when the selected voxel has an extreme intensity value compared to its surrounding. In this case, the difference measure will be high, however, the voxel's intensity may be more similar to its surrounding neighborhood. Therefore, the mean value of Pearson distance ($\overline{d_P}$) is additionally considered as a measure that gives information about the degree of similarity between the interpolated value and its surrounding. The mean value of Pearson distance is computed between the neighboring voxels inside the original volume, after 2D and 3D interpolations. In order to have a fair comparison, the calculation is done considering all the 3D neighboring voxels of the selected voxel for both 2D and 3D interpolations:

$$\overline{d_P}(u(x,y,z)) = \frac{1}{(2d+1)^3} \sum_{s_1=-d}^{d} \sum_{s_2=-d}^{d} \sum_{s_3=-d}^{d} \frac{[u(x,y,z) - u(x+s_1, y+s_2, z+s_3)]^2}{u(x+s_1, y+s_2, z+s_3)} \quad (4.2)$$

where $u(x, y, z)$ stands for the voxel's intensity before and after 2D and 3D interpolations.

The evaluation approach is as follows:

- A voxel is randomly selected inside the volume and its intensity is set to zero.
- $\overline{d_P}$ is computed in the original volume.
- The voxel's intensity is interpolated using a 2D block of size $[3, 3, 1]$ (i.e., $d = 1$) and a 3D block of size $[3, 3, 3]$.
- The difference measure and $\overline{d_P}$ are computed after the interpolation.
- This procedure is repeated for an arbitrary number of voxels.

The results of the comparison will be shown in chapter 5.

4.2.4. Data enhancement

The main purposes of this stage are to: a) reduce the speckle noise without affecting important information such as low contrasted defects, b) enhance the edges and c) weaken or remove small isolated artifacts.

Different enhancement techniques are proposed in the literature. Among most effi-

---
[2]Pearson distance is discussed in paragraph 3.

Figure 4.5.: Delamination appearing only on layers 24 and 25 in a CFRP inspected volume. In this volume, the voxel size ($[x, y, z]$ in mm) is $[1,1,0.5]$, i.e. the resolution in z direction is 0.5 mm.

cient approaches is the approach which exploits the redundancy information in the data [160]. Based on this reason, the NL-means filter [148] was considered as technique to enhance the corrected data. The NL-means filter will be compared with two other spatial filters: median filter, M3 filter [159].

Filtering is applied layer by layer in the depth direction. There are two main reasons for this choice:

- Typically a thin discontinuity perpendicular to the wave propagation, like delamination, can be seen only on one or two consecutive layers of the reconstructed volume (see figure 4.5). Thus, there is a risk to loose defects if the filtering is applied in 3D. While by filtering the layer at a certain depth z, the existing defect in the layer can be enhanced without having a high risk to loose it.

- Filtering in 2D needs less time computation than in 3D because the considered number of points inside the filtering kernel is less in 2D than in 3D. For instance, when applying a 2D median filter of size $[5, 5, 1]$, at each pixels position, the number of voxels is 25 instead of 125 voxels in case of 3D median filter of size $[5, 5, 5]$. The choice to filter in 2D has a vital influence on calculation time for the NL-means filter since time consumption is its main drawback.

Non Local Means filter The NL-means filter was first introduced by Buades et al. [160]. The concept of the filter is derived from the idea that there exists a certain degree of redundancy in any image. NL-means filter tries to take advantage of this redundancy.

To elaborate, for every current voxel (or pixel) of the volume, voxels with similar intensity values and similar neighborhood exist and are not necessarily in the immediate vicinity of the current voxel. Thus, a degree of similarity is evaluated between several neighborhoods not directly close to the voxel. The similarity degree is regarded as a weigh contributing in the final restored intensity of the current voxel. The restored value of the current voxel is a weighted average of all voxels in the

4.2.4 Data enhancement

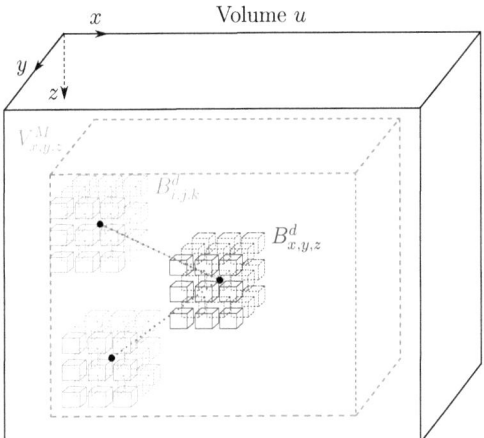

Figure 4.6.: Illustration of the NL-means filter: the restored intensity at voxel, of coordinates (x, y, z), center of the block $B^d_{x,y,z}$ is the weighted average of all intensities of voxels inside the search volume $V^M_{x,y,z}$.

image. The NL-means is claimed to allow the combination of two major important attributes of denoising algorithms: noise removal and edges preservation [166].

In the original definition of the NL-means filter, the similarity for each voxel is searched in the complete volume. Nevertheless for computational reasons, the search is limited only inside a search window $V^M_{x,y,z}$ of size $[2M+1, 2M+1, 2M+1]$ and centered at the current voxel of coordinates (x, y, z), (see figure 4.6).

Consider $\mathbf{u}(B^d_{x,y,z})$ and $\mathbf{u}(B^d_{i,j,k})$ as the vectors containing the intensities of voxels in the blocks $B^d_{x,y,z}$ and $B^d_{i,j,k}$ respectively centered at the current voxel of coordinates (x, y, z) and voxel of coordinates (i, j, k) (see figure 4.6). The restored intensity at (x, y, z) is defined as:

$$\widetilde{v}(x,y,z) = \sum_{(i,j,k) \in V^M_{x,y,z}} w_s\{u(x,y,z), u(i,j,k)\} \cdot u(i,j,k) \qquad (4.3)$$

where $w_s\{u(x,y,z), u(i,j,k)\}$ is the weight assigned to $u(i,j,k)$ in the restoration of $u(x,y,z)$. It measures the similarity between intensities in $B^d_{x,y,z}$ and $B^d_{i,j,k}$ under the assumption that:

$$w_s\{u(x,y,z), u(i,j,k)\} \in [0,1] \text{ and } \sum_{(i,j,k) \in V^M_{x,y,z}} w_s\{u(x,y,z), u(i,j,k)\} = 1.$$

Buades et al. [160] proposed to use the Gaussian weighted Euclidean distance, denoted by $\|\cdot\|^2_{2,\sigma}$ as a reliable measure for the comparison of similarity between blocks. This distance, adapted to any additive white noise [160], is a convolution of the L^2-norm with a Gaussian kernel of zero mean and standard deviation $\sigma > 0$. It is defined as [172]:

$$\|\mathbf{u}(B^d_{x,y,z}) - \mathbf{u}(B^d_{i,j,k})\|^2_{2,\sigma} = \sum_{s_1=-d}^{d}\sum_{s_2=-d}^{d}\sum_{s_3=-d}^{d} G_\sigma(s_1,s_2,s_3) \cdot$$
$$[u(x+s_1,y+s_2,z+s_3) - u(i+s_1,j+s_2,k+s_3)]^2$$

where $G_\sigma(s_1,s_2,s_3)$ is the 3D Gaussian kernel centered at (0,0,0) and of the same dimension as $\mathbf{u}(B^d_{x,y,z})$ and defined as:

$$G_\sigma(s_1,s_2,s_3) = \frac{1}{\sqrt{2\pi}\sigma} \exp\left(-\frac{s_1^2 + s_2^2 + s_3^2}{2\sigma^2}\right) \qquad (4.4)$$

The weight is then computed as:

$$w_s\{u(x,y,z), u(i,j,k)\} = \frac{1}{Z_{x,y,z}} \exp\left(-\frac{\|\mathbf{u}(B^d_{x,y,z}) - \mathbf{u}(B^d_{i,j,k})\|^2_{2,\sigma}}{h^2}\right) \qquad (4.5)$$

$Z_{x,y,z}$ is a normalization factor ensuring that the sum of all weights will be 1. It is computed as:

$$Z_{x,y,z} = \sum_{(i,j,k)\in V^M_{x,y,z}} \exp\left(-\frac{\|\mathbf{u}(B^d_{x,y,z}) - \mathbf{u}(B^d_{i,j,k})\|^2_{2,\sigma}}{h^2}\right) \qquad (4.6)$$

The parameter $h > 0$ is a smoothing parameter which controls the decay of the exponential function and thus the smoothing degree of the image. For very high values of h, the weights will be almost the same for all the voxels of $V^M_{x,y,z}$. In this case, the restored intensity $\widetilde{v}(x,y,z)$ will be the average intensity of voxels $V^M_{x,y,z}$ which represents a strong smoothing of the volume data. For very low values of h, the decay of the exponential will be strong which leads to negligible weights for voxels with not very similar neighborhood to the current voxel and significant weights for voxels with very similar neighborhood to the current voxel. Thus, the restored intensity will only be influenced by the latter voxels, this corresponds to a weak smoothing of the volume data.

As introduced in equation 3.17, the most recent model relating noise free intensities to noisy ones is: $u = v + v^\psi \cdot \eta$. Speckle is not an additive noise, rather it is a multiplicative noise. Thus, Coupé et al. [148] proposed to replace the $L2$-norm by Pearson distance which is more adapted to the multiplicative aspect of the speckle noise model. Pearson distance is given by:

$$d_P(u(x,y,z), u(i,j,k)) = \sum_{p=1}^{(2d+1)^3} \frac{[\mathbf{u}^{(p)}(B^d_{x,y,z}) - \mathbf{u}^{(p)}(B^d_{i,j,k})]^2}{(\mathbf{u}^{(p)}(B^d_{i,j,k}))^{2\psi}} \qquad (4.7)$$

As already cited in the noise study chapter, the factor ψ depends on ultrasound devices and additional processing related to image formation [148]. Based on the experimental estimation of the mean versus the standard deviation in Log-compressed

4.2.4 Data enhancement

images, Loupas et al. [152] showed that $\psi = 0.5$ is considered to be an adapted value to the model to better fit ultrasound data than the speckle multiplicative model (equation 3.16). This value was also adapted in the work presented in [148]. Thus, it appears relevant to keep using the value of $\psi = 0.5$ in our implementation of the NL-means (see algorithm 3).

Algorithm 3 NL-means algorithm in 2D

Size of the search window $[2M+1, 2M+1, 1]$ $\quad\triangleright$ Volume u has a size of $P \times S \times T$
Size of the block $[2d+1, 2d+1, 1]$
for $z \leftarrow 1 : T$ **do** $\quad\triangleright$ Filtering is done layer by layer
$\quad$ **for** $x \leftarrow M+1 : P-M$ **do**
$\quad\quad$ **for** $y \leftarrow M+1 : S-M$ **do** $\quad\triangleright$ Filtering voxels inside the layer
$\quad\quad\quad$ consider the block $B_{x,y,z}^{d,0}$ centered at (x,y,z)
$\quad\quad\quad$ consider the search window $V_{x,y,z}^{M,0}$ centered at (x,y,z)
$\quad\quad\quad$ $V_{x,y,z}^{M,0} = \bigcup_n B_{i_n,j_n,z}^{d,0}$, partition of the search window into overlapping blocks centered at (i_n, j_n, z) where $n \in \mathbb{N}$ is the distance between the centers of $B_{i_n,j_n,z}^{d,0}$
$\quad\quad\quad$ **for each** $B_{i_n,j_n,z}^{d,0}$ **do**
$\quad\quad\quad\quad$ compute its similarity weight with $B_{x,y,z}^{d,0}$ using Pearson distance (equation 4.7)
$\quad\quad\quad$ **end for each**
$\quad\quad\quad$ $\widetilde{v}(x,y,z) = \sum_{(i_n,j_n,z) \in V_{x,y,z}^{M,0}} w_s \{u(x,y,z), u(i_n,j_n,z)\} \cdot u(i_n,j_n,z)$
$\quad\quad$ **end for**
$\quad$ **end for**
end for

Median filter The median filter is commonly used to remove impulse noise. Depending on the kernel's size, it relatively preserves image edges and removes the isolated extreme values. Thus, it can be successful in reducing the speckle noise. It is easy to implement, to modify and was applied in numerous works to enhance the ultrasound data [173, 153, 174]. For a given layer at depth z, the median filter replaces the current voxel value $u(x,y,z)$ by the median value of its neighboring voxels in the layer.

$$\widetilde{v}(x,y,z) = \text{median}\{\mathbf{u}(B_{x,y,z}^{d,0})\} = \text{median}\left\{\mathbf{u}^{(p)}(B_{x,y,z}^{d,0});\ p = 1 : (2d+1)^2\right\} \quad (4.8)$$

At each kernel's position, the median value is found using the quick select algorithm [175]. It partially sorts the elements of $B_{x,y,z}^{d,0}$ and selects the median value.

M3 filter The M3 filter is a hybrid filter of the mean and the median filters. It replaces the current voxel value by the maximum value of the mean and median of its neighboring voxels. Intensity values of homogeneous regions are reduced and high frequency components are preserved [159]. Thangavel et al. [159] applied the M3 filter and 15 different noise removing algorithms, including the median filter, on medical ultrasonic images of prostate. Comparison between the different filters showed that the M3 filter performed better than all the other filters.

$$\widetilde{v}(x,y,z) = \max\{\text{mean}\{\mathbf{u}(B_{x,y,z}^{d,0})\};\ \text{median}\{\mathbf{u}(B_{x,y,z}^{d,0})\}\} \quad (4.9)$$

Data quality evaluation metrics

Different characteristics should be considered when evaluating the performance of an enhancement technique: noise reduction, details preservation, sharpness and contrast. While a qualitative visual analysis is a more subjective methodology, there is a need for an objective evaluation by means of quality metrics which can cover the different aspects of improvement in the enhanced data. Therefore, four statistical measures are computed to estimate the improvement in speckle noise reduction, details preservation and defects detectability after filtering. Since the filtering was done layer by layer in depth direction, the measures need to be computed in specific layers, where defects with low contrast are existing.

For a given depth z, let $l(x,y)$ be the original image and $L(x,y)$ the filtered image of size $N_x \times N_y$. σ_l^2 denotes the variance of the original image and σ_L^2 is the variance of the filtered images. The following metrics are computed:

- Root Mean Square Error (RMSE) measures the intensity change between the original and processed image and is defined as:

$$\text{RMSE} = \sqrt{\frac{\sum_{i=1}^{N_x} \sum_{j=1}^{N_y} [l(i,j) - L(i,j)]^2}{N_x N_y}}$$

    The RMSE is lower when pixels in the original and filtered image have close values.

- Noise Reduction Factor (NRF) measures directly the noise reduction and is computed as:

$$\text{NRF} = 10 \log_{10} \frac{\sigma_l^2}{\sigma_L^2}$$

    A higher NRF corresponds to a smoother image.

- Peak Signal to Noise Ratio (PSNR) is defined as:

$$\text{PSNR} = 20 \log_{10} \frac{g_{max}}{\text{RMSE}}$$

    where g_{max} is the maximum possible intensity value[3]. The PSNR is higher when the RMSE is low, i.e. when the intensities of the original and filtered image are close.

These first three metrics inform on the noise reduction or the global intensity change in the image. However, they do not inform on the compromise between noise reduction and edge preservation. Thus, another metric has been introduced, which is directly measured around a chosen defect's zone.

---

[3] $g_{max} = 2^{16} - 1$ for 16 unsigned bits images

4.2.5 Detection of entrance and backwall layers

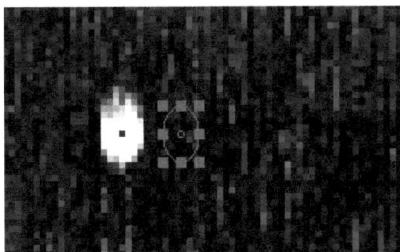

Figure 4.7.: CNR: defect zone and neighboring reference zone.

- Contrast to Noise Ratio (CNR) informs on the defect detectability after denoising and is defined as:

$$\text{CNR} = \frac{|M_{\text{def}} - M_{\text{background}}|}{\sqrt{\sigma_{\text{def}}^2 + \sigma_{\text{background}}^2}}$$

Where M_{def} and σ_{def}^2 are respectively the mean intensity value and variance of the defect's zone and $M_{\text{background}}$ and $\sigma_{\text{background}}^2$ are the corresponding mean and variance values of a neighboring reference background (see figure 4.7). A higher CNR indicates a better defect detectability.

4.2.5. Detection of entrance and backwall layers

The objective of this stage is to detect the layers which correspond to the entrance and backwall of the specimen. This allows to extract the inner volume denoted $\tilde{v}_{in}$ (volume of interest) located between the entrance and backwall layers.

The strong entrance and backwall echoes produced by the acoustic impedance mismatch between the coupling medium (water) and the inspected specimen appear over many consecutive layers in the reconstructed volume. Thus, they influence the intensity in the internal layers at depths near the surface and the end of the specimen. Moreover, in the settings of the inspection process, the inspection depth is manually set by the operator. For instance, for a part of 10 mm thickness, the expert can choose to inspect 15 mm in depth. Therefore in the reconstructed volume, the layers from 11 to 15 mm are not necessary and should be automatically eliminated from the total volume. By detecting the backwall layers, deeper layers will not be considered in the analysis. Additional important benefits can be gained by detecting the entrance and backwall layers. They are resumed as follows:

- Entrance and backwall layers contain valuable information which help into successfully distinguish defects from artifacts. For instance the shadowing effect, which can be clearly seen in the backwall layers (see figure 2.16), represents a clear indication of presence of a defect at a certain position z above the backwall layer.

- The detection of entrance and backwall echoes allows to estimate the thickness of the specimen without prior information.

- Entrance and backwall layers are characterized by higher intensity values compared to the inner volume. Therefore, it will be more simple to find an adequate threshold for $\widetilde{v}_{in}$ than to find the threshold considering the complete volume because in this case, the global histogram of the intensity values will be much influenced by the voxels of the entrance and backwall layers.

Indeed, the detection of entrance and backwall layers is a critical task because defects may be present near the surface or the backwall. In case when the corresponding layer(s) is (are) considered as entrance or backwall layer(s) then, those defects will not be detected. Therefore, an inner volume with a maximal size and less influenced by the strong entrance and backwall echoes is requested in order to detect all defects which appear in the input volume. In the reminder of this work, entrance and backwall layers will respectively be denoted by EE layers and BWE layers.

The detection of the EE and BWE layers can be seen as an edge detection issue where corresponding voxels are characterized by high intensities. The proposed algorithm will try to use this criterion by investigating the second derivative variation of intensity level in depth direction. To better explain the principle of the algorithm, let us again consider the CFRP volume shown in figure 2.16: the CFRP plate has a thickness of 8 mm, the volume dimensions ($[x,y,z]$) are $[345, 357, 161]$ voxels with a voxel size in z direction of 0.05 mm. By a visual evaluation of the data, it can be noticed that the EE layers begin at $z = 0$ and end at $z = 11$. At $z = 12$, the first defect starts to appear in the corresponding layer (see figure 4.8). The BWE layers start at $z = 146$ because high intensity values corresponding to strong echoes of the backwall start to clearly appear on this layer and end at $z = 160$ (see figure 4.9). Note that results shown in this stage will not be commented, they only serve to illustrate the explanations.

Proposed approach

The proposed approach to detect the EE and BWE layers relies on the mean value of intensity in each layer. By computing the mean intensity value of each layer, this approach will be restricted for specimens of planar geometries. Note, however, that the mechanical scanning system in the present experimental device can only be used to scan planar specimens (see figure 2.15). The obtained volume, containing the mean intensity of each layer, is shown in figure 4.10a. The corresponding mean value profile in depth direction is shown in figure 4.10b. Notice that the EE and BWE layers have higher mean values than other layers, but it is difficult to automatically specify where exactly do the EE layers and the BWE layers begin and end.

Thus, to detect the EE and BWE layers, the proposed procedure is as follows:

(1) Consider a single signal I gathering the mean intensity of each layer in the volume

4.2.5 Detection of entrance and backwall layers

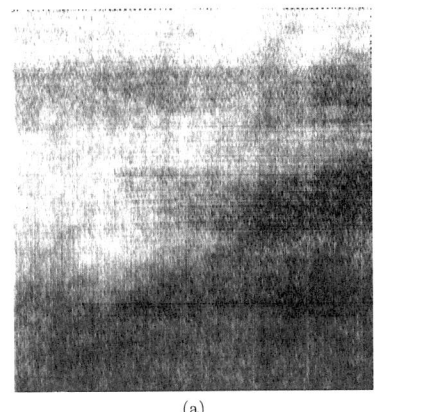
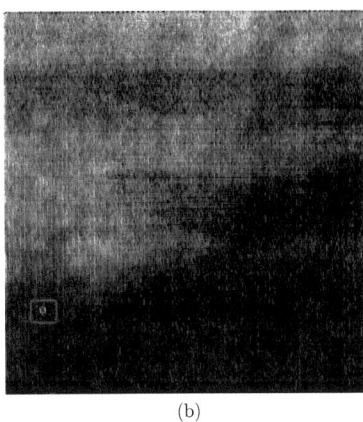

(a)   (b)

Figure 4.8.: (a) Last layer of the entrance layers. (b) First layer of the inner volume with the first defect (red box) starting to appear and the high intensity regions corresponding to strong echoes of the entrance fad out.

going from depth $z = 0$ to $z = T - 1$ (the end of the volume).

(2) Marr-Hildreth operator is applied on I.

Marr-Hildreth operator is an edge detection operator which consists of convolving the signal I with the Laplacian of Gaussian (LoG) function. It can be seen as an application first of a low pass filter (Gaussian function of zero mean) which at first stage will smooth the image followed by a high pass filter (Laplace operator) which will enhance the high frequencies. Remind that in one dimension, the Gaussian function is defined as:

$$G_\sigma(z) = \frac{1}{\sqrt{2\pi}\sigma} e^{-\frac{z^2}{2\sigma^2}}$$

The Laplacian of Gaussian is then:

$$\nabla^2 G_\sigma(z) = \frac{1}{\sqrt{2\pi}\sigma} \frac{z^2 - \sigma^2}{\sigma^4} e^{-\frac{z^2}{2\sigma^2}}$$

Applying the Marr-Hildreth operator corresponds to the convolution of $\nabla^2 G(x, \sigma)$ with the input signal I. The output signal is shown in figure 4.11.

$$I^*(z) = \nabla^2 G_\sigma(z) * I(z)$$

(3) The EE layers are finally to be searched between $z = 0$ and the middle of I^* ($z = \frac{T}{2}$) and the BWE layers are to be searched between $z = \frac{T}{2}$ and $z = T$. The end of the EE corresponds to the absolute maximum of the signal between 0 and $\frac{T}{2}$ and

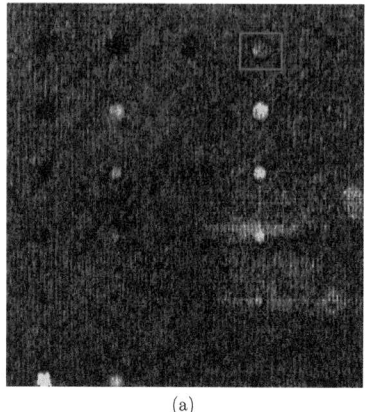 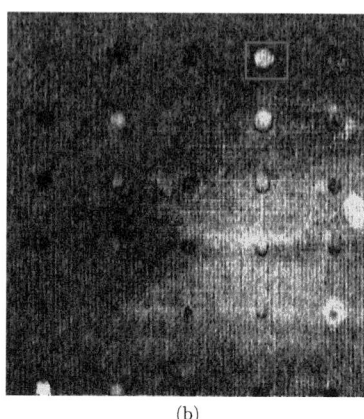

(a) (b)

Figure 4.9.: (a) Last layer of the inner layers. (b) First layer of the BWE where high intensity regions corresponding to echoes from the backwall start to strongly appear. Note that the defect at the top right (red box) is more intense in the BWE layer (b) than in the inner layer (a), thus there is a risk to miss such a defect which is very close to the backwall.

the start of the BWE corresponds to the absolute maximum of the signal between $\frac{T}{2}$ and T. The last backwall layer corresponds to the absolute minimum of $I^*(z)$ between $\frac{T}{2}$ and T. This layer is called BWE slice. The complete EE and BWE detection is resumed in algorithm 4.

The layers forming the entrance (same for backwall) are members of the EE volume (and BWE volume). Thus, the reconstructed 3D volume is divided at the end of this step into: EE volume, inner volume and BWE volume. The thickness of the specimen can be estimated as the difference between the z position of the BWE slice and the z position of the first layer of the EE volume.

4.2.6. Thresholding

Thresholding will be applied on the voxels of $\tilde{v}_{in}$ in order to divide them between background and foreground. Background voxels are not suspicious, thus, they are set to null. Foreground voxels are suspicious and are set to 1. Finding the optimal threshold is still not a trivial task even when working on the enhanced inner volume. Indeed, the noise will be reduced to a certain degree after filtering, however, it will not be completely removed. Furthermore, the remaining artifacts after filtering could have been amplified by the enhancement process. Thus, there will be foreground regions which correspond to false alarms, nevertheless mandatory is to have all existing defects as foreground even if they have weak contrast.

4.2.6 Thresholding

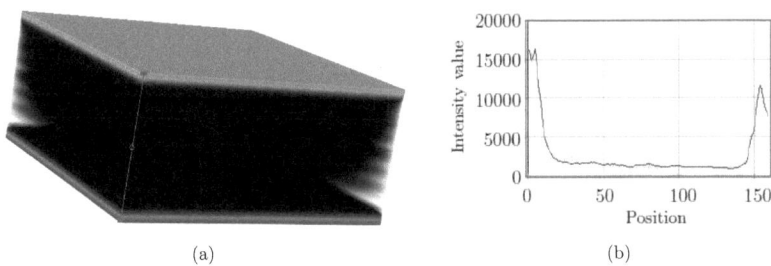

Figure 4.10.: (a) 3D view of the CFRP mean volume where the mean intensity of each layer is computed and presented. (b) Mean values profile along Z axis (signal I): EE is on the left position and BWE is on the right position.

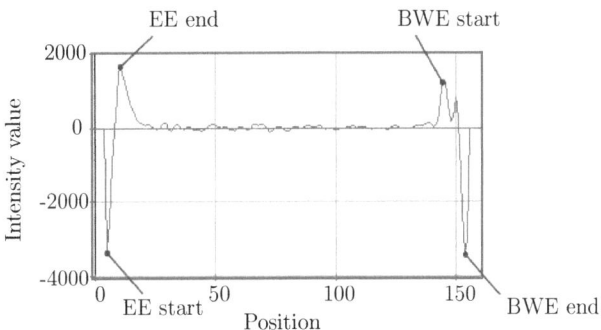

Figure 4.11.: Marr-Hildreth output signal where the end of EE and the start of BWE layers can be detected ($\sigma = 1$).

Algorithm 4 Entrance and backwall layers detection

$I = \text{Zeros}[T]$
$End_{EE} = 0$ ▷ Layer where EE ends
$Start_{BWE} = 0$ ▷ Layer where BWE starts
$End_{BWE} = 0$ ▷ Layer where BWE ends
  for $z \leftarrow 1 : T$ **do**
    $I(z) =$ mean intensity of layer z in $\tilde{v}$
  end for
Convolve I with LoG: $I^*(z) = \nabla^2 G_\sigma(z) * I(z)$
  for $z \leftarrow 1 : \frac{T}{2}$ **do**
    Search the maximum intensity value in $I^*(z)$ and save its position at End_{EE}
  end for
  for $z \leftarrow \frac{T}{2} : T$ **do**
    Search the maximum intensity value in $I^*(z)$ and save its position at $Start_{BWE}$
    Search the minimum intensity value in $I^*(z)$ and save its position at End_{BWE}
  end for

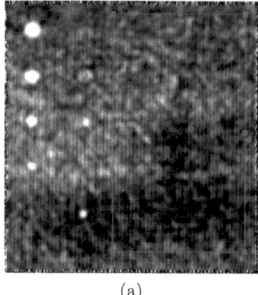 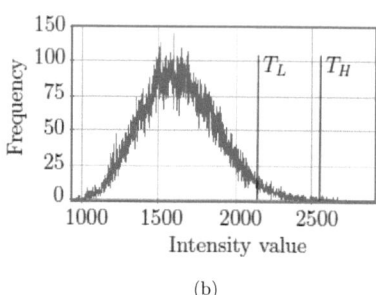

(a) (b)

Figure 4.12.: (a) Illustration of selection of a reference zone. (b) Histogram of intensities inside the reference zone: T_L and T_H are computed based on the statistics of intensity in the reference zone.

An attempt to automatically find a threshold without operator's intervention, by using the Otsu method [176], was done. Nevertheless, one major inconvenient of the Otsu method is that it gives a threshold even in the case where no defect exists in the volume. In addition, many low contrasted defects are lost with the automatic thresholding. Indeed, speckle noise can have a high contrast and can thus mask the presence of low contrasted defects. Therefore, a data dependent thresholding method is applied in order to keep all potential defects present in the volume.

Two thresholds are computed from the intensity statistics of the inner layers of a reference volume V_{ref}. The reference volume is a volume obtained by scanning a sample, without defects, of the same material type and geometry as the analyzed specimen. A high threshold $T_H \geq 0$ and a low threshold $0 \leq T_L \leq T_H$ can take values as follows:

$$T_L = M_{T_L} \cdot \text{mean}[V_{ref}] + S_{T_L} \cdot \text{std}[V_{ref}] \qquad (4.10)$$

$$T_H = M_{T_H} \cdot \text{mean}[V_{ref}] + S_{T_H} \cdot \text{std}[V_{ref}] \qquad (4.11)$$

where $\text{mean}[V_{ref}] \in \mathbb{R}_+$ and $\text{std}[V_{ref}] \in \mathbb{R}_+$ are the mean value and the standard deviation of intensities of the inner layers of V_{ref}, $M_{T_L}, M_{T_H}, S_{T_L}$ and S_{T_H} are weights of the mean intensity and standard deviation and take values $\in \{0, 1, 2, 3\}$.

For this work, no reference volumes were available. Therefore, the operator's intervention was necessary in order to manually select a reference zone Z_{ref} inside $\widetilde{v}_{in}$ in order to compute the thresholds. This is the only input required from the operator.

The two thresholds are then applied on all voxels of $\widetilde{v}_{in}$ as follows: voxels with intensity values higher than T_H are considered as foreground. Voxels with intensity values lower than T_L are attached to background. Voxels with intensity values higher than T_L and connected with a foreground voxel are finally considered as foreground. The advantage of this thresholding method, known as hysteresis threshold, is to

4.2.6 Thresholding

recover more precisely the size of suspicious regions (role of T_L) while preventing the noise detection as much as possible by application of the hard threshold T_H on intensity values.

Algorithm 5 Hysteresis thresholding algorithm

Binary Volume $V_B = \text{Zeros}[P, S, End_{BWE} - Start_{BWE} - 1]$ ▷ Volume V_B has a size of $\tilde{v}_{in}$
$Foreground = 255$
$Background = 0$
for $z \leftarrow 1 : End_{BWE} - Start_{BWE} - 1$ **do**
  for $x \leftarrow M + 1 : P - M$ **do**
    for $y \leftarrow M + 1 : S - M$ **do** ▷ non filtered border voxel will not be considered
      consider the block $B_{x,y,z}$ of size $d = 1$ centered at (x, y, z)
      if $\tilde{v}_{in}(x, y, z) \geq T_H$ **then**
        $V_B(x, y, z) = Foreground$
        for each voxel (i, j, k) inside $B_{x,y,z}$ **do**
          if $\tilde{v}_{in}(i, j, k) \geq T_L$ **then**
            $V_B(i, j, z) = Foreground$
          end if
        end for each
      end if
    end for
  end for
end for

After threshold application (algorithm 5), $\tilde{v}_{in}$ is divided into background and foreground. Voxels belonging to the same region are now to be connected to each other. For each foreground voxel at coordinates (x, y, z), the 26 neighboring voxels are checked and voxels which do belong to the foreground are connected to the voxel at (x, y, z). Connected voxels are grouped into one binary large object (blob) with a unique identification number (labeling) which additionally serves as an intensity level for the display of this label.

The selection of the optimal thresholds $\{T_L, T_H\}$ must be done in a training phase on a sample with a known number of defects. The approach is based on the quantitative analysis of the number of suspicious regions classified as defects versus the amount of false alarms.

In the case when the operator is not satisfied with the outputs given by the hysteresis thresholds, for example because a low contrasted defect is missing from the binary volume, another thresholding option (called manual threshold) is given. The idea is to manually select the low contrasted defect itself as a zone to compute the thresholds T_L and T_H. In this case, the default values of the hysteresis thresholds are set to $T_L = T_H = M_{\text{def}}$ where M_{def} is the mean intensity of the selected low contrasted defect.

4.2.7. Features extraction

After thresholding, each detected suspicious region will be characterized by a list of features. Computed features are centered principally around the measurement of the geometric properties and the intensity characteristics of detected blobs. Consequently, the measured features (names in italic) are divided into two categories:

Geometric features

- *BlobSize*: is the number of voxels of the blob.

- *BlobVolume*: knowing the Blobsize and the voxel size, the BlobVolume in mm^3 can be deduced.

- BlobPosition: the position of blob in 3D is given by the integer features *BlobPosX*, *BlobPosY* and *BlobPosZ*.

- Feret diameters: Feret diameters F_α serve to measure the features: length, width and elongation of suspicious regions. To compute the Feret diameters, 3D suspicious regions are projected into xy, xz and yz planes. Then in each 2D space, the Feret diameters are measured as the diameters of the projection over four directions: $\alpha = 0°$, $\alpha = 45°$, $\alpha = 90°$ and $\alpha = 135°$ (see figure 4.14). Afterward, the computation of length [in mm], width [in mm] and elongation in xy, xz and yz is done as follows:

    L_{xy}, L_{xz}, L_{yz} are the maximal values of Feret diameters in the respective xy, xz and yz planes.

    $$L = \max\{F_{0°}, F_{45°}, F_{90°}, F_{135°}\}$$

    W_{xy}, W_{xz}, W_{yz} are the minimal values of Feret diameters in the respective xy, xz and yz planes.

    $$W = \min\{F_{0°}, F_{45°}, F_{90°}, F_{135°}\}$$

    E_{xy}, E_{xz}, E_{yz} are given by: $E = \dfrac{L}{W}$.

- Maximum inscribing sphere (MIS) and minimum covering sphere (MCS): another way to describe the form in 3D of the blob is by finding the diameter d_1 of the maximum sphere which can be included inside the blob and the diameter d_2 of the minimum covering sphere which includes the blob. The corresponding features are then the radius *MISRadius* of the maximum inscribing sphere and the radius *MCSRadius* of the minimum covering sphere (see figure 4.14).

4.2.7 Features extraction

- *MISToMCSRatio* is the ratio between d_1 and d_2. It represents the distance between the form of the suspicious region and a 3D sphere, for which this feature is equal to 1. In addition, the ratio between the size of the minimum covering sphere and the BlobSize is computed, *MCSToBlobSizeRatio*.

- *BlobFillingLevel*: is the ratio between the blob and the size of the minimum covering 3D square which includes the blob. This is also another distance between the form of the suspicious region and a 3D square.

Intensity characteristics

- Intensity characteristics measured on the filtered volume $\widetilde{v}(x,y,z)$: for each blob, the mean and standard deviation of intensity values of the blob's voxels are measured. The blob's intensity characteristics are called *MeanValueOfBlob* and *StdOfBlob*.

  Moreover, the intensity characteristics of the neighborhood of the blob are computed. The neighborhood is specified using a mask of fixed size. For instance a mask size of 11 means that the blob is dilated by a $[11,11,11]$ 3D structuring element. Then, the neighboring region to the blob is computed by subtracting the blob from the obtained dilation. Obtained features for the neighborhood are the mean intensity value called *MeanValueOfNeighbourhood* and the standard deviation of intensity values *StdOfNeighbourhood*.

  Then, the feature *MeanBlobContrast* is measured as the difference between *MeanValueOfNeighbourhood* and *MeanValueOfBlob*.

- Contrast statistics of the blob (CS) are measured using $\widetilde{v}$ and a reference volume V_{ref}: in this case the blob of the filtered volume $\widetilde{v}$ and the corresponding zone of the reference volume are considered. This zone has the same size and spatial location as the blob. Afterward, the difference between the mean, minimum, maximum, standard deviation are computed. In addition, the difference between each voxel of the two zones is computed and stacked inside a buffer called MaximumBlobDifference (MBD). The outputs are the following contrast measures:

$$CSMean = |\text{mean}[V_{ref}] - MeanValueOfBlob|$$
$$CSMin = |\min[V_{ref}] - \min[\text{blob}]|$$
$$CSMax = |\max[V_{ref}] - \max[\text{blob}]|$$
$$CSStd = |\text{std}[V_{ref}] - \text{std}[\text{blob}]|$$
$$MBDMin = |\min[MBD]|$$
$$MBDMax = |\max[MBD]|$$
$$MBDMean = |\text{mean}[MBD]|$$
$$MBDStd = \text{Std}[MBD]$$

$$MBDVar = \text{Var}[MBD]$$

In the case when no reference volume is available, the reference zone Z_{ref}, selected in the thresholding stage (paragraph 4.2.6) can be used to compute the features which require a reference volume. In this case, the minimum, maximum, mean, standard deviation and variance of Z_{ref} are used in the calculus.

- *Shadow*: shadows are indeed traces of presence of discontinuities above them, this information is very valuable and is used as a feature called shadow. The simplest way to compute the shadow is by projecting the blob on the backwall (see figure 4.13), then to consider the mean intensity of the zone occupied by the projection in the BWE layer (zone called BWE_{blob}) and divide it by the mean intensity of the complete BWE layer (see figure 4.14).

$$\text{mean}[BWE_{blob}] = \frac{\sum\limits_{(x,y,z)\in BWE_{blob}} \widetilde{v}(x,y,z)}{|BWE_{blob}|}$$

where $|BWE_{blob}|$ is the number of voxels in the BWE_{blob} zone.

$$\text{mean}[BWE] = \frac{\sum\limits_{(x,y,z)\in BWE} \widetilde{v}(x,y,z)}{|BWE|}$$

where $|BWE|$ is the number of voxels in the BWE layer.

$$Shadow = \frac{\text{mean}[BWE_{blob}]}{\text{mean}[BWE]}$$

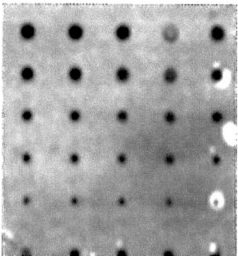

Figure 4.13.: BWE layer where shadows corresponding to defects can be clearly seen.

- *Damage index*: the damage index (DI) is defined as the ratio between the mean intensity of the 3D blob and the mean intensity of the zone (called EE_{blob}) occupied by the blob projection on the EE layer (see figure 4.14).

$$MeanValueOfBlob = \frac{\sum\limits_{(x,y,z)\in blob} \widetilde{v}(x,y,z)}{BlobSize}$$

4.3 Classification procedure

$$\mathrm{mean}[EE_{blob}] = \frac{\sum\limits_{(x,y,z) \in EE_{blob}} \tilde{v}(x,y,z)}{|EE_{blob}|}$$

$$DI = \frac{\mathrm{mean}[blob]}{\mathrm{mean}[EE_{blob}]}$$

Resumed in tables B.1 and B.2, in total 35 features are computed for each blob. They will form the input of the classification procedure described in the next section.

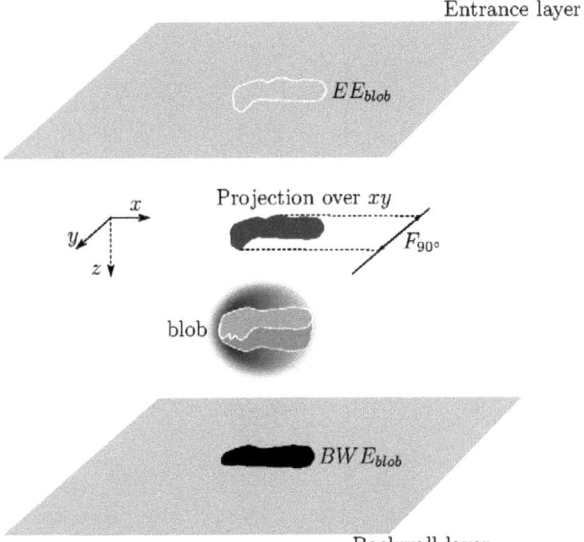

Figure 4.14.: Illustration of features in 3D space: the dark zone (BWE_{blob}) under the blob corresponds to its projection over xy in the BWE layer (defect's shadow), the projection of the blob over xy in the entrance layer corresponds to the EE_{blob} zone. The $F_{90°}$ is the Feret diameters in xy plane for a 90° angle. The minimum covering 3D sphere is also illustrated.

4.3. Classification procedure

The input data of the classification procedure is a list of segmented suspicious regions, among which some are true defects, while others are false alarms. Thus, the issue is to classify them into one of the two classes: class H_1=True Defect (TD) or H_2=False Defect (FD). A third class is introduced in order to take into account the ignorance, $H_3 = \{H_1, H_2\}$. This class allows us to model the part of doubt or uncertainty existing when the available information is not sufficient to decide between H_1 and H_2.

This type of uncertainty can be considered as epistemic uncertainty[4] which is due to a lack of knowledge. The Bayesian model of the probability theory represents a classical framework for reasoning with uncertainty. Nevertheless, the main disadvantage of this model is its inability to represent ignorance. Accordingly, last decades have seen the appearance of other theories such as the possibility theory proposed by Zadeh [178] and the theory of evidence, initiated by Dempster [179] and further developed by Shafer [180] and then Smets [181, 182, 183] under the name Transferable Belief Model (TBM).

The Dempster-Shafer evidence theory forms a theoretical framework for uncertain reasoning and has the particular advantage to enable handling of uncertain, imprecise and incomplete information. It overcomes the limitation of conventional probability theory .

4.3.1. Basic concept and definitions

In evidence theory, a fixed set of J hypotheses, called the frame of discernment, is defined and symbolized by $\Theta = \{H_1, H_2, \cdots, H_J\}$, where $J \in \mathbb{N}$. In Dempster-Shafer (DS) theory, all hypotheses are considered mutually exclusive[5] and exhaustive[6]. The frame of discernment Θ defines the working space for the application being considered since it consists of all propositions for which the information sources can provide evidence through the so-called confidence measure or mass function m. The mass function m is defined as a mapping from the power set 2^Θ, called the fusion space[7], to $[0,1]$ and it verifies the property that $\sum_{A \subseteq \Theta} m(A) = 1$, A is a subset of Θ.

$$m: \quad 2^\Theta \longrightarrow [0,1]$$
$$A \longmapsto m(A)$$

Here, A designates a single hypothesis H_i or a union of simple hypotheses (composite hypothesis). The value $m(A)$ represents a measure of belief that is assigned to subset $A \subseteq \Theta$ by a source of information and that cannot be committed to any strict subset of A [184]. An information source assigns mass values only to those hypotheses, for which it has a direct evidence. That is, if an information source cannot distinguish between two hypotheses A_i and A_j, it assigns a mass value to the set including both

---

[4]Epistemic uncertainty represents a lack of knowledge about the appropriate value to use for a quantity [177].
[5]$H_i \cap H_j = \varnothing$ for any $i \neq j$
[6]i.e., at least one hypothesis has to be true
[7]E.g., if $\Theta = \{H_1, H_2, H_3\}$, the power set 2^Θ of Θ is the set of all hypotheses and all possible unions of hypotheses: $(\varnothing, H_1, H_2, H_3, \{H_1, H_2\}, \{H_1, H_3\}, \{H_2, H_3\}, \{H_1, H_2, H_3\})$ where $\varnothing$ is the empty set and $m(\varnothing) = 0$.

4.3.1 Basic concept and definitions

hypotheses $(A_i \cup A_j)$. This point is precisely the reason for us to choose the DS theory because it reflects the hesitation between two hypotheses.

Every subset $A \subseteq \Theta$ such that $m(A) > 0$ is called a focal set of m. If all focal sets are singletons (the cardinality of A denoted $|A|$ is 1), then the mass function is equivalent to a probability distribution. In fact, the main difference between the probability theory and DS theory is that, a mass function gives the possibility to assign a measure of belief to non singleton subset of Θ. Thus, a mass function can be seen as a generalized probability distribution.

A mass function m is:
- *Bayesian* if all focal elements are singleton. In this case, the mass function is equivalent to a probability distribution.
- *Vacuous* if the only focal set is Θ (total ignorance).
- *Simple* if it has only two focal sets including Θ.

A simple mass function m such that [185]:

$$\begin{cases} m(A) = 1 - w_A, & \forall A \subset \Theta \\ m(\Theta) = w_A \end{cases} \quad (4.12)$$

where $w_A \in [0,1]$, can be in this case be denoted as A^{w_A}. Consequently, a vacuous mass function can be denoted as A^1, $\forall A \subseteq \Theta$.

Equivalent representation of the mass function m are belief *bel*, plausibility *pl*, commonality q and conjunctive weight function w [185]. They are respectively defined, for all A and $B \subseteq \Theta$, as follows:

$$\begin{aligned} bel : \quad 2^\Theta &\longrightarrow [0,1] \\ A &\longmapsto bel(A) \end{aligned} \quad (4.13)$$

where $bel(A) = \sum\limits_{\varnothing \neq B \subseteq A} m(B)$, $\forall A \subseteq \Theta$.

$$\begin{aligned} pl : \quad 2^\Theta &\longrightarrow [0,1] \\ A &\longmapsto pl(A) \end{aligned} \quad (4.14)$$

where $pl(A) = \sum\limits_{B \cap A \neq \varnothing} m(B)$, $\forall A \subseteq \Theta$.

$$\begin{aligned} q : \quad 2^\Theta &\longrightarrow [0,1] \\ A &\longmapsto q(A) \end{aligned} \quad (4.15)$$

where $q(A) = \sum\limits_{B \supseteq A} m(B)$, $\forall A \subseteq \Theta$.

$$\begin{aligned} w : \quad 2^\Theta \setminus \Theta &\longrightarrow (0, +\infty) \\ A &\longmapsto w(A) \end{aligned} \quad (4.16)$$

The weights $w(A)$ for every $A \subset \Theta$ can be obtained from the commonalities q using the following formula [185]:

$$w(A) = \prod_{B \supseteq A} q(B)^{(-1)^{|B|-|A|+1}}$$
$$= \begin{cases} \dfrac{\prod_{B \supseteq A, |B| \notin 2\mathbb{N}} q(B)}{\prod_{B \supseteq A, |B| \in 2\mathbb{N}} q(B)} & \text{if } |A| \in 2\mathbb{N} \\ \dfrac{\prod_{B \supseteq A, |B| \in 2\mathbb{N}} q(B)}{\prod_{B \supseteq A, |B| \notin 2\mathbb{N}} q(B)} & \text{otherwise} \end{cases} \quad (4.17)$$

where $|A|$ and $|B|$ are the cardinals of A and B and $2\mathbb{N}$ denotes the set of even natural numbers.

4.3.2. Information combination

Depending on the independence and reliability conditions of available information sources, there exist different combination rules to combine mass functions given by different sources and defined on the same frame of discernment Θ.

Dempster orthogonal combination rule

The orthogonal combination rule of Dempster, denoted by $\oplus$, assumes that the information sources are independent (i.e., they are assumed to provide distinct, non overlapping pieces of evidence (i.e., mass values) [185]) and reliable. Mass functions m_1, m_2 from two different sources combined with Dempster's orthogonal rule result in a new function $m_1 \oplus m_2$, which carries the joint information, about hypothesis $A \subseteq \Theta$, provided by the two sources:

$$m_{1 \oplus 2}(A) = \begin{cases} 0 & \text{if } A = \varnothing \\ \dfrac{\sum_{B \cap C = A} m_1(B) m_2(C)}{1 - K} & \text{Otherwise} \end{cases} \quad (4.18)$$

$K = \sum_{B \cap C = \varnothing} m_1(B) m_2(C)$ is the mass assigned to the empty set $\varnothing$. It is interpreted as a measure of conflict between sources and it is introduced in equation 4.18 as a normalization factor. The larger K is, the more the sources are conflicting and the less makes sense to combine their mass values. As a consequence some authors, Smets in particular [181], require the use of the Dempster combination rule without normalization, the obtained new rule is called conjunctive combination. Indeed, when the conflict increases, the fused mass increases although it is not related to an increase of confidence.

Thus, the conjunctive rule $\bigcirc$, as proposed by Smets [181], also assumes that the sources are independent and reliable. Resulting mass function by usage of the conjunctive combination rule is denoted $m_1 \bigcirc\!\!\!\!\!\cap\, m_2$ and defined for all $A \subseteq \Theta$ as:

$$m_1 \bigcirc\!\!\!\!\!\cap\, m_2(A) = \sum_{B \cap C = A} m_1(B) m_2(C) \tag{4.19}$$

The conjunctive rule is thus equivalent to Dempster's rule without normalization. Both rules are commutative and associative.

Cautious conjunctive combination

In case when the sources of information are dependent, Denoeux [185] introduced the cautious conjunctive combination rule $\bigcirc\!\!\!\!\!\wedge$ to be applied in this case. For this combination rule, mass functions m_1 and m_2 are considered to be separable, i.e. they can be decomposed as conjunctive combinations of simple mass functions [180, 183, 185]:

$$m_1 = \bigcirc\!\!\!\!\!\cap_{A \subset \Theta} A^{w_1(A)} \tag{4.20}$$

$$m_2 = \bigcirc\!\!\!\!\!\cap_{A \subset \Theta} A^{w_2(A)} \tag{4.21}$$

where $A^{w_1(A)}$ and $A^{w_2(A)}$ are simple mass functions and weights $w_1(A)$ and $w_2(A) \in (0,1]$ for all $A \subset \Theta$. The combination of m_1 and m_2 using the cautious rule is given by:

$$m_1 \bigcirc\!\!\!\!\!\wedge\, m_2(A) = \bigcirc\!\!\!\!\!\cap_{A \subset \Theta} A^{w_1(A) \wedge w_2(A)} \tag{4.22}$$

In this equation, the operator $\wedge$ is the minimum operator. The cautious rule in addition to being commutative and associative, is idempotent, i.e. $m \bigcirc\!\!\!\!\!\wedge\, m = m$. Moreover it is distributive with respect to $\bigcirc\!\!\!\!\!\cap$:

$$(m_1 \bigcirc\!\!\!\!\!\cap\, m_2) \bigcirc\!\!\!\!\!\wedge\, (m_1 \bigcirc\!\!\!\!\!\cap\, m_3) = m_1 \bigcirc\!\!\!\!\!\cap\, (m_2 \bigcirc\!\!\!\!\!\wedge\, m_3) \tag{4.23}$$

The distributivity property explains why the cautious rule is more relevant than the conjunctive rule when combining dependent mass functions since the shared mass m_1 in equation 4.23 is not computed twice [185].

In a recent paper [184], the evidence theory was used in the study done on the fault diagnosis of railway track circuits. Condition of railway track circuits was examined using an inspection vehicle that delivered a measurement signal which needed to be classified into three classes: fault free, medium defect and major defect. Authors used the evidence theory framework to build the classifier and they compared the performance of cautious rule with the performance of conjunctive rule in the classification of defects of railways track circuits and found out that the cautious rule outperforms the conjunctive rule.

4.3.3. Data fusion classification

The data fusion classification (DFC) method [186] is based on the DS theory and has the goal to automatically classify each input segmented suspicious region as defect

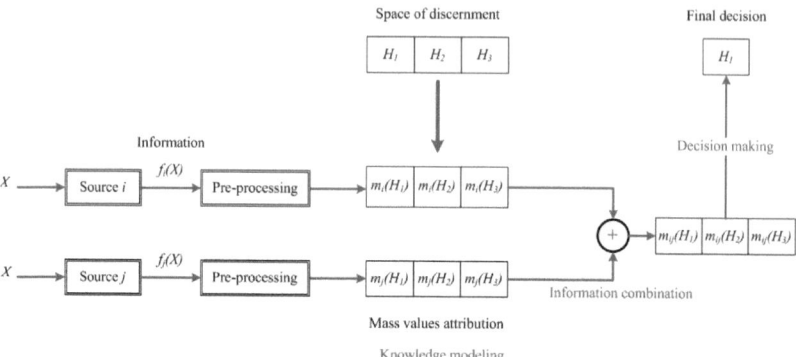

Figure 4.15.: Illustration of the data fusion classification steps in case of two sources: knowledge modeling, information combination and decision making.

or not, without expert supervision. This is done by analyzing the feature values extracted from an input region, assigning to it a confidence level (or mass value) and then combining mass values obtained from different features. Once the mass values are combined, a decision must be taken based on a threshold applied on the final mass (see figure 4.15).

In this work, the extracted features measured on each suspicious region (denoted X) represent the sources of information (denoted f_k, where $k = 1 \cdots 35$). Thus, in order to permit the fusion of these sources, feature values must be translated into mass values which will be assigned to the hypotheses of the frame of discernment $\Theta = \{H_1, H_2\}$. The adopted power set 2^Θ contains the following hypotheses:

- H_1: suspicious region is a defect.
- H_2: suspicious region is a false defect (i.e, false alarm).
- $H_3 = \Theta = \{H_1, H_2\}$: ignorance.
- $\varnothing$: empty set.

Conflict will occur when a source classifies a region as a defect and another source considers the region as false alarm. To avoid the conflict in our modeling approach, a source can give a mass value m only to the hypothesis H_1 and the rest is assigned to H_3, i.e. no mass is assigned to H_2. Thus, simple mass functions are obtained:

$$\begin{cases} m(H_1) = m \\ m(H_2) = 0 \\ m(H_3) = 1 - m \\ m(\varnothing) = 0 \end{cases}$$

The proposed approach consists of a learning phase and a validation phase, which are described hereafter. The approach will be illustrated using two classes of normally

4.3.3 Data fusion classification

distributed data points: 500 data points of class A standing for true defects (TDs) and 500 data points of class B standing for false defects (FDs). Let $X \in [1, 1000]$ be a random input data point which can be either element of class A or B. Let f_k be an information source: $f_k(X) \in \mathbb{R}$ represent the feature value of X.

Learning phase

The learning is conducted on a set of input data points (i.e., suspicious regions) of known classes (see figure 4.16). The learning phase can be decomposed into several steps:

Step 1: building regions of confidence which permit the translation from feature values to mass values.

Step 2: combining the mass values using different rules of combination.

Step 3: application of a decision rule on the obtained mass values.

Step 4: performance measurement and selection of the combinations with optimum classification rates..

The first step of the learning phase will be described in more details as it is the crucial step of the method. For each feature (i.e., information source f_k), the translation from feature values to mass values is done as follows:

- Computation of histogram of feature values for the two classes: class A (TDs) and class B (FDs) takes place. Each histogram is divided into 100 bins or intervals (see figure 4.16).

- In each histogram interval i, the proportion of points of class A is computed and denoted by $P_{A,B}(i) \in [0, 1]$.

$$P_{A,B}(i) = \frac{h_A(i)}{h_A(i) + h_B(i)} \quad (4.24)$$

where $h_A(i)$ and $h_B(i)$ are respectively the number of data points of class A (TDs) and class B (FDs) inside the interval $i \in [1, 100]$.

- Let $\Delta P_{A,B}$ be the derivative of $P_{A,B}$ computed as:

$$\Delta P_{A,B}(j) = |P_{A,B}(j+1) - P_{A,B}(j)| \quad (4.25)$$

where $j \in [1, 99]$. Consecutive intervals j and $j+1$ are merged into one region R_j if $\Delta P_{A,B}(j)$ is lower than a threshold DV:

$$\Delta P_{A,B}(j) < \text{DV} \quad (4.26)$$

The standard value of DV is fixed at 20%.

- In order to have significant regions (called regions of confidence), a minimum number of data points (N_c) inside each region R_j is imposed (a threshold, denoted by Perc, on the percentage of points inside each region is applied). Let N_M be the maximal number of data points found inside one region after merging consecutive intervals based on equation 4.26. The minimal number of points to be respected inside each region of confidence is:

$$N_c = \text{Perc} \cdot N_M \qquad (4.27)$$

The standard value of Perc is fixed at 10%.

Let T_R, $1 \leq T_R \leq 100$, be the total number of obtained regions of confidence. Each region R_j is characterized by the proportion of points of class A ($P_{A,B}(R_j)$) inside it.

- Mass values are attributed to each region of confidence as follows:

$$\begin{cases} m(H_1) = m(R_j) = P_{A,B}(R_j) \\ m(H_2) = 0 \\ m(H_3) = 1 - m(H_1) \\ m(\varnothing) = 0 \end{cases}$$

The regions of confidence obtained for the example of figure 4.16 are illustrated on figure 4.17.

- Fuzzy transitions are defined between consecutive regions of confidence: a fuzzy set is attributed to each region with corresponding membership functions. Then, the final mass of the input data point X is obtained by the mass of each region of confidence weighted by the degree of membership of the feature value of X to the region (see figure 4.17). The mass attributed by the source (or feature) f_k to the input X is:

$$m(X \in H_1/f_k) = \sum_{j=1}^{T_R} \mu_j(f_k(X)) \cdot m(R_j) \qquad (4.28)$$

$$\sum_{j=1}^{T_R} \mu_j(f_k(X)) = 1$$

where R_j is the region of confidence and $\mu_j(f_k(X)) \in [0,1]$ is the degree of membership of the feature value of X to R_j.

In the second step, the obtained mass values are combined using:

- The conjunctive combination rule is used to combine sources pairwise, to combine the three sources which give the maximal mass values[8] (called DSF{3 max mass}) or all sources together (called DSF{all sources}).

---

[8]Each suspicious region has 35 single mass values given by the information sources (features). For each suspicious region, the maximal three mass values of individual features are found and combined using the conjunctive rule.

4.3.3 Data fusion classification

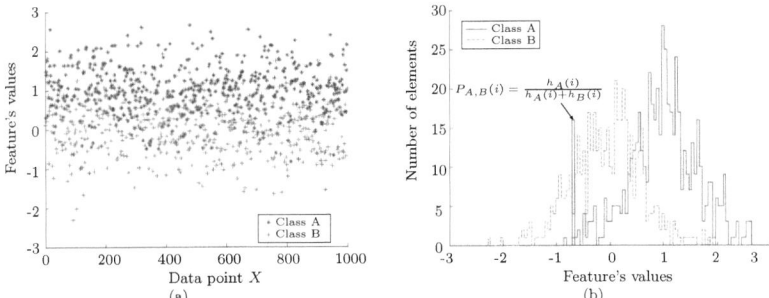

Figure 4.16.: Illustration of the starting step of the DFC method on two normal distributions. (a) For one feature, the values measured for the objects are represented. The overlapping between the two classes A (blue star) and B (red cross) is obvious. (b) The histogram of the values obtained for this feature is represented, class A (full line) and class B (dotted line), where the overlapping is also clearly visible.

- The cautious rule.

- The statistical combination rules: mean mass and median mass. The mean mass is the mean value of all the mass values attributed to X. It gives a sort of equal influence to the different sources. The median mass is the median value of all the mass values attributed to X. It allows to discount some sources when they are not in accordance with the others.

With a total number of 35 features, 635 different combinations are obtained including: each feature alone, all the DS combinations (pairwise, 3 sources and all sources), the cautious combination and the statistical combinations.

In the third step, the decision rule is applied:

- A decision threshold S_m is applied on the mass value $m(X \in H_1)$ of X to classify it as: an element of class A (TD) if $m(X \in H_1) \geqslant S_m$ or an element of class B (FD) if $m(X \in H_1) < S_m$

The last step of the learning phase is to select the optimal combinations:

- The combinations which classify at best the true and false defects are chosen based on selection criteria which are explained after the next paragraph.

Validation phase

The validation is done on a test database with input suspicious regions of known class and the following steps take place:

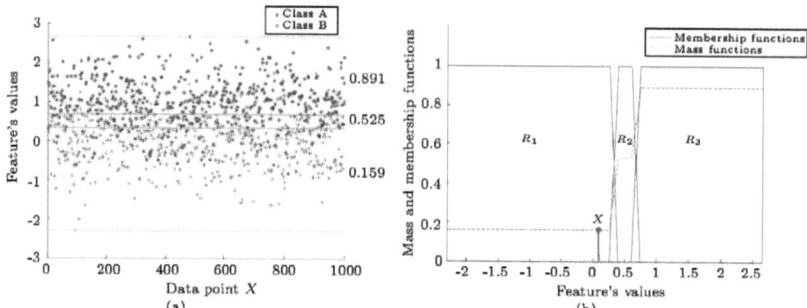

Figure 4.17.: a) Illustration of the regions of confidence and their corresponding mass values $m(H_1)$ in the right side of the graph. (b) Membership (blue full line) functions defined to obtain a fuzzy transition between the regions of confidence and mass function $m(H_1)$ (red dotted line) obtained after weighting the initial mass of the region by the membership function. In this example: $m(R_1) = 0.159$, $m(R_2) = 0.525$ and $m(R_3) = 0.891$. $\mu_1(f_k(X)) = 1$ and $\mu_2(f_k(X)) = \mu_3(f_k(X)) = 0$.

- First, features extraction is performed via the segmentation procedure.

- Then, the translation from feature values to mass values is done using the relation in equation 4.28 given in learning phase of the DFC method.

- Afterward, the optimal combinations selected in the learning phase are used here. Note here that there is no need to compute all the 35 features if the analysis chain user is only interested in detecting defects without more details about all their characteristics. In this case, only features which contribute in the selected combination need to be computed.

- Performances on the test database are then compared with the performances obtained during the learning phase.

Performance evaluation

To evaluate the performance of a source in discriminating between two classes, the well known Receiver Operating Characteristics (ROC) graphs and some statistical classification rates are used. Additionally, a global classification rate dedicated to industrial applications is proposed.

First let us consider two classes: true defects (i.e., positives) and false defects (i.e., negatives). Let: NP be the total number of positives, NN be the total number of negatives, NTP be the total number of positives correctly classified (i.e., true positives), NTN be the total number of negatives correctly classified (i.e., true negatives), NFN

4.3.3 Data fusion classification

be the total number of positives incorrectly classified as negative (i.e., false negatives) and NFP be the total number of negatives incorrectly classified as positives (i.e., false positives).

Receiver operating characteristics curves ROC curves are useful for organizing classifiers and visualizing their performance. One of the earliest adopters of ROC curves in machine learning was Spackman [187], who demonstrated the value of ROC curves in evaluating and comparing algorithms. Recent years have seen an increase in the use of ROC curves in the machine learning community, in part due to the realization that simple classification accuracy is often a poor metric for measuring performance [188]. In addition to being a generally useful performance graphing method, they have properties that make them particularly useful for domains with skewed class distribution and irregular classification error costs. These characteristics have become increasingly important as research continues into the areas of cost-sensitive learning and learning in the presence of unbalanced classes [188].

ROC curves are two-dimensional graphs in which false positives rate fp is plotted on the x-axis and true positives rate tp is plotted on the y-axis. Following are the definitions of tp and fp:

$$\text{tp} = \frac{\text{NTP}}{\text{NP}} \tag{4.29}$$

$$\text{fp} = \frac{\text{NFP}}{\text{NN}} \tag{4.30}$$

The higher the value of area under the ROC curve is, the better is the ability by using the corresponding source to separate between two classes. In figure 4.18 are presented the ROC curve of the illustration example of figure 4.16, using feature values (figure (a)) and using mass values (figure (b)) to construct the ROC curves. Each point of the ROC curve corresponds to a different decision threshold applied either on the feature values or on the mass values. A high threshold yields a low number of false positives rate, but also a rather low number of true positives (left part of the ROC curve). The area under ROC curve (A_{ROC}) can be used to select the pertinent (or accurate) sources. An $A_{ROC} = 1$ represents a perfect classifier; an $A_{ROC} = 0.5$ represents a worthless classifier.

Performance measures In order to measure the performance of a source (can be a feature or a combination of features), a threshold S_m is first applied to the mass value $m(X \in H_1)$. Remind that each input data point (i.e., suspicious region) whose mass $m(X \in H_1) \geqslant S_m$ is classified as a true defect, otherwise it is classified as a false defect. The classification results are then compared to the true decision given by the expert (human inspector) and the following rates are computed:

- Correct decisions rate PCD (also called accuracy by [188]):

$$\text{PCD} = \frac{\text{NTP} + \text{NTN}}{\text{NP} + \text{NN}} \tag{4.31}$$

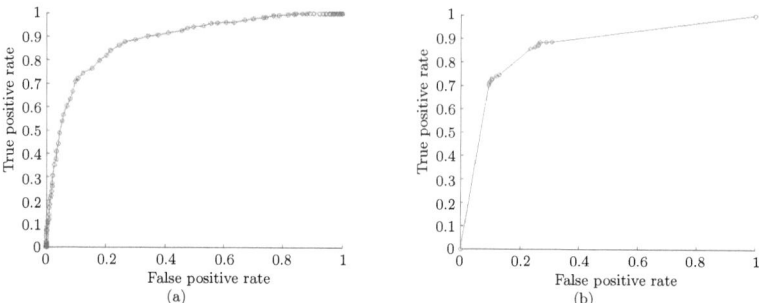

Figure 4.18.: (a) ROC curve obtained for the example of feature values shown in figure 4.16. (b) ROC curve obtained for the same feature, after mass attribution.

- True defects classification rate PTD, already defined as true positive rate tp:

$$\text{PTD} = \frac{\text{NTP}}{\text{NP}} = \text{tp} \qquad (4.32)$$

- False defects classification rate PFD:

$$\text{PFD} = \frac{\text{NTN}}{\text{NN}} = 1 - \text{fp} \qquad (4.33)$$

- Apart from those classical classification rates, a new measure called overall classification rate R is introduced in order to summarize the performance in one single value, industrially relevant. It is defined as:

$$\text{R} = \frac{W_{tp} \cdot \text{PTD} + W_{tn} \cdot \text{PFD} + W_c \cdot \text{PCD}}{W_{tp} + W_{tn} + W_c} \qquad (4.34)$$

The use of $W_{tp} \geqslant 0$, $W_{tn} \geqslant 0$ and $W_c \geqslant 0$ to compute the overall classification rate R is driven by industrial requirements. It is very important in industrial inspection to detect as many real defects as possible, while preventing the increase in the false alarm rate. Thus, the overall rate R is computed with $W_{tn} = W_c = 1$ and $W_{tp} = 5$ in order to put higher emphasis on true defects.

Related DFC results

The obtained results using DFC method were published during the doctoral thesis in two journal papers [186, 189] and in conferences (appendix ??). In the following, the published work is briefed.

In reviewed publication [186], the DFC method was introduced and applied to classify 2D radioscopy images. It was compared with the Automatic X-ray Inspection

4.3.3 Data fusion classification

System (ISAR) [190]. Obtained results in [191] showed that the use of DFC leads to a significant improvement of classification performances with respect to the actual system especially in false defects classification.

The paper presented at the 10th European Conference on Non-Destructive Testing (ECNDT) [192] studied the stability and the optimization of DFC by changing two internal parameters (derivation variation DV, percentage of points inside regions of confidence Perc and the threshold S_m applied on the mass function). The optimum parameters were investigated using the same radioscopy database used in [186]. The optimal performance was given by DV=0 and Perc=0.1 and S_m had a small influence on the optimization of the system. The DFC results outperformed the Support Vector Machine (SVM) and ISAR.

The DFC method was additionally used to classify 3D Computed Tomography (CT) datasets. Results showed high classification rates, of defects and false defects, and they were reported in the conference paper [193] presented in the International Symposium on Digital Industrial Radiology and Computed Tomography.

The most recent reviewed publication [189] reported about the possibility to improve the DFC performance. The improvement approach was based on the selection of most pertinent features based on the area under their corresponding ROC curves. Performance was studied on 3D CT datasets and compared to SVM, where DFC method showed comparable performance.

Lately, results given by applying the complete analysis chain proposed in this chapter to segment and classify ultrasound SPA volumes of CFRP specimens were presented in the International Symposium on Ultrasound in the Control of Industrial Processes [194]. The classification of suspicious regions was done using the DFC method. The paper will appear in the AccessIOP Conference Series: Materials Science and Engineering published by the Institute of Physics Publishing in the United Kingdom.

Cautious and conjunctive rules comparison

The DFC method uses the non normalized Dempster rule (i.e., the conjunctive rule) to combine the information sources. This rule assumes that sources are independent and reliable. The reliability of the sources is not doubted in this research. Interested readers can find more information about sources reliability in [195]. Concerning the independence condition between sources (i.e., a piece of evidence is not shared by more than one source), this condition is not always guaranteed. The cautious rule [185] was proposed to overcome the independence assumption about combined sources. This is due to the distributivity property of the cautious rule which implies that a shared evidence is not counted twice (see equation 4.23). This paragraph presents a comparison of the conjunctive rule with Cautious rule for the case of the DFC method.

Let m_1 and m_2 be the two simple mass functions shown in table 4.1 attributed

A	$m_1(A)$	$m_2(A)$	$q_1(A)$	$q_2(A)$	$w_1(A)$	$w_2(A)$	$w_{1\wedge 2}(A)$	$m_{1\varowedge 2}(A)$	$m_{1\varobigcirc 2}(A)$
$\varnothing$	0	0	1	1	1	1	1	0	0
H_1	a	b	1	1	$1-a$	$1-b$	$1-b$	b	$a+b-ab$
H_2	0	0	$1-a$	$1-b$	1	1	1	0	0
H_3	$1-a$	$1-b$	$1-a$	$1-b$				$1-b$	$(1-a)(1-b)$

Table 4.1.: Table of combinations of mass functions using conjunctive and cautious rules: $0 \leqslant a \leqslant 1$; $0 \leqslant b \leqslant 1$ and $a \leqslant b$.

to the hypotheses $\varnothing$, H_1, H_2 and H_3 by two reliable sources. In this comparison, m_1 and m_2 are simple mass functions (our case). Commonalities $q_1(A)$ and $q_2(A)$ can be computed from the mass functions using equation 4.15. For example, the commonality given by the first source to hypothesis H_1 can be computed as follows:

$$q_1(H_1) = \sum_{B \supseteq H_1} m(B) = m_1(H_1) + m_1(H_3) = 1.$$

Weights are computed using equation 4.17. For example, the weight $w_1(H_1)$ is given as:

$$w_1(H_1) = \frac{\prod_{B \supseteq H_1, |B| \in 2\mathbb{N}} q(B)}{\prod_{B \supseteq H_1, |B| \notin 2\mathbb{N}} q(B)} = \frac{q_1(H_3)}{q_1(H_1)} = 1 - a$$

Considering that factor $a \leqslant b$ will not reduce the generality of the demonstration. In this case $w_1(H_1) = 1 - a$ is greater than $w_2(H_1) = 1 - b$, and $w_{1\wedge 2}(H_1)$ is thus equal to $1 - b$.

Thus, using the notation introduced in (4.12), $H_1^{w_{1\wedge 2}} = H_1^{1-b}$ yields the following final mass values:

$$\begin{cases} m_{1\varowedge 2}(H_1) = 1 - (1-b) = b \\ m_{1\varowedge 2}(H_3) = 1 - b \end{cases}$$

Thus, the cautious rule in our case, simply selects the maximal mass value given to the hypothesis H_1. The rest is assigned to H_3. This fact can be generalized to the case of combination of all sources of information where the cautious rule will select the maximum mass value from all available mass values (for simple mass functions as ours).

As for the mass combination using the conjunctive rule, the application of equation 4.19 yields:

$$m_{1\varobigcirc 2}(H_1) = m_1(H_1)m_2(H_1) + m_1(H_1)m_2(H_3) + m_1(H_3)m_2(H_1) = a + b - ab$$

$$m_{1\varobigcirc 2}(H_3) = m_1(H_3)m_2(H_3) = (1-a)(1-b)$$

The cautious rule will be used in the fusion step of the DFC method and will be compared with the conjunctive rule. Moreover, the performance of the DFC method will be compared with SVM classifier using the performance measures introduced in equations 4.31–4.34.

Support vector machine

Support Vector Machines (SVM) are a new generation learning system based on recent advances in statistical learning theory. Support Vector Machines are among the standard tools for machine learning and data mining [196].

They work in a two step process. The first is the training (with representative learning data) where the support vectors are generated determining the optimal separating hyperplane or set of hyperplanes with the maximum distance to these support vectors. The second step is the regression/classification of unknown data in the features space. Support Vector Machines can handle two or more classes. A Support Vector Machine is a maximal margin hyperplane in feature space, built by using a kernel function in input space. A detailed theoretical introduction to SVM can be found in [197] and a good overview of two categories classification using SVM is presented in [198].

The SVM classifier used in this work, was obtained from [199] and is implemented in a software library. The library includes different SVM kernels. It also includes a routine to select the optimal kernel for different applications.

4.4. Conclusion

This chapter has introduced and explained the algorithms proposed to evaluate the reconstructed 3D ultrasound data. The complete analysis chain is composed of a segmentation followed by a classification procedure. The output of the chain is a list of detected defects inside the volume with a features list describing the geometrical and intensity properties of each defect. Next chapter will present the experimental evaluation of the chain.

saaaa

5. Experimental evaluation of the proposed segmentation and classification method

Contents

5.1.	Experimental environment	91
	5.1.1. 3D ultrasound datasets of CFRP specimens	92
	5.1.2. Ultrasound data segmentation tool	93
	5.1.3. Data fusion classification tool	93
5.2.	Experimental results of the segmentation procedure . .	95
	5.2.1. Data correction results	95
	5.2.2. Data enhancement results	98
	5.2.3. Entrance and backwall layers detection results	107
	5.2.4. Thresholding results	109
	5.2.5. Features extraction results	118
5.3.	Experimental results of the classification procedure . . .	119
	5.3.1. Results for CFRP-14	119
	5.3.2. Results for CFRP-8	124
5.4.	Discussion	126

This chapter presents the results obtained using the proposed analysis chain. Next section will be devoted to explain the experimental environment of the work. The remaining of the chapter is dedicated to present the experimental results of different stages of the chain. The chapter ends with a discussion section.

5.1. Experimental environment

By experimental environment are meant the available datasets on which the analysis chain is tested and the developed tools used for data segmentation and classification.

5.1.1. 3D ultrasound datasets of CFRP specimens

The proposed approach is tested on the following two CFRP specimens:

- Specimen (denoted CFRP-8) of 8 mm thickness, presented in figure 5.1, which contains:
  - 25 circular shaped artificial defects (bottom drilled circular holes) with diameters ranging from 7 mm to 20 mm and positions in z direction from 0.6 mm to 6 mm.
  - 5 border rectangular shaped artificial Iron (Fe) inclusions of size 13x30 mm^2.

  The specimen was scanned from the side without drilled holes.

- Specimen (denoted CFRP-14) of 14 mm thickness which contains 24 rectangular shaped artificial defects, including delamination, at different z positions: at 0.6 mm, at 7.2 mm and at 13.7 mm (see figure 5.2).

Defects close to the surface and to the end of the specimens are considered difficult to detect due to the influence of the entrance echo and backwall echo signals. Thus, these two specimens are representative examples to show the performance of SPA technology and the proposed chain for detecting and classifying defects which are present in the reconstructed volume.

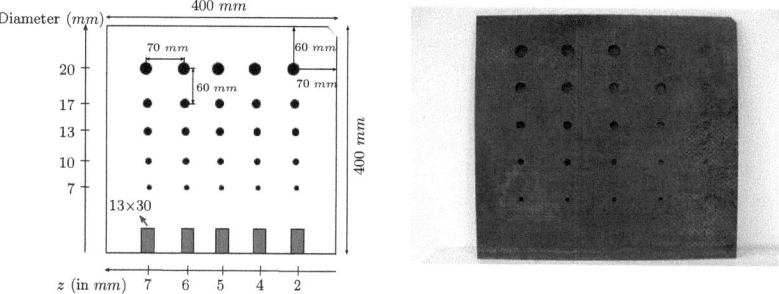

Figure 5.1.: CFRP specimen of thickness 8 mm (CFRP-8): circular defects and rectangular inclusions.

The available volumetric data for this work are from two sources: EZRT and IZFP laboratories. The volumes are presented in table 5.1 with their corresponding identification names (ID) and all available technical information. As it can be noticed, different resolution, applied gain, volume dimensions and inspection speed are used.

5.1.2 Ultrasound data segmentation tool

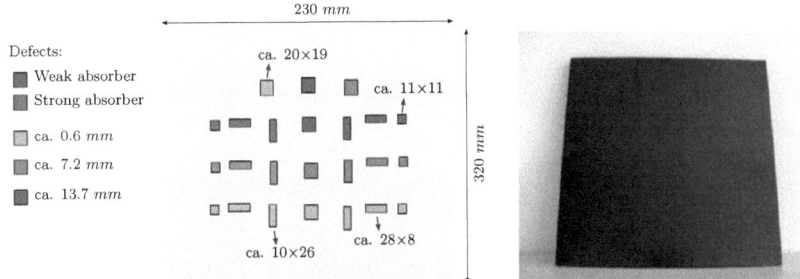

Figure 5.2.: CFRP specimen of thickness 14 mm (CFRP-14): defects at 0.6 mm, at 7.2 mm and at 13.7 mm z location.

ID	Specimen	Dimensions $[x,y,z]$	Resolution [mm³]	Gain [dB]	Scan speed [mm/s]	F [MHz]	Technique
V14-15	CFRP-14	[310, 265, 31]	[1, 1, 0.5]	14	15	5	SPA 1 × 16
V14-70	CFRP-14	[310, 265, 31]	[1, 1, 0.5]	17.5	70	5	SPA 1 × 16
V14-100	CFRP-14	[310, 265, 31]	[1, 1, 0.5]	17.5	100	5	SPA 1 × 16
V14-IZFP	CFRP-14	[316, 301, 341]	[1, 1, 0.05]	-	-	5	SPA 1 × 16
V8-21	CFRP-8	[339, 359, 43]	[1, 1, 0.2]	21	30	5	SPA 1 × 16
V8-22	CFRP-8	[345, 357, 161]	[1, 1, 0.05]	22	10	5	SPA 1 × 16
V8-24	CFRP-8	[339, 359, 46]	[1, 1, 0.2]	24	30	5	CPA

Table 5.1.: Available 3D ultrasound data of CFRP specimens. The SPA 1 × 16 refers to the sampling phased array technique mode were one element transducer sends and all elements receive. The CPA refers to the use of the conventional phased array technique.

5.1.2. Ultrasound data segmentation tool

The proposed algorithms of the segmentation approach are developed in C++ code and integrated in a graphic user interface (GUI) framework. The GUI is developed using Microsoft Foundation Class Library (MFC). The obtained tool, called Ultrasonic ImageProcessing, is shown in figure 5.3. Each step of the segmentation can be called using the corresponding field in the image processing menu bar.

5.1.3. Data fusion classification tool

The classification approach based on data fusion is developed into a tool called Data Fusion Classification (DFC) system. The tool is composed of C++ kernels integrated in GUI developed using Qt application framework (see figure 5.4).

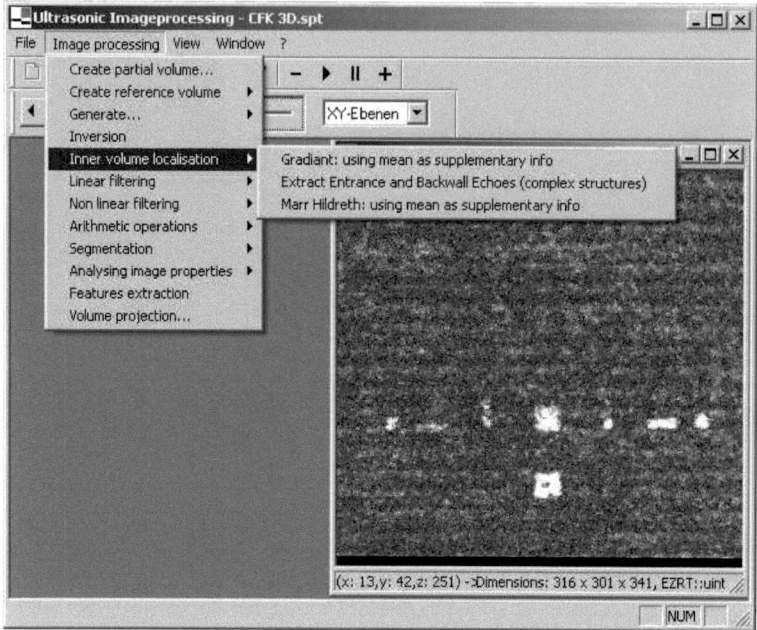

Figure 5.3.: GUI of the ultrasound image processing tool with the image processing menu including inner volume localization (i.e., detection of entrance and backwall layers) and other segmentation steps.

The input of the DFC tool is the list of features measured during the segmentation procedure. The translation from features values to mass values is done automatically after loading the features. The user has the possibility to control all the classification approach parameters (i.e., DV, Perc etc.). The tool can combine the mass values given by different information sources using the following rules: conjunctive rule, cautious rule and the statistical combination rules. The user has the possibility to specify the decision threshold S_m which is applied on the mass value $m(H_1)$.

Moreover, the DFC tool gives the possibility to specify the required classification rates (PTD, PFD, and R). The tool selects all the combinations which have a performance higher or equal to the required performance. It furthermore selects the combination which has the highest PTD, the combination which has the highest PFD and the combination which gives the optimal overall rate R. In addition, the DFC tool allows to test the performance of selected sources on a testing dataset.

5.2 Experimental results of the segmentation procedure

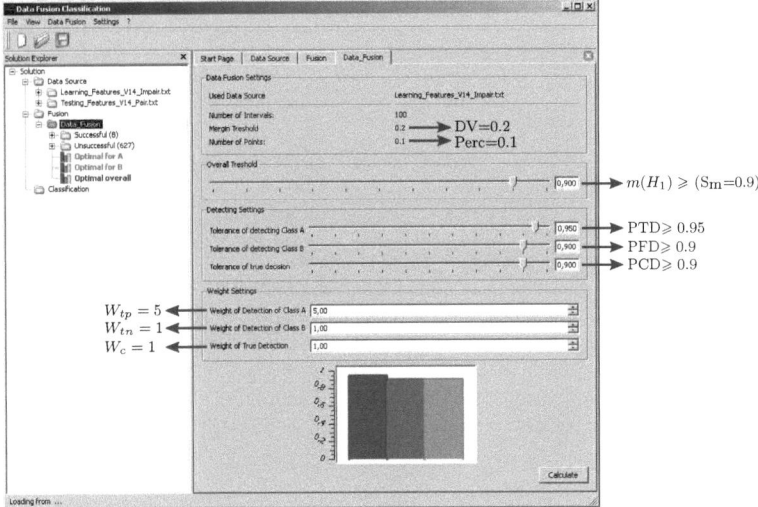

Figure 5.4.: GUI of the DFC tool.

5.2. Experimental results of the segmentation procedure

The segmentation steps are systematically applied on all input volumes. Illustrative results will be shown for V14-IZFP, V14-70 and V8-22 CFRP volumes. The segmentation results for the other volumes are in the corresponding appendixes.

5.2.1. Data correction results

First step of the segmentation procedure is the data correction. The interpolation can be either applied in 2D or 3D. However, it is important to remind that the 3D interpolation does not allow to interpolate all layers in the volume due to boundaries issues. Following the 2D and 3D interpolations are to be quantitatively compared in order to investigate the difference between both methods.

The volume V14-IZFP, acquired in IZFP laboratory, contains no invalid voxels. Therefore, it can serve to evaluate the influence of the interpolations on real data instead of simulated data. Table 5.2 reports the results obtained for 10 randomly selected voxels inside the volume. Three important remarks can be elaborated from this table:

- When the selected voxel is in a homogeneous region, such as voxel at coordinates

5.2 Experimental results of the segmentation procedure

	Original volume		2D interpolation			3D interpolation		
(x, y, z)	Intensity	$\overline{d_P}$	Intensity	Difference	$\overline{d_P}$	Intensity	Difference	$\overline{d_P}$
(51, 63, 9)	14686	348.46	14685	-1	348.52	32767	240	337.43
(199, 210, 278)	32767	0	32767	0	0	32767	0	0
(170, 183, 51)	3475	204.22	3724	249	230.69	3198	-277	214.01
(251, 264, 320)	23558	5469.3	14711	-8847	1262	12775	-10783	1415.9
(83, 26, 288)	13251	1675.6	8908	-4343	955.5	9445	-3806	865.6
(221, 190, 18)	3798	467.4	2577	-1221	156.7	2735	-1063	146.8
(269, 46, 87)	2581	502.4	1635	-946	392.8	1717	-864	369.7
(98, 272, 57)	1171	798.1	2310	1139	194.2	2336	1165	196.2
(248, 223, 90)	2494	467.6	3630	1136	220.9	3556	1062	213.3
(272, 206, 63)	5274	572.6	4212	-1062	279.9	4212	-1062	279.9

Table 5.2.: Original intensity of a randomly selected voxel at coordinates (x, y, z), 2D and 3D interpolated intensities using a 2D and 3D modified median filter ($d = 1$). For each interpolation, two parameters are given: the difference between the original and interpolated intensities and the similarity measure $\overline{d_P}$ between the voxels in the neighborhood of the considered voxel, before and after interpolation. A null dp means that the region is homogeneous.

(199, 210, 278), both 2D and 3D interpolations are able to interpolate the exact intensity of the voxel. Notice that $\overline{d_P}$ is null in the original volume, i.e. the voxel is in a completely homogeneous neighborhood.

- When the intensity of the voxel is much different than the neighboring voxels, such as voxel at coordinates (83, 26, 288), the interpolated intensity values are far from the original intensity. Thus, the difference between the interpolated 2D and 3D intensities and original intensity is high. However, values of $\overline{d_P}$ in 2D and 3D are much less than in the original volume. Therefore, the interpolated intensity is more similar to its surrounding.

- Although modifying the original intensity, the 2D and 3D interpolations improve the similarity measure by giving in most cases a lower $\overline{d_P}$ than in the original volume.

Thus, the interpolations would either reduce the extreme values in the volume or give a close interpolation to the original value in cases of homogeneous volumes. Figures 5.5 and 5.6 present respectively the difference and similarity measures obtained in case of 30 randomly selected voxels. It can be clearly noticed that the difference measures given by the 2D and 3D interpolations have globally similar values. Concerning the similarity measures, both interpolations could repeatedly improve the similarity of intensity to the surrounding.

Since the 2D and 3D interpolation have similar performance, later on, the data correction will be carried out using the 2D interpolation. Illustrative result of the data correction step is presented in figure 5.7. The figure shows a layer at position $z = 25$ of the V8-22 volume. Notice that before correction (figure 5.7a), invalid voxels are affecting the complete original layer including the defects zone. Invalid voxels cause

5.2.1 Data correction results

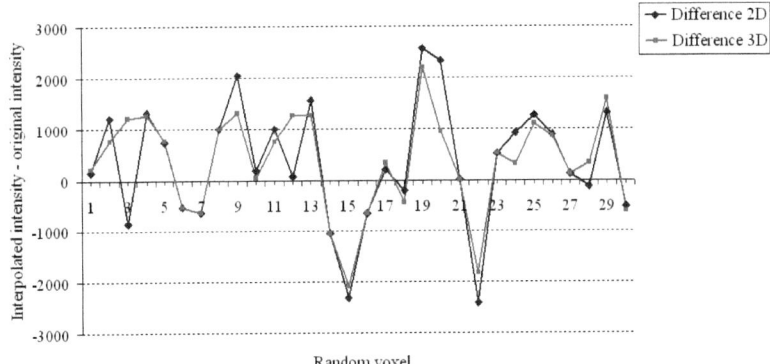

Figure 5.5.: Difference between the 2D and 3D interpolated intensity values and the original intensity values of 30 voxels randomly selected in the volume V14-IZFP.

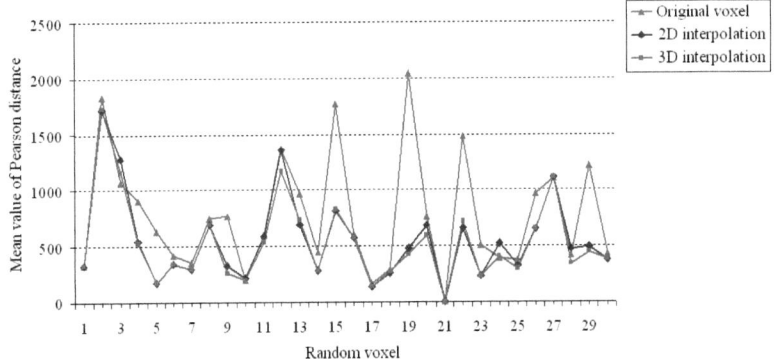

Figure 5.6.: Similarity measure between the 2D and 3D interpolated intensity values of the selected voxel and the intensity values of the voxel's surrounding neighborhood.

sudden falls to zero inside the defects intensity values zone. The output of the data correction algorithm, presented in figure 5.7b shows the successful removal of all invalid voxels.

It is worth noting that the map of all corrected voxels is kept in memory in order that after the whole processing, the final decision about a defect's zone can be compared with the map. If too many voxels of the defect belong to the map, the decision can be considered as non valid.

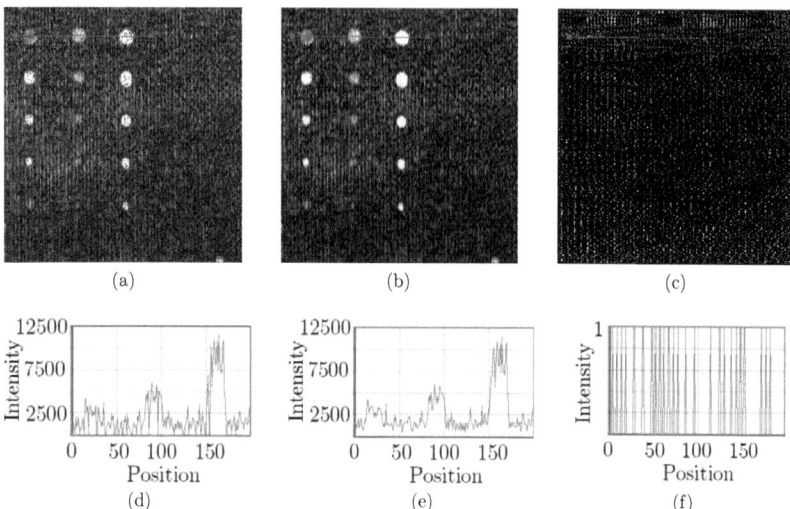

Figure 5.7.: V8-22: (a) xy view of the original layer at depth $z = 25$. (b) Corrected layer (c) Map of the position of the interpolated voxels in the layer. (d) Intensity profile corresponding to the red line tracker on the original layer. (e) The intensity profile after correction. (f) Positions in the map of the interpolated voxels along the line tracker.

5.2.2. Data enhancement results

After invalid voxels interpolation, the corrected volume is then filtered by considering separately median, M3 and NL-means filters applied with different kernels size. Significant layers (i.e., low contrasted defects and high noise) of V14-IZFP and V8-22 will be used to select the optimal filters. The validation of the selected filters will be done on a layer of V14-70.

Optimal filter selection on V14-IZFP

Median filter The median filter is applied on the corrected input layer of V14-IZFP. Visual comparison is presented in figure 5.8. Median filters are qualitatively (visual analysis) efficient in removing the impulsive noise. Nevertheless, the image structures are lost especially at structures corners when the kernel size exceeds the size [7,7,1] (i.e., $d = 3$).

Quantitative comparison is achieved via the data quality evaluation metrics. The results of RMSE, NRF, PSNR and CNR are given in table 5.3. CNR is measured

5.2.2 Data enhancement results

on the upper right side defect[1] (red box in figure 5.8a). The maximal CNR value is obtained using the kernel of size $[7, 7, 1]$ (i.e., $d = 3$). Consequently, the use of this kernels to filter the image should permit a better detection of defects inside the image (however the maximal CNR value is rather low). As for NRF, it only measures the noise reduction. Thus, NRF increases with the increase of the kernel size.

Median kernel	RMSE	NRF	PSNR	CNR	M3 kernel	RMSE	NRF	PSNR	CNR
0	-	-	-	0.98	0	-	-	-	0.98
1	3.31	3.23	37.72	1.35	1	3.25	3.43	37.87	1.55
2	3.94	5.44	36.21	1.36	2	3.93	6.02	36.24	1.36
3	4.15	6.93	35.76	1.38	3	4.15	6.93	35.76	1.38
4	4.31	8.04	35.43	1.29	4	4.31	8.04	35.43	1.29
5	4.41	8.88	35.22	1.09	5	4.41	8.88	35.22	1.08

Table 5.3.: Quantitative evaluation metrics of the median and M3 filters on a layer of the V14-IZFP volume for $d = \{1, 2, 3, 4, 5\}$.

The metrics PSNR and RMSE should be interpreted simultaneously because the computation of the PSNR is based on the RMSE. When the kernel size increases, the filtered image becomes more smoothed and more homogeneous in terms of noise repartition. However, more smoothing corresponds to a higher loss of details in the image. This means that the similarity between the original image and the filtered image decreases. RMSE measures the degree of dissimilarity between images. Thus, it increases (i.e., PSNR decreases) with the increase of the kernel's size.

M3 filter Application of the M3 filter on the input layer yields the results presented in the right part of table 5.3. Figure 5.9 gives a visual illustration. The M3 with a kernel size $[3, 3, 1]$ (i.e., $d = 1$) gives the best performance with the highest CNR, PSNR and the lowest RMSE. Nevertheless, it has the lowest NRF.

Note that for $d \geq 3$, filters M3 and median give the same result. This is related to the definition of the M3 filter which is the maximal value between the mean and median intensity inside the filtering block.

NL-means filter Based on the optimization work done by Coupé et al. [166], the NL-means filter is tested for $M = \{3, 4, 5\}$, corresponding respectively to searching windows of size $[7, 7, 1]$, $[9, 9, 1]$ and $[11, 11, 1]$. The block size varies between $d = \{1, 2, 3\}$. The following notation is considered in order to facilitate the presentation of results for all NL-means: NLMW$_i$B$_j$ stands for a NL-means filter of a search window with $M = i$ and a block with $d = j$.

The block size specifies the local kernel around the voxel to process and the searching window is the global zone inside which all the local neighborhoods are considered for similarity measurement. Ideally, the bigger is the searching window size, the better

---
[1]This is the smallest defect in the image and has a low contrast.

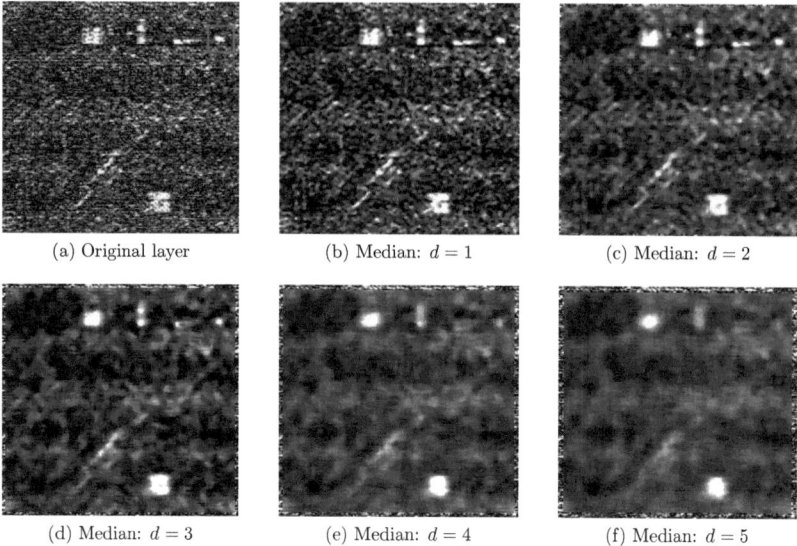

Figure 5.8.: Results obtained using median filters of different kernels size $[2d+1, 2d+1, 1]$ to filter a layer of the V14-IZFP volume. Important details and low contrasted defects are lost when the kernel size exceeds $[7,7,1]$. The red box in (a) corresponds to the zone where CNR is calculated.

NL-means	RMSE	NRF	PSNR	CNR
Initial Image	-	-	-	0.98
NLMW3B1	3.7	5.38	36.67	1.92
NLMW3B2	3.14	3.71	38.17	1.55
NLMW4B1	3.94	6.51	36.21	2.12
NLMW4B2	3.78	5.5	36.56	1.99
NLMW4B3	3.15	3.71	38.14	1.54
NLMW5B1	4.09	7.36	35.88	2.56
NLMW5B2	4.01	6.65	36.05	2.18
NLMW5B3	3.8	5.54	36.51	1.94
NLMW5B4	3.16	3.72	38.12	1.52

Table 5.4.: Quantitative evaluation metrics of the NL-means filter on a layer of the V14-IZFP volume.

is the filtering. However, for computational reasons, it is necessary to limit it. The block size is more interesting to analyze because it corresponds more to the scale of the similarity that is expected. The optimal block size is the one for which a lot of similar neighborhoods can be found.

5.2.2 Data enhancement results

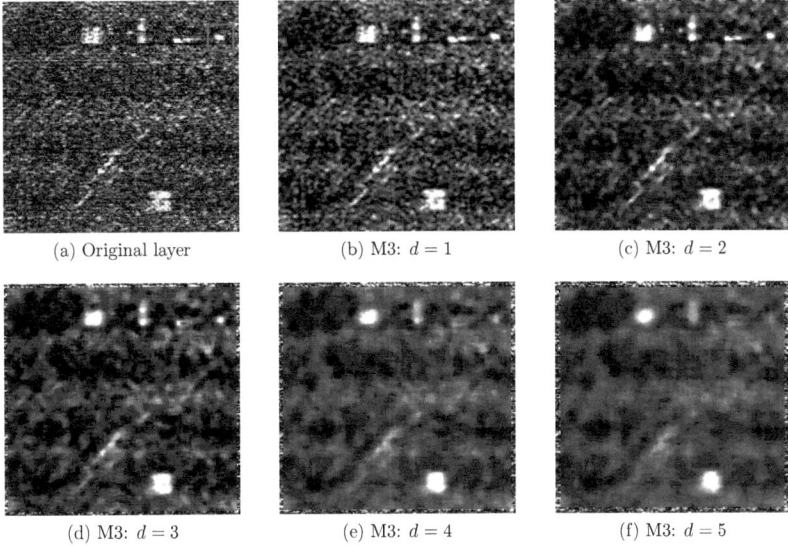

Figure 5.9.: Results obtained with different kernels size M3 filters on a layer of the V14-IZFP measure of CFRP-14. The red box in (a) corresponds to the zone where CNR is calculated.

Visual comparison is provided in figure 5.10 which presents the output of the configurations of the NL-means filter. As for quantitative evaluation, table 5.4 resumes the obtained data quality evaluation metrics. It can be noticed that the NLMW5B1 gives the highest CNR and NRF.
The RMSE metric increases (i.e., PSNR decreases) when the window size increases. Inversely, RMSE decreases when the block size increases. The same tendency is observed for NRF. This can be interpreted by the fact that the filter is more severe (higher smoothing) when the searching window increases, but only for a small block size. When the block size is too high, there are no more similar neighborhoods in the searching zone. Visually, it is clear that when d increases, the smoothing of the image does not increase. The smoothing of the image (i.e. the severity of the filter) increases when M increases for $d = 1$ only.

CNR measures simultaneously the defect's contrast and the noise reduction. Thus, CNR describes better the objective of the data enhancement step. Consequently, the final decision about the optimal filter will be principally based on CNR.

The values of the evaluation metric CNR in table 5.4 suggest that, the NL-means filter NLMW5B1 ($M = 5$ and $d = 1$) gives the optimal performance with a CNR=2.56. This CNR value is higher than all CNR values given by the median, M3 and other NL-means configurations.

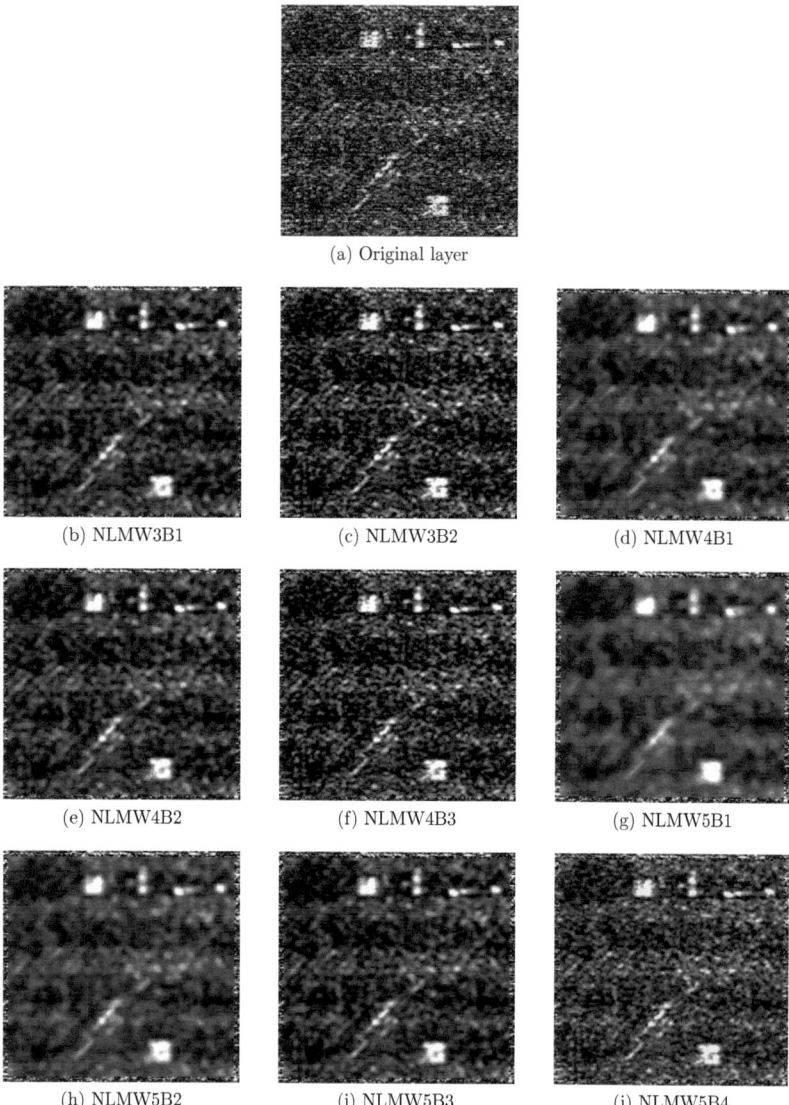

Figure 5.10.: Results obtained with different configurations of the NL-means filter on a layer of the V14-IZFP volume. The red box in (a) corresponds to the zone where CNR is calculated.

5.2.2 Data enhancement results

Optimal filter selection on V8-22

The same procedure is followed for the V8-22 volume, where a noisy layer containing defects of different sizes is considered. In this layer appears the smallest defect in the CFRP-8 specimen. The metric CNR is measured for this defect which has a diameter of 7 mm (see figure 5.11a).

First, results obtained by applying the median and M3 filters are presented. Both filters have similar effects on this layer. Visual assessment, as given in figure 5.11 and 5.12, reveals a strong blurring and defects distortion with the increase of the kernel size.

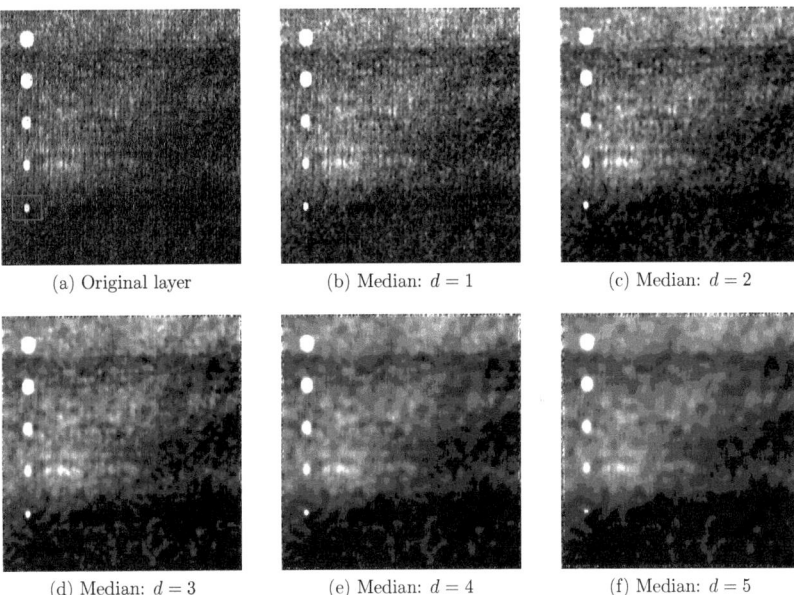

(a) Original layer   (b) Median: $d = 1$ (c) Median: $d = 2$

(d) Median: $d = 3$ (e) Median: $d = 4$ (f) Median: $d = 5$

Figure 5.11.: Results obtained using median filters of different kernels size to filter a layer of the V8-22 volume of CFRP-8. The 7 mm defect (red box) is severely eroded and the image becomes very blurred when the kernel size exceeds [7,7,1].

Quantitative evaluation metrics for the median and M3 filters are presented in table 5.5. Clearly, the M3 filter for $d = 1$ has the best performance in comparison with other configurations of the M3 and median filters. Moreover, notice the reduction in CNR which occurs when the size of the filtering kernel increases.

As for the NL-means filter, figure 5.13 is given for visual comparison. Quantitative

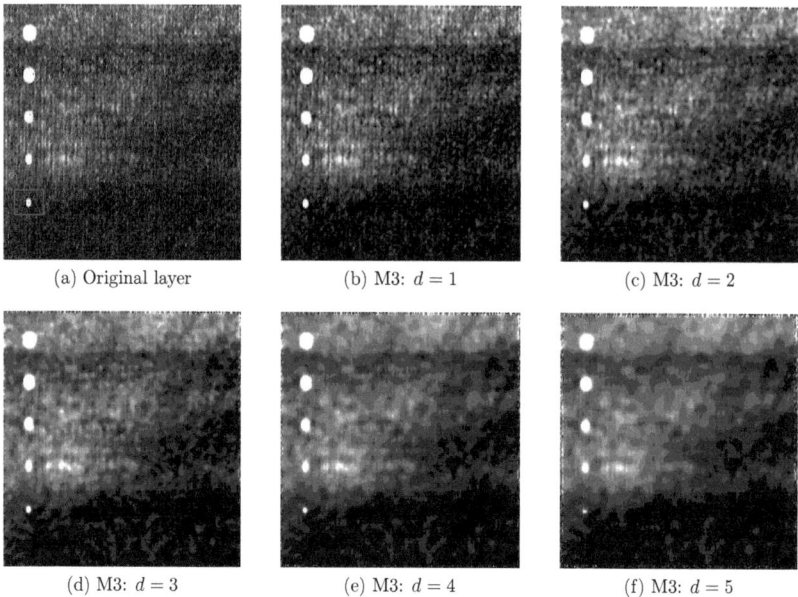

Figure 5.12.: Results obtained using M3 filters of different kernels size to filter a layer of the V8-22 volume. The 7 mm defect (red box) is severely eroded and the image becomes very blurred when $d > 3$.

Median kernel	RMSE	NRF	PSNR	CNR	M3 Kernel	RMSE	NRF	PSNR	CNR
0	-	-	-	1.64	0	-	-	-	1.64
1	1.87	0.84	42.67	1.76	1	1.82	0.86	42.88	2.03
2	1.94	1.25	42.36	1,6	2	1.93	1.31	42.37	1.6
3	2.12	1.65	41.58	1.38	3	2.12	1.65	41.58	1.38
4	2.2	2.05	41.27	1.28	4	2.2	2.05	41.27	1.28
5	2.35	2.5	40.68	1.25	5	2.35	2.5	40.68	1.25

Table 5.5.: Quantitative evaluation metrics of the median and M3 filters on a layer of the V8-22 volume.

comparison is presented in table 5.6. Yet again, NLMW5B1 gives the highest value of CNR=3.22.

Validation on V14-70

The analysis of the previously shown results indicates that the NLMW5B1 is the optimal filter for data enhancement. As for the median and M3 filters, it appears that the M3 of size $[3, 3, 1]$ gives the best performance between all configurations of

5.2.2 Data enhancement results

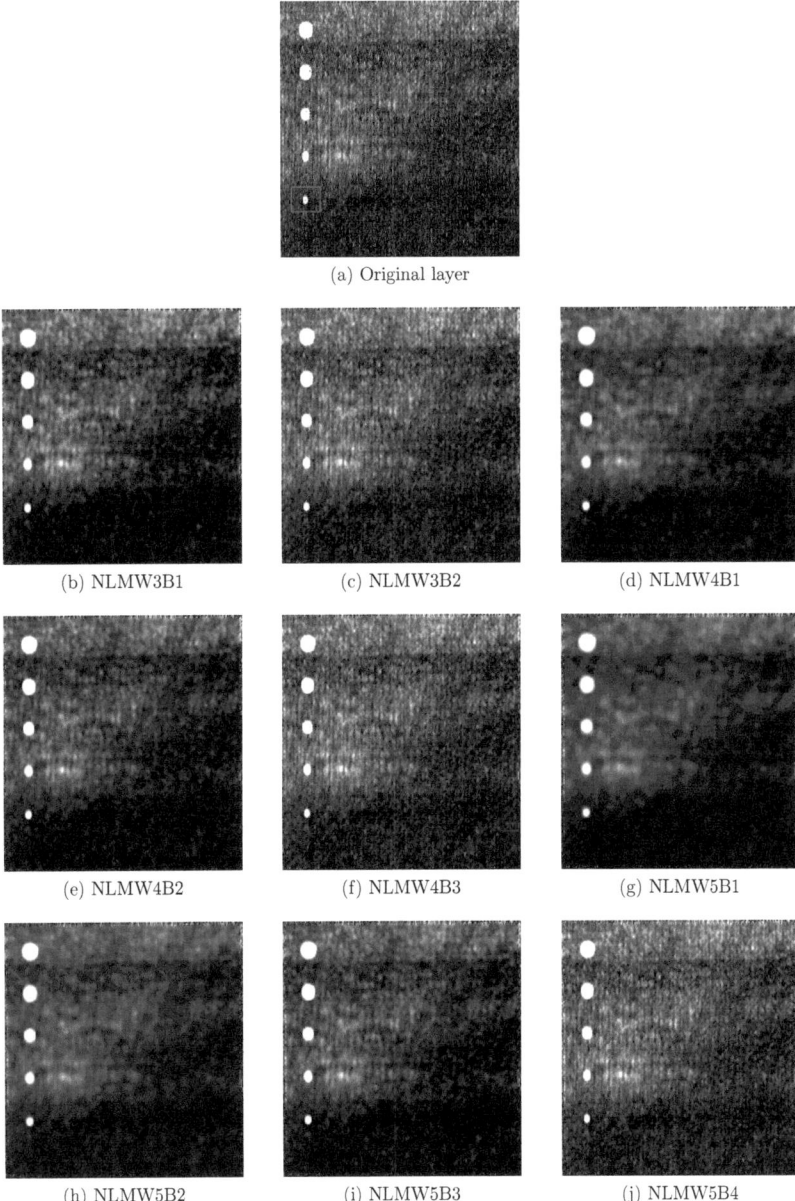

Figure 5.13.: Results obtained with different configurations of the NL-means filter on a layer of V8-22.

NL-means	RMSE	NRF	PSNR	CNR
Initial Image	-	-	-	1.64
NLMW3B1	1.97	1.29	42.2	2.59
NLMW3B2	1.85	0.98	42.78	2.2
NLMW4B1	2.15	1.53	41.47	2.84
NLMW4B2	2	1.33	42	2.69
NLMW4B3	1.85	0.98	42.74	2.17
NLMW5B1	2.18	1.76	41.33	3.22
NLMW5B2	2.18	1.58	41.33	3.19
NLMW5B3	2.01	1.35	42.04	2.72
NLMW5B4	1.86	0.98	42.73	2.19

Table 5.6.: Quantitative evaluation metrics of the NL-means filter on a layer of the V8-22 volume.

these two filters.

To validate the obtained results, the NLMW5B1 and M3 of size $[3, 3, 1]$ are tested on a layer of the V14-70 volume. Low contrasted defects, large artifacts and high noise exist in this layer as shown in figure 5.14a.

Visual comparison of the filtered layers can be seen in figure 5.14. Qualitatively, it is clear that the NLMW5B1 filter effectively removes the noise, while the M3 filter partially removes the noise. Nevertheless, the NL-means filter tends to dilate the borders of structures as it can be seen in the difference image. When the defect is close to an artifact, the dilation caused by the NL-means could provoke the attachment of their voxels. In this case, there is a risk to wrongly classify this defect as a false alarm.

Quantitatively (see table 5.7), the NLMW5B1 much improves the defects detectability with a CNR=4.75 instead of a CNR=1.15 in the original image. The M3 filter has lower CNR value (CNR=2.16).

Later on, the NLMW5B1 filter is used in the data enhancement step of the analysis chain.

NL-means	RMSE	NRF	PSNR	CNR
Initial Image	-	-	-	1.15
M3 $(d = 1)$	14.88	0.95	24.67	2.16
NLM $(M = 5, d = 1)$	16.37	1.11	23.84	4.75

Table 5.7.: Data enhancement evaluation metrics for the NL-means filter NLMW5B1 ($M = 5$, $d = 1$) and M3 ($d = 1$) obtained on the validation layer of the V14-70 volume.

5.2.3 Entrance and backwall layers detection results

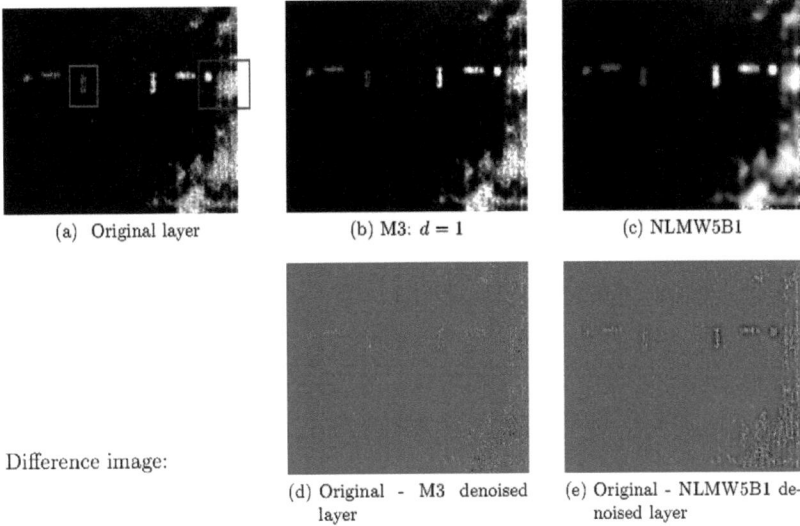

Difference image:

Figure 5.14.: Comparison of the M3 filter and the NL-means filter on a layer of the V14-70 measure of CFRP-14. The CNR is measured on the defect inside the red box. The blue box surrounds a defect which is close to a large artifact. The NLMW5B1 dilates this defect which could provoke the attachment of voxels of the defect and the artifact.

5.2.3. Entrance and backwall layers detection results

Using the NL-means filtered volume $\tilde{v}$, the mean volume is first computed. Afterward, the EE and BWE layers are to be automatically located.

Next, results of the EE and BWE layers detection are discussed only for the V14-IZFP volume. Results for the remaining volumes are presented in appendix C. Table 5.8 resumes the results of this step.

V14-IZFP

This volume corresponds to the 14 mm thick CFRP specimen. It has a voxel size of $[1,1,0.05]$ mm^3, thus 20 layers in z direction represent 1 mm of thickness. The first layer of the volume is at $z = 0$. The backwall slice (last layer of the backwall) should be at $z = 279$ which corresponds to a thickness of $(279 + 1) \cdot 0.05 = 14$ mm.

Applying the proposed algorithm yields the output presented in figure 5.15: the last layer of the BWE is at $z = 269$ which means that the thickness of the specimen is

ID	Resolution in z [mm]	start of $\widetilde{v_{in}}$ [mm]	end of $\widetilde{v_{in}}$ [mm]	BWE slice [mm]	Estimated thickness [mm]	Error [mm]
V14-15	0.5	1	13.5	13.5 to 14	14	0
V14-70	0.5	1	13.5	13.5 to 14	14	0
V14-100	0.5	1	13.5	13.5 to 14	14	0
V14-IZFP	0.05	0.8	13.1	13.45 to 13.5	13.5	-0.5
V8-21	0.2	0.4	7.4	7.6 to 7.8	7.8	-0.2
V8-22	0.05	0.06	7.3	8 to 8.05	8.05	+0.05
V8-24	0.2	0.8	7.2	7.6 to 7.8	7.8	-0.2

Table 5.8.: Results of EE and BWE detection obtained on all the input volumes.

13.5 mm; Thus, there is a 0.5 mm thickness estimation error. Defects within this depth will not be detected. Remind that layers after the BWE slice are not useful, they are present in the volume because the maximal depth ($z = T$) in the sampling software is set to a value higher than the specimen's thickness.

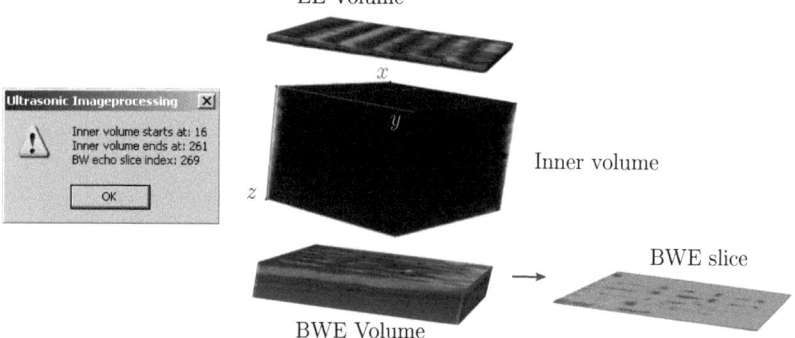

Figure 5.15.: Outputs of the Ultrasound Image processing tool for the volume V14-IZFP: the EE volume, the inner volume z start and z end, the BWE volume and the position z of the BWE slice (last layer of the backwall at $z = 269$ (13.45 to 13.5 mm).

Notice in figure 5.16 the remaining effect of the BWE (traces) in the inner volume. These BWE traces have high contrast and could form large artifacts and potentially get attached to some nearby defects, especially because the NL-means filter tends to dilate structures. This issue will be addressed later on.

Although minimal errors in locating EE and BWE remain (see table 5.8), the important point for us is to keep all defects present in the specimens in the inner volume. Among all the acquisitions, only one inclusion was missed as it was considered part of the BWE volume. This occurred in the volume V8-24 which might be due to the CPA acquisition mode which apparently is less favorable to such defects which are close to the end of the specimen.

5.2.4 Thresholding results

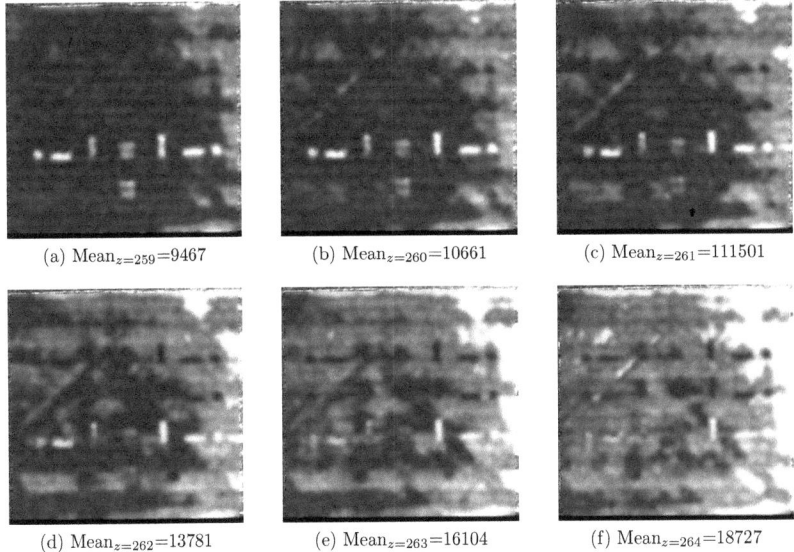

(a) Mean$_{z=259}$=9467　　(b) Mean$_{z=260}$=10661　　(c) Mean$_{z=261}$=111501

(d) Mean$_{z=262}$=13781　　(e) Mean$_{z=263}$=16104　　(f) Mean$_{z=264}$=18727

Figure 5.16.: V14-IZFP: comparison of last three layers of the inner volume (a,b,c) and first three layers of the BWE (d,e,f). Notice the strong influence of the BWE echoes which affects layers close to the end of the specimen.

5.2.4. Thresholding results

First, the thresholding step requires to select a reference zone (without defect) inside the filtered inner volume. Afterward, the hysteresis thresholds T_L and T_H can be computed.

In order to find the optimal thresholds selection, a study (manual classification) of all output labeled volumes obtained for every thresholds selection was carried out. Here, from the total number of suspicious regions, the number of detected defects (NTP) and the number of false positives[2] (NFP) were computed and analyzed. The optimal thresholds selection should give the highest value of NTP and the lowest value of NFP. Next, the results for the three illustrative volumes are discussed. Results for the remaining volumes can be found in appendix D. Note that the possible thresholds selections which did not provide an NTP higher than 90 % of the total number of positives (NP) will not be mentioned in the tables.

---

[2]Reminder: a false positive (i.e., false alarm) is a suspicious region which is not a defect but was misclassified as a defect by the classifier.

V14-IZFP

The selected reference zone Z_{ref} inside $\widetilde{v_{in}}$ is presented in figure 5.17a. The hysteresis threshold dialogue box is presented in figure 5.17b. It allows to specify the dimensions of the reference zone, to select the values of T_L and T_H and needs the dimensions of the enhancing filter (i.e., NLMW5B1) as additional information. This information is required in order to specify the borders of the filtered volume. The non filtered borders are excluded from the binary volume. Remind that, in this volume the number of defects is NP=24. Table 5.9 resumes the output of the thresholding step for selections of T_L and T_H which satisfy the condition on the number of NTP.

Hysteresis thresholds	NTP	NFP
$T_L = 2 \cdot \text{mean}[Z_{ref}]$, $T_H = 3 \cdot \text{mean}[Z_{ref}]$	22	18
$T_L = 3 \cdot \text{mean}[Z_{ref}]$, $T_H = 3 \cdot \text{mean}[Z_{ref}]$	22	25

Table 5.9.: Number of defects (NTP > 21) and false positives (NFP) obtained by hysteresis thresholds applied on the volume V14-IZFP.

On the first hand, it can be surprising that low thresholds did not provide enough high NTP. Indeed, a low threshold should allow to detect all true defects, at the expense of a high number of false alarms. This is not the case here because a very low threshold effectively detect the defects, however, they are all connected to large artifacts (such as BWE artifacts) and thus, they are manually classified as false defects.

Results proved that for this volume, a T_L equal to double of the mean intensity and a T_H equal to triple of the mean intensity inside Z_{ref} give the optimal results. The output of the thresholding method is presented in figure 5.18, where the number of found suspicious regions (labels) is: NTP+NFP=40. Notice that the amount of artifacts dramatically increases in layers at the end of the inner volume because of the influence of the BWE traces. This is the reason behind the loss of two defects which are located near the backwall.

In fact, for the selection of $T_L = 2 \cdot \text{mean}[Z_{ref}]$ and $T_H = 3 \cdot \text{mean}[Z_{ref}]$, all defects do appear (i.e., set as foreground) in the binary volume. Nevertheless, two of them get attached to nearby large artifacts and they are labeled with the artifact as one suspicious region.

To further explain the effect of the BWE traces, let us take a look on 2D views of the layers presented in figure 5.19. The BWE traces have high intensity values and are set as foreground. While some artifacts corresponding to the BWE traces are isolated, other large artifacts get attached to the neighboring two defects. This cause the loss (see red dotted box) of these two defects. Another smaller artifact distorts the shape of another defect (see red box).

5.2.4 Thresholding results

Figure 5.17.: (a) V14-IZFP: selection of the reference zone using the red rectangular tracker. (b) Dialogue box corresponding to the hysteresis thresholding method containing the possibilities: to select the reference zone, setting T_L and T_H and the specify the borders of the filtered volume. The non filtered borders are excluded from the binary volume.

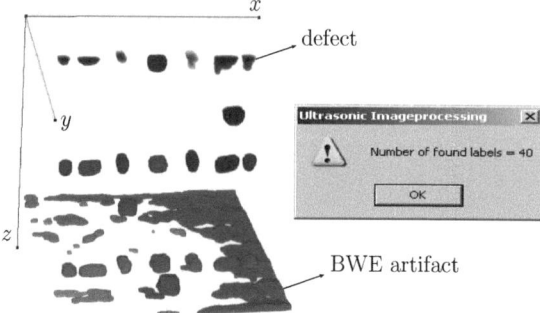

Figure 5.18.: V14-IZFP: 3D view of labeled suspicious regions (label=intensity value) where defects and artifacts can be seen. Total number of suspicious regions (NTP+FTP) is 40.

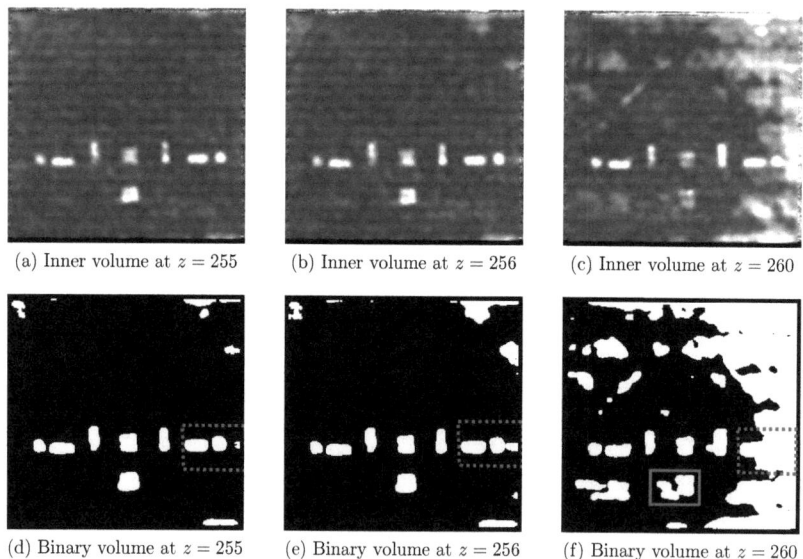

(a) Inner volume at $z = 255$ (b) Inner volume at $z = 256$ (c) Inner volume at $z = 260$

(d) Binary volume at $z = 255$ (e) Binary volume at $z = 256$ (f) Binary volume at $z = 260$

Figure 5.19.: V14-IZFP: Artifacts caused by the BWE traces in the inner volume at different z locations close to BWE (a,b,c) and their corresponding binary layers (d,e,f). Two defects (dotted box) are lost because they get connected to the voxels of the remaining traces of the BWE. Another smaller artifact distort the shape of the defect surrounded by a red box (still considered as true defect).

5.2.4 Thresholding results

V14-70

The results of the hysteresis thresholds applied on the inner volume intensities of V14-70 indicated that the hysteresis thresholds selection which gave the required NTP is again: $T_L = 2 \cdot \text{mean}[Z_{ref}]$ and $T_H = 3 \cdot \text{mean}[Z_{ref}]$ (table 5.10). For this output volume, the number of suspicious regions is 45. However, two defects were missed: a) as presented in figure 5.20, one very low contrasted defect does not appear in the binary volume when using this thresholds selection. b) one defect near the backwall get attached to the backwall artifact.

The manual threshold option was used to ensure the appearance of the low contrasted defect. Figure 5.21 shows the result where the low contrasted defect is clearly visible. Nevertheless, as presented in figure 5.22, the number of detected suspicious regions increases to 105 (NTP=23 and NFP=82) due to the less hard threshold applied on the intensity values. This of course gives more artifacts set as foreground.

Note that in this case, the user needs to select another reference zone in order to measure the features which need a reference zone. Figure 5.23 shows the results after thresholding for the first two layers and the last layer of the inner volume. It can be seen that in the last layer, one defect is attached to the artifact of the BWE.

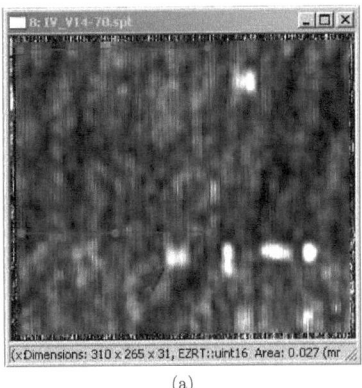
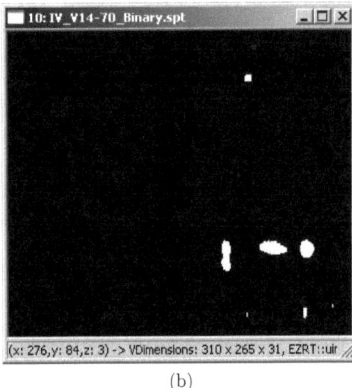

(a)   (b)

Figure 5.20.: (a) V14-70: selection of the reference zone without defects. (b) View of the corresponding layer in the obtained binary volume using $T_L = 2 \cdot \text{mean}[Z_{ref}]$ and $T_H = 3 \cdot \text{mean}[Z_{ref}]$. The low contrasted defect (pointed at by the blue arrow) is missing in the binary volume.

Hysteresis thresholds	NTP	NFP
$T_L = 2 \cdot \text{mean}[Z_{ref}]$, $T_H = 3 \cdot \text{mean}[Z_{ref}]$	22	23

Table 5.10.: Number of defects (NTP>21) and false positives (NFP) obtained by the hysteresis threshold applied on the volume V14-70.

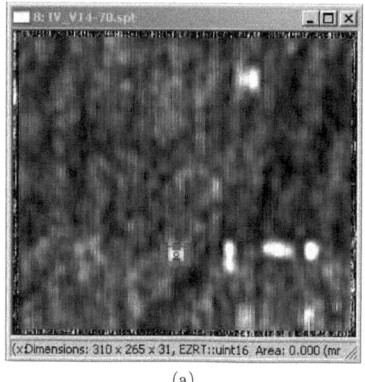
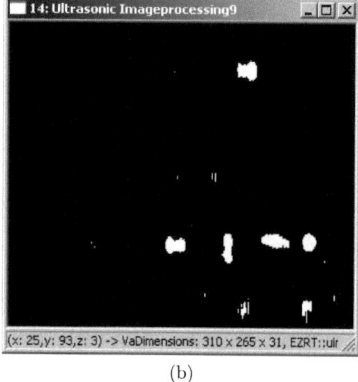

Figure 5.21.: (a) V14-70: selection of the low contrasted defect to compute T_H and T_L as $T_H = T_L = M_{\text{def}}$. (b) View of the binary layer where all defects are seen.

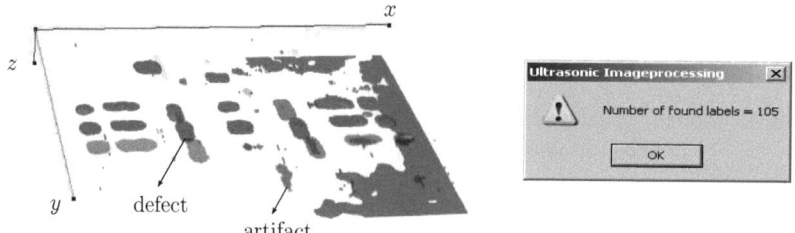

Figure 5.22.: V14-70: 3D view of labeled suspicious regions (label=intensity value) obtained using the low contrasted defect to select the thresholds. Total number of suspicious regions is 105.

5.2.4 Thresholding results

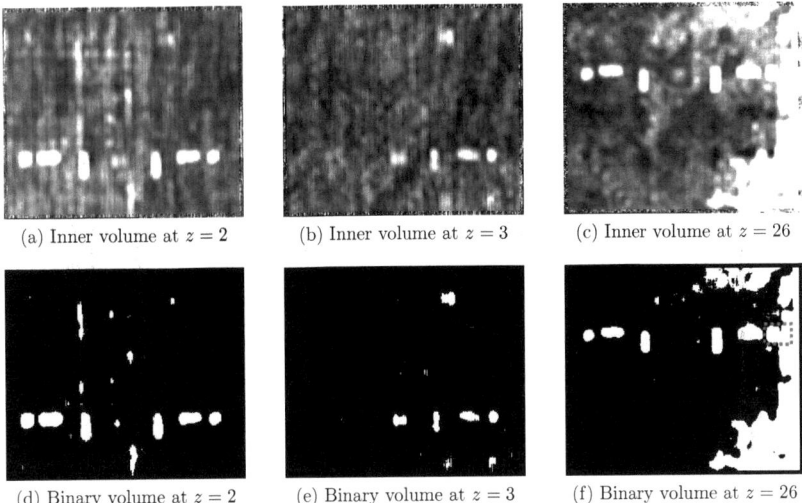

(a) Inner volume at $z = 2$
(b) Inner volume at $z = 3$
(c) Inner volume at $z = 26$
(d) Binary volume at $z = 2$
(e) Binary volume at $z = 3$
(f) Binary volume at $z = 26$

Figure 5.23.: V14-70: (a,b) first and second layers in the inner volume (near the EE volume). (c) Last layer of the inner volume near the BWE slice (at $z = 27$). (d,e) binary layers obtained for the first two layers of the inner volume. (f) Binary layer near the backwall slice. Note that one defect gets attached to the BWE artifact (red dotted box).

V8-22

The number of defects inside this volume is NP=30. The selected reference zone Z_{ref} without defects is presented in figure 5.24. As reported in table 5.11, three selections allowed to have NTP=30. Nevertheless, two selections gave the lowest NFP, one of them is the selection of: $T_L = 2 \cdot \text{mean}[Z_{ref}]$ and $T_H = 3 \cdot \text{mean}[Z_{ref}]$. For this selection, all defects are seen, even their ghosts (i.e., reverberations of reflectors) appear when their amplitude is higher than the threshold T_H.

Hysteresis thresholds	NTP	NFP
$T_L = \text{mean}[Z_{ref}]$, $T_H = 3 \cdot \text{mean}[Z_{ref}]$	30	17
$T_L = 2 \cdot \text{mean}[Z_{ref}]$, $T_H = 3 \cdot \text{mean}[Z_{ref}]$	30	17
$T_L = 3 \cdot \text{mean}[Z_{ref}]$, $T_H = 3 \cdot \text{mean}[Z_{ref}]$	30	19

Table 5.11.: Number of defects (NTP $\geq$ 27) and false positives (NFP) obtained by different hysteresis thresholds selections applied on the volume V8-22.

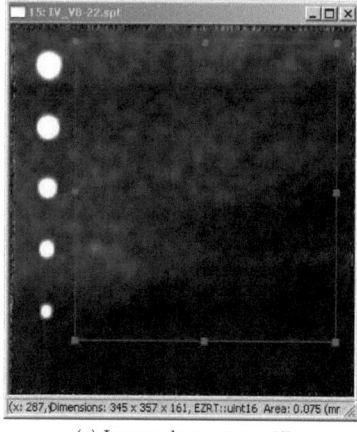

(a) Inner volume at $z = 17$ (b) Binary volume at $z = 17$

Figure 5.24.: V8-22: (a) Selection of the reference zone used to compute the hysteresis threshold T_L and T_H. (b) Output binary layer for $T_L = 2 \cdot \text{mean}[Z_{ref}]$ and $T_H = 3 \cdot \text{mean}[Z_{ref}]$

Figure 5.26 shows the 3D binary volume, where in total 47 suspicious regions were detected. Note that, for layers at $z = \{12, 13, 14\}$, not all five defects which are present in these layers appear in the corresponding binary layers. The selected hysteresis threshold failed to set them as foreground in these layers. However, all five defects start to appear in the binary layer at depth $z = 15$ (see figure 5.25).

Thresholding results for the other volumes can be found in appendix D.

The analysis of all obtained results revealed that the following thresholds selection: $T_L = 2 \cdot \text{mean}[Z_{ref}]$ and $T_H = 3 \cdot \text{mean}[Z_{ref}]$ gives very good results (high NTP and low FTP). Only three low contrasted defects were missed from the inner volumes when applying this selection. Those defects were successfully detected by selecting them as zones to compute the thresholds such that: T_L and T_H are equal to the mean intensity inside the selected defect's zone. Naturally, this came at the cost of larger amount of false positives.

For the next stages, it was decided to take the thresholding selections for which all existing defects inside the input inner volumes were considered as foregrounds. This means more artifacts that needs to be distinguished from the real defects. However, the aim of the classification procedure is to successfully classify these artifacts as false defects. Table 5.12 resumes the results considered for the ulterior stages.

5.2.4 Thresholding results

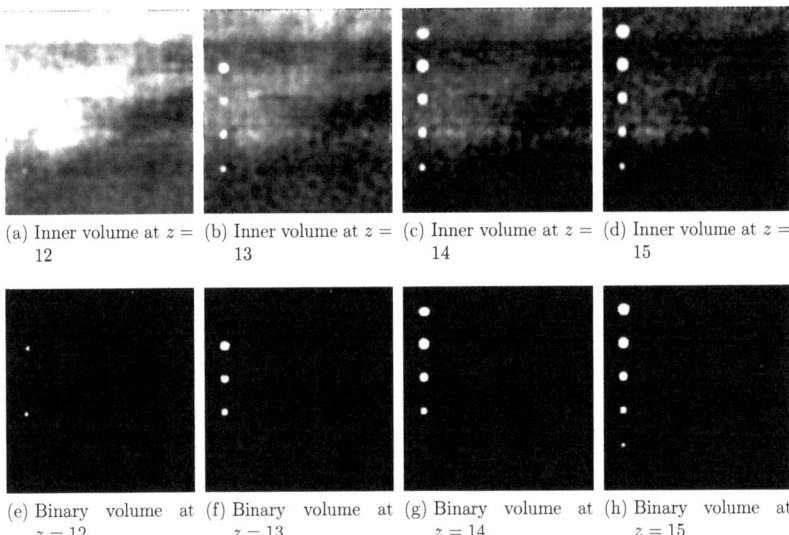

(a) Inner volume at $z = 12$
(b) Inner volume at $z = 13$
(c) Inner volume at $z = 14$
(d) Inner volume at $z = 15$

(e) Binary volume at $z = 12$
(f) Binary volume at $z = 13$
(g) Binary volume at $z = 14$
(h) Binary volume at $z = 15$

Figure 5.25.: V8-22: (a,b,c,d) Layers of the inner volume near the EE layers. (e,f,g,h) Binary layers obtained using $T_L = 2 \cdot \mathrm{mean}[Z_{ref}]$ and $T_H = 3 \cdot \mathrm{mean}[Z_{ref}]$. Some defects are not seen in the binary volume until $z = 15$.

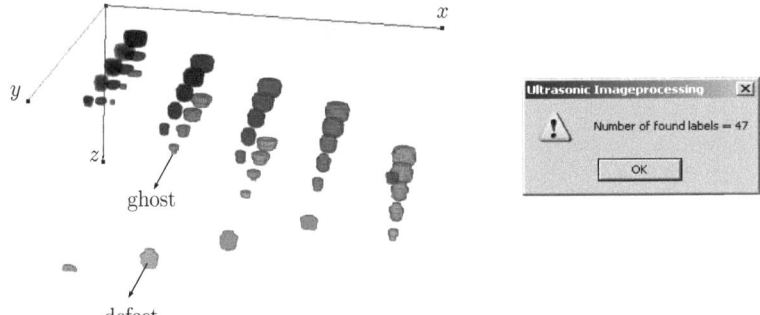

Figure 5.26.: V8-22: 3D view of labeled suspicious regions (label=intensity value) where defects and their ghosts can be seen. Total number of suspicious regions is 47.

ID	T_L	T_H	suspicious regions	NTP	NFP	lost defects	reason of loss
V14-15	M_{def}	M_{def}	94	23	71	1	attachment to a BWE artefact
V14-70	M_{def}	M_{def}	105	23	82	1	attachment to a BWE artefact
V14-100	M_{def}	M_{def}	180	23	157	1	attachment to a BWE artefact
V14-IZFP	$2 \cdot \text{mean}[Z_{ref}]$	$3 \cdot \text{mean}[Z_{ref}]$	40	22	18	2	attachment to a BWE artefact
V8-21	$2 \cdot \text{mean}[Z_{ref}]$	$3 \cdot \text{mean}[Z_{ref}]$	77	30	47	0	-
V8-22	$2 \cdot \text{mean}[Z_{ref}]$	$3 \cdot \text{mean}[Z_{ref}]$	47	30	17	0	-
V8-24	$2 \cdot \text{mean}[Z_{ref}]$	$3 \cdot \text{mean}[Z_{ref}]$	36	29	7	1	defect is part of the BWE volume

Table 5.12.: Results of thresholding obtained for all the input volumes.

5.2.5. Features extraction results

The final step of the segmentation procedure is to characterize each suspicious region by a list of features in order to classify it as defective or not. Illustrative features, damage index (DI) and elongation in yz plane (E_{yz}), are presented in figures 5.27 and 5.28 for V14-70 and V8-22. In figure 5.27, it can be seen that defects have a high DI and artifacts (false defects) have a low DI. Defects in V14-70 have high $E_{yz} = L_{yz}/W_{yz}$ values while defects in V8-22 has low E_{yz} values. The reason is that, defects in V14-70 are thin delaminations (elongated shape with thin width and high length). While in V8-22, most defects are bottom drilled circular holes which have nearly the same length and width (elongation values are around 1).

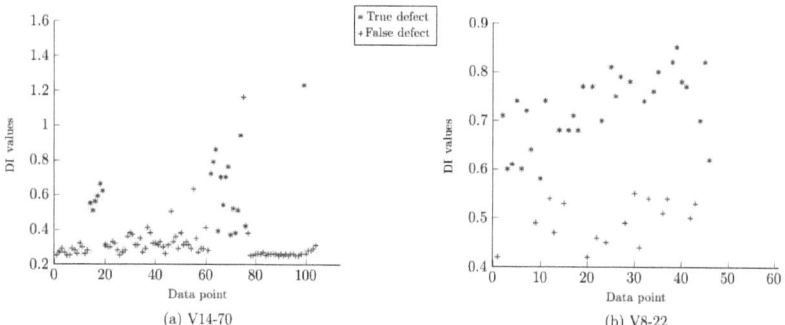

Figure 5.27.: (a) Damage Index (DI) values of suspicious regions found in the volume V14-70. (b) DI values for suspicious regions found in V8-22.

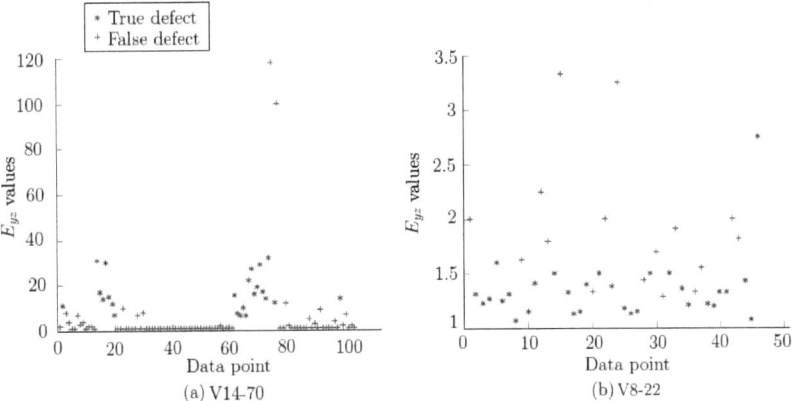

Figure 5.28.: (a) Elongation in yz plane (E_{yz}) values of suspicious regions found in the volume V14-70. (b) E_{yz} values for suspicious regions found in V8-22.

5.3. Experimental results of the classification procedure

The classification methods DFC and SVM are supervised processes. They need to be trained and tested on inputs of known classes. Thus, suspicious regions were manually classified into TD or FD.

The classification procedure will be conducted separately for the CFRP-14 specimen (V14-IZFP, V14-15, V14-70, V14-100) and for the CFRP-8 specimen (V8-21, V8-22, V8-24). The methodology, for each specimen, is to merge all the suspicious regions (or potential defects) of the corresponding input volumes into one dataset. Afterward, the resulting dataset is divided (separation: odd IDs, even IDs) into two datasets on which the learning and testing phases are done.

5.3.1. Results for CFRP-14

The suspicious regions obtained for segmented volumes V14-15, V14-70, V14-100 and V14-IZFP are merged into one dataset forming a total of 419 potential defects. The dataset contains 91 TDs and 328 FDs. Next, it is divided into learning and testing datasets:

- Learning dataset: 212 potential defects consisting of 164 FDs and 48 TDs.
- Testing dataset: 207 potential defects consisting of 164 FDs and 43 TDs.

At first ROC curves are built, for the learning dataset, to give us a primary idea about the accuracy of the measured features. The ROC curves for feature values are built using thresholds on the feature values. The ROC curves for mass values are build using thresholds on the obtained mass values from the learning phase. Remind that the first step of the learning phase is the elaboration of the regions of confidence which allow the translation from feature values to mass values. An example of the output of this step is presented in figure 5.29.

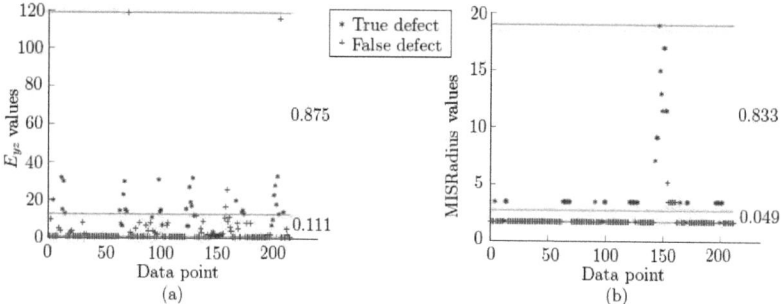

Figure 5.29.: Regions of confidence elaborated during the learning phase (DV=0 and Perc=0.1) for the features: (a) E_{yz}. (b) MISRadius.

The A_{ROC} for all sources of information (using original feature values and mass values to build the ROC curves) is presented in figure 5.30. In this figure, features are referred to by their identification numbers (see tables B.1 and B.2). Remind that the A_{ROC} informs about the accuracy of the source and corresponds to the probability of correctly identifying the TDs and FDs [200]. Thus, the A_{ROC} will be used to select features which satisfy the condition ($A_{ROC} \geq 0.9$). The aim of this selection is to improve the classifiers performance [189].

Classification using all features

The learning phase for DFC and SVM is at first done using all measured features. Afterward, the testing phase takes place. The optimal performance for the DFC system is given for values of DV=0 and Perc=0.1 as demonstrated in [186]. Concerning the threshold S_m on the mass value, different thresholds are applied $S_m = \{0.6, 0.7, 0.8, 0.9\}$. The threshold which gives the best performance is specified.

Results obtained by the DFC method are reported in table 5.13.

On the learning dataset: the statistical combination rules have very high FDs classification rates (PFD). However, they have low TDs classification rates (PTD). The reason is that the majority of the individual sources (features) assign low mass values to the true defect hypothesis (H_1) and they assign high mass values to the ignorance

5.3.1 Results for CFRP-14

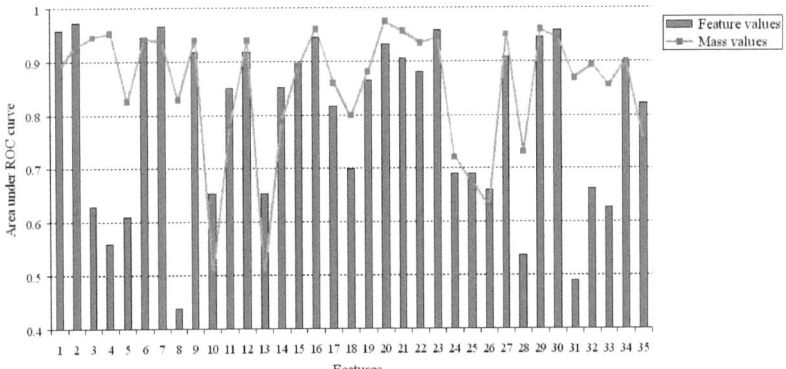

Figure 5.30.: CFRP-14: Area under ROC curves for feature values and their corresponding mass values. Mean value of the area under ROC curves for features is 0.791. Mean value of the area under ROC curves for mass values is 0.85.

hypothesis.

The DS fusion (DSF) of all the sources almost classify all inputs as TDs. It has a PFD close to zero. In fact, using the Dempster rule for the whole set of 35 features is wrong here because they are not all independent sources. Thus, if several sources are dependent, the same piece of information can be counted twice which yields a higher mass on the hypothesis H_1.

The DSF of the three maximal mass values is compared with the cautious rule. In fact, in DFC method, the cautious rule selects the maximal mass value among all mass values attributed to H_1 by the sources of information. Comparison of the results show that the cautious rule has an overall rate (R) which overcomes the R given by the DSF{3 max mass}.

The best source for TDs classification is the DSF of features 14 (E_{yz}) and 15 (MIS-Radius) with a PTD=1. This combination also has the highest overall rate R=0.984. Note that these two features do not have $A_{ROC} \geq 0.9$. However, when combined, they give the optimal performance. Another remark is that, these two features are indeed independent. The DSF of features 12 (E_{xy}) and 29 (CSMax) gives the highest FDs classification (PFD=0.981) rate. Those two features are independent (geometric/intensity features) and both got an $A_{ROC} > 0.9$.

On the testing dataset: the statistical combination rules have the same behavior. They give a high PFD and a low PTD. Same for DSF{all sources}, its performance is the same as on the learning dataset. Concerning the DSF{3 max mass} and cautious rule, it is clear that both combinations have a drop in their PFDs rates. However, the cautious rule is still giving a better overall rate than the DSF{3 max mass}.

The overall rate for the DSF {14&15} is slightly reduced because of the drop in the PFD, nevertheless PTD is kept at value 1, which means a perfect classification of

DV=0, Perc=0.1	Learning phase			Testing phase		
Source	PTD	PFD	R	PTD	PFD	R
DSF{12&29} [S_m=0.8]	0.958	0.981	0.964	1	0.93	0.982
DSF{14&15} [S_m=0.8]	1	0.94	0.984	1	0.896	0.973
Cautious rule [S_m=0.9]	0.979	0.975	0.979	1	0.786	0.945
DSF{3 max mass} [S_m=0.9]	1	0.756	0.938	1	0.6	0.89
DSF{all sources} [S_m=0.9]	1	0.05	0.76	1	0.06	0.759
Median mass [S_m=0.6]	0.66	0.99	0.749	0.465	0.981	0.597
Mean mass [S_m=0.6]	0.395	1	0.548	0.209	1	0.411

Table 5.13.: CFRP-14: performance of DFC combinations using all available features for learning and testing of DFC method. Combinations are sorted by decreasing overall rate R obtained on the testing dataset.

true defects.
For DSF{12&29} which represents the best source for FDs classification, the PTD increases to 1 on the testing dataset while PFD decreased, still the overall rate R for this source increased due to the increase in the PTD rate. The fact that these last two combinations could give a perfect TDs classification while maintaining a classification rate of FDs (PFD$\geq$ 0.89) is a very promising result for industrial applications. Still some optimization could be done to improve PFD. A further important remark is the fact that both sources have a stable overall performances despite the fact that the datasets are unbalanced. This is also interesting for industrial applications where usually there is a lack of TDs comparing to the large amount of FDs.

The performance of the SVM on the testing dataset, after being trained on the same learning dataset, is presented in table 5.14. The PTD given by the SVM on the testing dataset is limited to 0.976 while it gives a PFD higher than the PFD values given by the sources of DFC system. However, the overall rate for the SVM is lower than the R given by DSF{12&29}.

Testing phase	PTD	PFD	R
SVM	0.976	0.957	0.971

Table 5.14.: CFRP-14: SVM performance on the testing dataset using all available features.

Classification using selected features

In the next section, selected features with $A_{ROC} \geq 0.9$ are used to train the classifiers.

Selection from feature values The analysis of values of the area under ROC for feature values, in figure 5.30, reveals that 14 features (1, 2, 6, 7, 6, 9, 12, 16, 20, 21,

5.3.1 Results for CFRP-14

23, 26, 27, 29, 30 and 34) have an $A_{ROC} \geq 0.9$, thus they are considered to be more reliable sources of information. As in the previous section, learning and testing takes place but this time only using these features. Performances for DFC and SVM are respectively reported in tables 5.15 and 5.16.

DV=0, Perc=0.1	Learning phase			Testing phase		
Source	PTD	PFD	R	PTD	PFD	R
DSF{12&29} [S_m=0.8]	0.958	0.981	0.964	1	0.93	0.982
Cautious rule [S_m=0.9]	0.979	0.975	0.979	1	0.871	0.967
DSF{all sources} [S_m=0.9]	1	0.841	0.959	1	0.762	0.939
DSF{3 max mass} [S_m=0.8]	1	0.871	0.967	1	0.75	0.935
Median mass [S_m=0.6]	0.833	0.987	0.872	0.837	0.957	0.867
Mean mass [S_m=0.6]	0.833	0.987	0.872	0.813	0.969	0.853

Table 5.15.: CFRP-14: performance of DFC combinations using features with $A_{ROC} \geq 0.9$ for learning and testing of DFC method. Combinations are sorted by decreasing overall rate R obtained on the testing dataset.

Testing phase	PTD	PFD	R
SVM	0.976	0.981	0.978

Table 5.16.: CFRP-14: SVM performance on the testing dataset using features with $A_{ROC} \geq 0.9$.

For the DFC method, notably the performances of all the combinations was improved. This is certainly due to the fact that the independence of the sources is better respected here. The mean and median combinations became much more reliable. This is because all the sources are reliable. They assign a high mass value to TDs and a low mass value to FDs. This reason is also behind the amelioration of DSF{all sources} and DSF{3 max mass}. As for the cautious rule source, its overall rate increased due to the improvement in the PFD. Still, the optimal performance is given by the features combination DSF{12&29} having the same performance as presented in table 5.13. The SVM performance (table 5.16) had a slight improvement in the overall rate because of the increase in the PFD rate. However, the PTD rate given by the SVM did not improve. This result is different to what was obtained in our previous study [189]. In [189], a great improvement in the SVM's PTD rate was achieved when the SVM was trained on pertinent features which were selected based on the A_{ROC} of feature values.

Selection from mass values By using the mass values to build the ROC curves, 16 features (2, 3, 4, 6, 7, 9, 12, 16, 20, 21, 22, 23, 27, 29, 30 and 34) become more reliable ($A_{ROC} \geq 0.9$). Globally, the pertinence of the majority of the sources is improved. In fact, the mean value of all areas under ROC curves for feature values (mean(A_{ROC} for feature values)=0.791) is less than the mean value of all areas under ROC curves for all mass values (mean(A_{ROC} for mass values)=0.85). Thus, the translation from feature values to mass values via the proposed mass attribution method [186] improves the pertinence of several features. Results for the DFC system and SVM are respectively reported in tables 5.17 and 5.18.

DV=0, Perc=0.1	Learning phase			Testing phase		
Source	PTD	PFD	R	PTD	PFD	R
DSF{12&29} [S_m=0.8]	0.958	0.981	0.964	1	0.93	0.982
Cautious rule [S_m=0.9]	0.979	0.975	0.979	1	0.81	0.953
DSF{3 max mass} [S_m=0.8]	1	0.865	0.966	1	0.743	0.934
DSF{all sources} [S_m=0.9]	1	0.804	0.95	1	0.695	0.921
Median mass [S_m=0.6]	0.854	0.987	0.88	0.837	0.975	0.872
Mean mass [S_m=0.6]	0.791	0.987	0.841	0.79	0.975	0.838

Table 5.17.: CFRP-14: performance of DFC combinations using features with A_{ROC} for mass values higher or equal to 0.9 for learning and testing of DFC method. Combinations are sorted by decreasing overall rate R obtained on the testing dataset.

Testing phase	PTD	PFD	R
SVM	0.976	0.969	0.974

Table 5.18.: CFRP-14: SVM performance on the testing dataset using features with A_{ROC} for mass values higher or equal to 0.9.

While the DSF{12&29} is still the source with the optimal performance, the overall rate of the cautious rule source decreased (lower PFD rate) compared to the previous results obtained using features with $A_{ROC} \geq 0.9$ for feature values. Same is the case for DSF{all sources} and DSF{3 max mass}. However, all DFC combinations were improved compared to the case when the training was done using all features.

As for the SVM classifier, it was noticed that its performance slightly decreased (lower PFD rate) compared with the performance obtained using features with $A_{ROC} \geq 0.9$ for feature values. Still, the SVM's performance was slightly improved compared with the performance obtained using all features to train the SVM. In all cases, SVM could not outperform the DSF{12&29} given by the DFC method.

5.3.2. Results for CFRP-8

Difficulty for the CFRP-8 specimen case is the presence of ghost artifacts inside the corresponding measured volumes. These artifacts need to be classified as FDs despite

5.3.2 Results for CFRP-8

the fact that they have very similar characteristics to real defects. Therefore, they are difficult to distinguish from TDs by machine learning.

First, all the suspicious regions obtained by segmenting volumes V8-21, V8-22 and V8-24 are merged in order to form the learning and testing datasets for DFC and SVM. Obtained sets are as follow:

- Learning dataset: 81 potential defects including 36 FDs and 45 TDs.

- Testing dataset: 79 potential defects including 35 FDs and 44 TDs.

The A_{ROC}, for features values and mass values, obtained on the learning dataset is presented in figure 5.31. Only 5 features, (10, 13, 23, 29, 30), have a $A_{ROC} \geq 0.9$. While by using mass values to build the ROC curves, 16 features become pertinent (10, 13, 15, 17, 19, 20, 21, 22, 23, 27, 29, 30, 31, 32, 33 and 34). The same

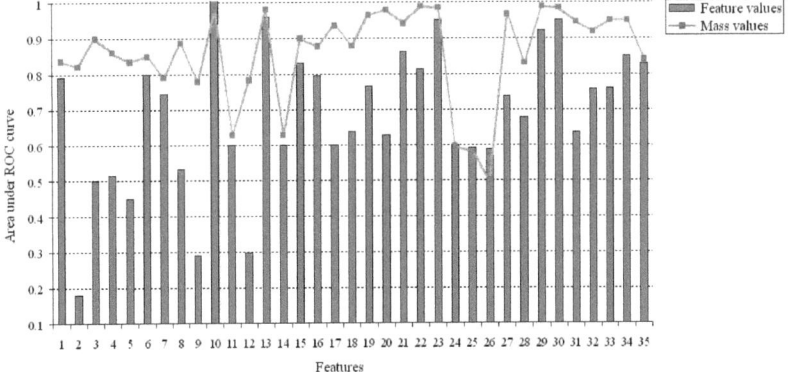

Figure 5.31.: CFRP-8: Area under ROC curves for feature values and their corresponding mass values. Mean value of the area under ROC curves for features is 0.685. Mean value of the area under ROC curves for mass values is 0.859.

procedure applied for CFRP-14, in the classification of potential defects and optimization of DFC and SVM performance using ROC curve, is followed for CFRP-8. Therefore without detailing each steps, only the optimal performances given by each combination and the corresponding necessary information about DV, Perc, S_m and the features used in the training will be reported. Results for DFC and SVM are resumed in tables 5.19 and 5.20.

For the DFC method: different combinations gave very good rates on the learning dataset with all combinations achieving an overall rate R≥0.96. However, R dropped for all the combinations on the testing dataset mostly because of the decrease in the PFDs rates. This reflects the difficulties encountered by the combinations to distinguish ghosts from defects. The best performance given by the cautious rule occurs when it is trained using only the selected features having $A_{ROC} \geq 0.9$ for feature values.

DV=0, Perc=0.1	Learning phase			Testing phase		
Source	PTD	PFD	R	PTD	PFD	R
Cautious rule [S_m=0.7]	1	0.941	0.987	0.976	0.6	0.898
DSF{3 max mass} [S_m=0.6]	1	0.852	0.969	0.976	0.6	0.898
DSF{all sources} [S_m=0.6]	1	0.852	0.969	0.976	0.6	0.898
Median mass [S_m=0.6]	1	1	1	0.9	0.8	0.884
DSF{23&34} [S_m=0.7]	1	1	1	0.88	0.71	0.848
Mean mass [S_m=0.6]	1	1	1	0.79	0.885	0.81

Table 5.19.: CFRP-8: Optimal performance of cautious rule, DSF{3 max mass} and DSF{all sources} are obtained using features with $A_{ROC} \geq 0.9$ for learning and testing of the DFC method. The statistical combinations (median and mean mass) give their optimal performances when using all features. The best performance of the conjunctive rule DSF{23&34} was given using features with $A_{ROC} \geq 0.9$ for mass values.

For the SVM: its best performance is given when using all features to train and test the classifier. Results show that the SVM outperforms the DFC method for the case of CFRP-8.

Testing phase	PTD	PFD	R
SVM	0.953	0.8	0.921

Table 5.20.: CFRP-8: SVM performance on the testing dataset using all available features.

5.4. Discussion

In this chapter were presented the experimental results obtained using the proposed analysis chain. The beginning was with the experimental CFRP volumes which were available for this work. Then, a brief description of the developed segmentation and classification tools was given. Each step of the segmentation procedure was closely studied and the corresponding results obtained on each input volume were presented and discussed.

The first step of the segmentation procedure was the interpolation of defect voxels. The interpolation was done using a 2D and a 3D modified median filter. A quantitative study proved that both methods gave similar results.

5.4 Discussion

Afterward, the input volumes were filtered using NL-means, median and M3 filter. The NL-means filter ($M = 5$ and $d = 1$) was most successful in enhancing the image and improving the detectability of defects. In fact, the CNR metric suggested that the NLMW5B1 filter largely improves the detectability of low contrasted defects. However, it was also noticed that this filter tends to dilate the borders of structures. The dilation effect caused minor number defects to get attached to backwall's large artifacts. Another note concerns the computation time of NLMW5B1 filter. While the median and M3 filter need seconds to filter the input volume, the NLMW5B1 has a computation time which is roughly about an hour for a [300,300,200] volume. Thus, the filter needs to be accelerated in order to permit its usage in real time application. A good solution was proposed in [165], where the authors proposed a Graphics Processing Unit (GPU) implementation of the NL-means algorithm.

Concerning the difficulties encountered in detecting the entrance and backwall layers: the mechanical scanning system is assumed to be parallel to the surface of the specimen, which must be planar in the present experimental device. This means that the water thickness is assumed to be constant. However, misalignment can occur, or the sample's surface can be not ideal. Consequently, the EE and/or BWE layers can have distorted appearance in the measured data. Another cause of distortion, precisely in the BWE appearance, is the speed of sound (see figure 5.32). The speed of sound can be slightly different from one region to another in the anisotropic CFRP structure.

As a consequence of the non planar appearance of the EE and BWE layers, large artifacts (called EE and BWE traces) were present in the layers near the entrance and the backwall of the specimen.

Hysteresis thresholds $T_L = 2 \cdot \text{Mean}[Z_ref]$ and $T_H = 3 \cdot \text{Mean}[Z_ref]$ successfully led to the setting of all defects as foreground. The only exception was in the case of the volumes V14-15, V14-70 and V14-100. In these volumes, one low contrasted defect was set as a background. This is possibly caused by the wrong setting of the voxel size in the image. In fact, the voxel size in z direction was set to 0.5 mm, which is almost equal to the wavelength (0.576 mm). This emphasizes the importance of the right choice of the voxel size for a given wavelength.

After thresholding, foreground voxels were connected to form labeled suspicious regions. Each region was characterized by geometric and intensity features.

The measured features were used in the classification procedure in order to distinguish true defects from false defects. The classification was carried out using the DFC method and the SVM classifier. The performance of the classifiers was quantified in terms of correct classification rates, respectively for TDs and FDs and also using ROC. The area under ROC curves allowed to select the most pertinent features and to compare the discrimination performance by directly using the feature or mass values.

The obtained results for the CFRP-14 specimen showed a very good performance of the classification chain where all defects were correctly classified (PTD=1) with only 7 % error in false defects classification (PFD=0.93). This result was obtained by the

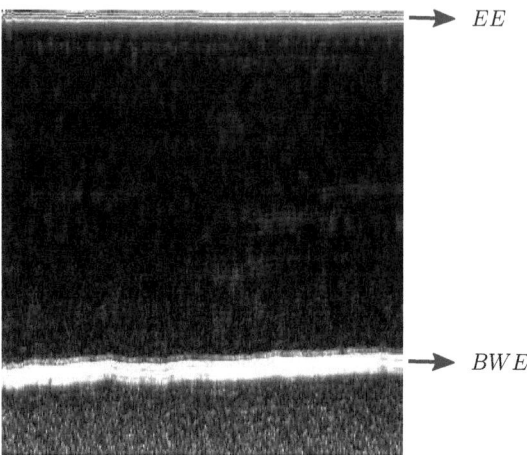

Figure 5.32.: A B-scan (xy view) of the V14-IZFP volume: the difference of the speed of sound in the anisotropic CFRP material cause the non planar appearance of the BWE. Notice that the EE and BWE of the specimen are seen over many layers in the reconstructed volume due to the strong reflected echoes from the entrance and the backwall of the specimen.

conjunctive combination of two independent features (DSF{12&29}) which gave an overall classification rate R=0.982. The performance given by the cautious rule was close to the performance given by the conjunctive combination. Cautious rule gave a maximal overall classification rate R=0.967 when using features with $A_{ROC} \geq 0.9$ to train and test the DFC method. As for the SVM, its best performance was given as well when using features with $A_{ROC} \geq 0.9$. SVM gave an R=0.978 and had a higher false defects classification rate than the DFC method. Nevertheless, SVM did not correctly classify all true defects. Thus, the DFC method performed better on the CFRP-14 reconstructed volumes.

The presence of ghost artifacts in the CFRP-8 reconstructed volumes induced a reduction in the performance of the both classifiers. The DFC method gave at best a overall classification rate R=0.898 using the cautious rule of combination, although the false defects detection rate was low (PFD=0.6). SVM performed better than the DFC on this dataset. It had a better performance on false defects classification (PFD=0.8) and gave an overall rate R=0.921. However, the true defects classification rate given by SVM (PTD=0.953) was less than what was achieved by the DFC method (PTD=0.976).

6. Summary and outlook

6.1. Summary

With the vast application of ultrasound technology in industry and the need to conduct large scale inspection tasks, an increasing need to automate the inspection procedure arises. While the main focus was on the technique itself, there is an imminent need to complete the inspection system with an analysis chain that can automatically interpret the large amount of produced data.

This thesis proposed a complete analysis chain dedicated to segment and classify defects in 3D ultrasound volumes. The work also included a study of the speckle noise in SPA volumes. The analysis chain was experimentally evaluated on CFRP volumes. The chain was stable and gave promising results. The segmentation and classification algorithms of the analysis chain were successfully implemented in two prototype softwares.

Speckle noise formation, distribution estimation and reduction techniques were the subject of chapter 3. Theoretical and empirical speckle models were reviewed and discussed in the first section of this chapter. Then, the pdf of the 4P-$G\Gamma D$ distribution was proposed as a model which fits the noise distribution in SPA data. The model was tested on SPA 3D volumes of three different materials: CFRP, aluminum and ceramic. The obtained results showed that the proposed model successfully fits the noise in CFRP and ceramic ultrasound data. In case of aluminum material, the model was in the second rank after the 3P-Lognormal pdf. After studying in detail the nature of noise, the speckle noise reduction techniques were tackled, where a review of the state of the art techniques employed to enhance ultrasound images was presented. The out coming conclusion was that filters which exploits the redundancy in the image, such as the NL-means filter, appear to be among the most successful approaches.

In chapter 4, the analysis chain formed of segmentation and classification procedures was proposed. The objective of the segmentation procedure was to detect all potential defects inside the volume. Difficulties were mostly encountered when defects are close to the entrance and backwall layers. The segmentation procedure is composed of different stages. First, an algorithm to interpolate the invalid voxels inside the reconstructed volume was proposed . Then objective was to reduce the noise and enhance the image by means of spatial filtering techniques. NL-means, median and M3 filters were separately applied in 2D over each layer of the volume. Afterwards, a method to automatically detect the entrance and the backwall was presented. This method is based on the second derivative of the mean intensity in depth direction. After the detection of the entrance and the backwall layers, the inner volume was extracted. The hysteresis thresholding was applied on the inner volume in order to separate voxels into background and foreground. Two hysteresis thresholds were computed using the statistical mean intensity of a selected reference zone inside the inner volume. The outputs of the thresholding stage were 3D suspicious regions, each labeled by a unique identifier. Geometric and intensity characteristics of these regions were measured. In total, 35 features were measured including two proposed features which are especially dedicated for ultrasound data (shadow and damage index). Features extraction formed the last stage of the segmentation procedure, output suspicious regions were to be classified by the classification procedure.

The classification procedure was based on the theory of evidence which allows to reason with uncertainty. The data fusion classification method (DFC) considered each measured features as a source of information. Different sources of information were combined together in order to improve the true classification rates of true defects and false alarms of the classification method. To make the sources combination possible, first a translation from the features space into a common space (mass values space) was done. Then, features were combined using the non normalized Dempster rule (conjunctive rule) and the cautious rule. The cautious rule is more tolerant to the independence between sources. The DFC method was intended to be compared with the well known Support Vector Machine classifier.

Chapter 5 was dedicated to the experimental evaluation of the analysis chain. Seven input volumes, with different acquisition parameters, size and resolution were used to test the chain. Here, the segmentation procedure was successful in detecting the majority of defects existing in the inner volumes (180 from 186 defects) with minor losses (6 defects) caused by the backwall echo remaining influence in the inner volume. The problem was identified as scan alignment problem where the backwall is not over one layer. The origin of this problem was due to the non ideally parallel contact between the transducer and the planar specimen and to the anisotropy (i.e., speed of sound is not constant) of the CFRP medium. The backwall influence started to appear over layers close to the end back of the specimen causing minor mistakes in detecting the end of the specimen. This led to minor losses of some defects which either get attached to a remaining backwall artifact inside the inner volume or were considered as part of the backwall volume.

The classification procedure gave very promising results when no ghost artifacts were among the suspicious region. The DFC method outperformed the SVM classifier and could reach 100 % classification of true defects with only 7 % error in false defects classification. In case when ghost artifacts are among the suspicious region, both classifiers had difficulties mainly in distinguishing false defects.

6.2. Outlook

This research activity had the aim to propose an analysis chain to segment and classify 3D ultrasound SPA volumes. The chain showed promising results when evaluated on CFRP specimen. However, different points can be further optimized.

The data correction algorithm needs to be compared with some more complex inpainting algorithms.

The elaborated speckle model can be potentially used to optimize the filtering step. This point can represent an interesting subject of a future research activity.

The entrance and backwall echoes/layers misalignment caused difficulties in the detection of the layers corresponding to the entrance and the end of the specimen. This led in some cases to a marginal failure in the estimation of the part thickness. Correction of this effect can be done by using reference signals for scan alignment. This will reduce the error in the BWE and EE locations and should result in more accurate indications about defects. Moreover, a Computer Aided Design (CAD) model of the specimen could help in having a more accurate evaluation. In fact, for non planar specimens, the use of a CAD model could give information on the positions of the EE and BWE of the specimen.

The backwall volume can be furthermore processed. Indeed, shadows can serve as verification if all the defects in the inner volume were found by the analysis chain.

A reference volume obtained on a sample without defects will allow to reduce the user intervention. The volume can be used to automatically compute the hysteresis thresholds and in the extraction of features which need a reference volume.

The presence of strong absorbers in the 8 mm thick CFRP (circular holes) caused the appearance of ghost artifacts in the corresponding reconstructed volumes. A decrease was noticed in the classifiers performance when trained and tested on this specimen. Indeed, it is difficult to distinguish the defects from their ghosts because of the strong similarity between them. It appears that a solution, in a future work, could be to compute features between the blobs (such as distance between the blobs or difference in contrast). Another possibility is to train the classifier on a third class corresponding to ghosts in addition to the other two classes: true defects or false alarms. This could help into improving the classification results.

A future development could incorporate the image processing and data classification codes in a single software. The software can be integrated into the inspection system and then eventually, the automated inspection system (acquisition + data analysis) can be part of the production chain.

The analysis chain was evaluated on specimens with artificial defects. Nevertheless, different defects types and shapes were present including delamination, inclusions and voids of different sizes (down to 7 mm diameter). Future work could be the testing of the evaluation method on parts with real defects. The type of defects has not been investigated in this work. Hence, the follow up of this research could involve the determination of the type of defects such as delamination and gas porosities using the geometrical and intensity characteristics which could help to distinguish different defect types.

Our work has included 3D ultrasound and X-ray tomography techniques [189]. The association of these two inspection modalities, using data fusion techniques, represents a promising research subject.

A. Definitions

Necessary definition of topics covered in this thesis and other aspects related to the physics of ultrasound waves are presented in this appendix.

A.1. Ultrasonic imaging concepts

Ultrasound waves are generated by electrical excitations of a piezoelectric transducer. Propagating inside a medium, these acoustical waves are scattered by discontinuities (figure A.1) due to a change in the acoustic impedance between the propagation medium and the discontinuities. The acoustic impedance is a measure relating the sound pressure P_{ac} to the particle velocity ϑ as $Z = \frac{P_{ac}}{\vartheta}$. A discontinuity at distance z from the transducer causes an echo at time $t = \frac{2z}{c}$, where c is the speed of sound inside the medium. Reflected waves received by the transducer at time t are associated with the discontinuity at depth $z = \frac{ct}{2}$. The reflected waves detected by the transducer are converted into an electrical signal.

A.1.1. Reflection and transmission coefficients

Consider an ultrasound wave propagating at a speed c_1 in a homogeneous medium (1) of acoustic impedance Z_1 as presented in figure A.2. The wave reaches a planar boundary, with an incidence angle θ_i, separating medium (1) from a homogeneous medium (2) of acoustic impedance Z_2. Part of the incident wave is reflected into medium (1), while another part is transmitted/refracted into medium (2). Let P_{ac_i} denote the pressure of the incident wave, P_{ac_r} the pressure of the reflected wave and P_{ac_t} the pressure of the transmitted wave. In addition, let ϑ_i, ϑ_r and ϑ_t be the corresponding particle velocities provoked by the (progressive) incident and transmitted waves and the (regressive) reflected wave. The continuity conditions on the sound pressure and particle velocity across the boundary interface permit to write:

$$P_{ac_i} + P_{ac_r} = P_{ac_t} \tag{A.1}$$

and

$$\vartheta_i \cos\theta_i + \vartheta_r \cos\theta_r = \vartheta_t \cos\theta_t \tag{A.2}$$

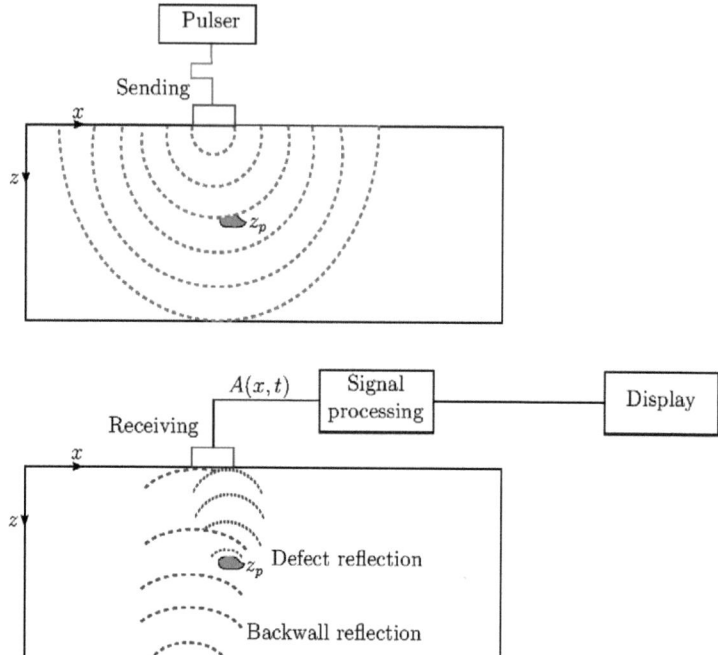

Figure A.1.: Ultrasound simple transducer sending and receiving reflected waves.

where $\theta_r = -\theta_i$.

While the Snell-Descartes law states that:

$$\frac{\sin \theta_i}{\sin \theta_t} = \frac{c_1}{c_2} \quad \text{(A.3)}$$

The acoustic impedance of the medium (1) is given by:

$$Z_1 = \frac{P_{ac_i}}{\vartheta_i} = -\frac{P_{ac_r}}{\vartheta_r} \quad \text{(A.4)}$$

The acoustic impedance of the medium (2) is given by:

$$Z_2 = \frac{P_{ac_t}}{\vartheta_t} \quad \text{(A.5)}$$

Substituting the acoustic impedance into particle velocity condition in equation A.2 yields that:

$$\left(\frac{P_{ac_i}}{Z_1} - \frac{P_{ac_r}}{Z_1}\right) \cos \theta_i = \frac{P_{ac_t}}{Z_2} \cos \theta_t \quad \text{(A.6)}$$

A.1.1 Reflection and transmission coefficients

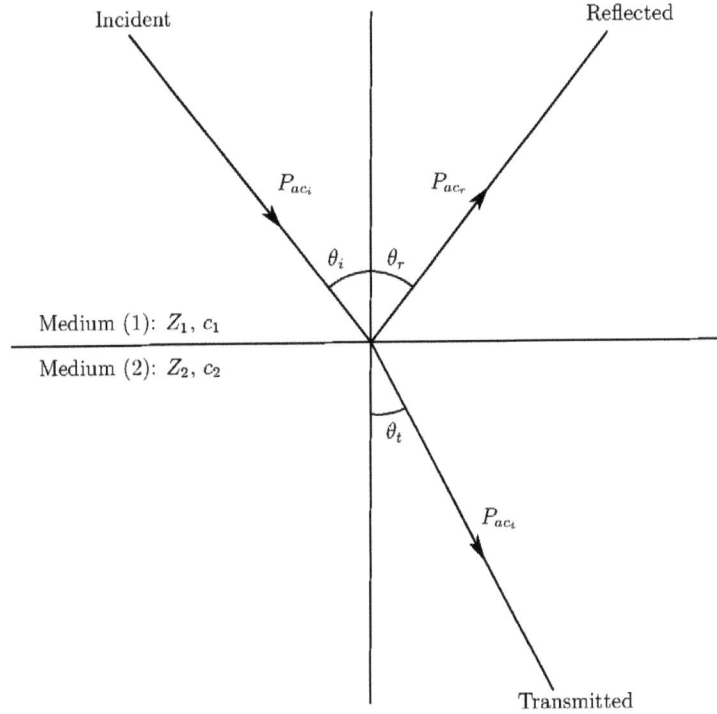

Figure A.2.: Incident ultrasound wave reaching a separation boundary at a speed of sound c_1 and angle θ_i. Part of the wave is reflected back inside medium (1) and another part is transmitted into medium (2).

Taking into consideration the equation A.1, equation A.6 can be formulated as:

$$\frac{1+C_r}{1-C_r} = \frac{\cos\theta_i\, Z_2}{\cos\theta_t\, Z_1} \tag{A.7}$$

where $C_r = \dfrac{P_{ac_r}}{P_{ac_i}}$ is the pressure reflectivity at the boundary. Using the latter equation, C_r can be expressed as:

$$C_r = \frac{Z_2 \cos\theta_i - Z_1 \cos\theta_t}{Z_1 \cos\theta_t + Z_2 \cos\theta_i} \tag{A.8}$$

For inspection tasks, only the surfaces parallel to the wavefront reflect waves back to the transducer (other surfaces reflect away from the transducer). The incidence angle for these surfaces is null: $\theta_i = \theta_r = \theta_t = 0$. Finally the reflection coefficient for waves at normal incidence to surface is:

$$C_r = \frac{P_{ac_r}}{P_{ac_i}} = \frac{Z_2 - Z_1}{Z_1 + Z_2} \tag{A.9}$$

In addition, the transmission coefficient defined as $C_t = \frac{p_t}{p_i}$ can be expressed as:

$$C_t = \frac{P_{ac_t}}{P_{ac_i}} = \frac{P_{ac_i} + P_{ac_r}}{P_{ac_i}} = \frac{2Z_2}{Z_1 + Z_2} \quad (A.10)$$

For a strong absorber (like air voids), the acoustic impedance $Z_2 << Z_1$ which means that the transmission coefficient is very low while the reflection coefficient is close to -1. Therefore shadows occur behind such discontinuities.

A.1.2. Ultrasound display formats

A.1.3. A-scan displays

Amplitude modulation scan, referred to as an A-scan, is a simple one dimensional presentation showing the amplitude of the received envelope signal (or energy) versus the time (or depth). Figure A.3 is an illustrative example of the A-scan obtained when the transducer is at the position showed in figure A.1. In an A-scan display, the depth of a reflector can be determined by the position of its corresponding peak on the horizontal sweep. The size of a reflector can be also estimated by comparing the signal amplitude obtained from it to that from a known reflector.

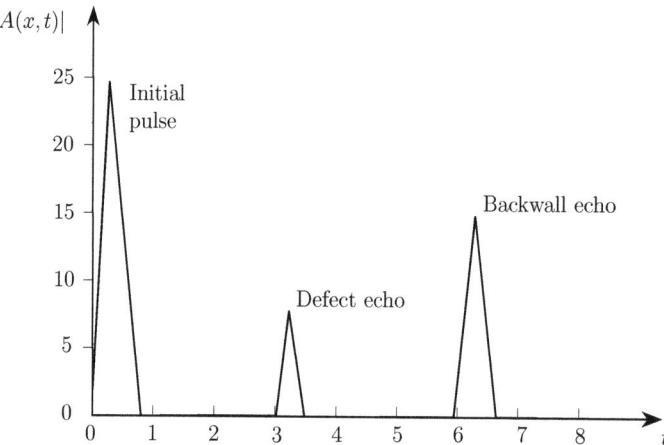

Figure A.3.: Illustration of the display format: A-scan.

A.1.4. B-scan displays

Consider that the transducer is moving over the surface of the specimen in a straight line at a uniform speed from point x_1 to x_2 (figure A.4). The brightness scan (B-scan) is a profile view (xz view) of the specimen, where the time of flight (or depth) is displayed versus the linear position of the transducer. from the B-scan, the depth and linear dimensions of the reflectors can be approximated. A typical method to produce B-scans is by establishing a trigger gate on the A-scans: when the signal intensity is large enough to trigger the gate, a bright point is produced on the B-scan. The gate can be triggered by the reflections coming from the backwall (BW) and reflecting discontinuities inside the medium. The pulse line is caused by the transducer's initial pulses at each sending. They appear in the B-scan when the inspection is done via contact mode. In immersion control, the initial pulses can be gated out and thus they do not appear in the displayed B-scan.

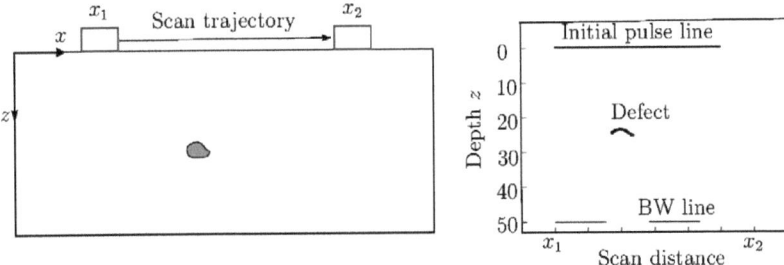

Figure A.4.: Illustration of the display format: B-scan obtained by a horizontal movement of the transducer from x_1 to x_2.

A.1.5. C-scan display

A Computerized scan (C-scan) can be considered as a planar view of the medium's inner structure at a particular depth. C-scans can be constructed by gating the A-scan signal and recording the amplitude of the gated signal (or time of flight) at regular intervals as the transducer is scanned over the specimen. The relative signal amplitude is displayed for each of the positions where data was recorded. In the C-scan, the form of the reflecting surface of the defect can be seen (figure A.5).

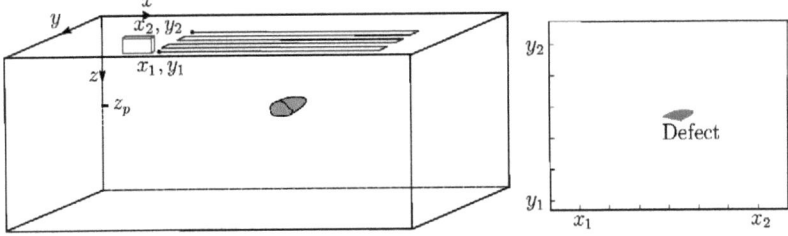

Figure A.5.: Illustration of the display format: C-scan at depth z_p.

B. List of features

B.1. Input data format for the DFC method

The data format required by the DFC method is as follows:

ID	Expert decision	Feature 1	Feature 2	...
1	0 or 1	...	...	...	...

B.2. Features characterizing suspicious regions

Identifier	Geometric features	Unit	2D	3D	Need a reference zone/volume
1	BlobSize	-	-	✓	-
2	BlobVolume	mm^3	-	✓	-
3	BlobPosX	-	-	✓	-
4	BlobPosY	-	-	✓	-
5	BlobPosZ	-	-	✓	-
6	Length in xy plane: L_{xy}	mm	✓	-	-
7	Length in xz plane: L_{xz}	mm	✓	-	-
8	Length in yz plane: L_{yz}	mm	✓	-	-
9	Width in xy plane: W_{xy}	mm	✓	-	-
10	Width in xz plane: W_{xz}	mm	✓	-	-
11	Width in yz plane: W_{yz}	mm	✓	-	-
12	Elongation in xy plane: E_{xy}	-	✓	-	-
13	Elongation in xz plane: E_{xz}	-	✓	-	-
14	Elongation in yz plane: E_{yz}	-	✓	-	-
15	MISRadius	mm	-	✓	-
16	MCSRadius	mm	-	✓	-
17	MISToMCSRatio	-	-	✓	-
18	MCSToBlobSizeRatio	-	-	✓	-
19	BlobFillingLevel	-	-	✓	-

Table B.1.: Geometric features measured for each suspicious region. MIS and MCS are abbreviations for maximum inscribing sphere and minimum covering sphere.

Identifier	Intensity features	unit	2D	3D	Need a reference zone/volume
20	Shadow	-	-	✓	-
21	Damage Index: DI	-	-	✓	-
22	MeanValueOfBlob	-	-	✓	-
23	StdOfBlob	-	-	✓	-
24	MeanValueOfNeighbourhoodOfBlob	-	-	✓	-
25	StdOfNeighbourhoodOfBlob	-	-	✓	-
26	MeanBlobContrast	-	-	✓	-
27	CSMean	-	-	✓	✓
28	CSMin	-	-	✓	✓
29	CSMax	-	-	✓	✓
30	CSStd	-	-	✓	✓
31	MBDMin	-	-	✓	✓
32	MBDMax	-	-	✓	✓
33	MBDMean	-	-	✓	✓
34	MBDStd	-	-	✓	✓
35	MBDVar	-	-	✓	✓

Table B.2.: Intensity based features measured for each suspicious region. CS and MBD are abbreviations for contrast statistics and maximum blob difference.

C. Experimental results: Entrance and Backwall layers detection

C.1. Results for the CFRP-14 volumes

The acquisition conditions, including the resolution in z direction ($0.5\ mm$), are the same for V14-15, V14-70 and V14-100. The scanning speed is different, however the results of the EE and BWE detection algorithm are the same for these volumes. Thus, results are presented only for the volume V14-70.

The EE and BWE detection algorithm gives the output presented in figure C.1a. The BWE slice is at $z = 27$, which means that the estimated thickness is equal to the real thickness $((27+1) \cdot 0.5 = 14 mm)$ of the CFRP component (figure C.1f). The inner volume starts at $z = 2$, this means that the defects at depth $0.7\ mm$ are part of the EE layer at $z = 1$. Main reason is because of the EE strong echo (figure C.1b). Nevertheless, these defects still appear in the layers $z = \{2, 3\}$, thus they are detected (figure C.1c and C.1d).

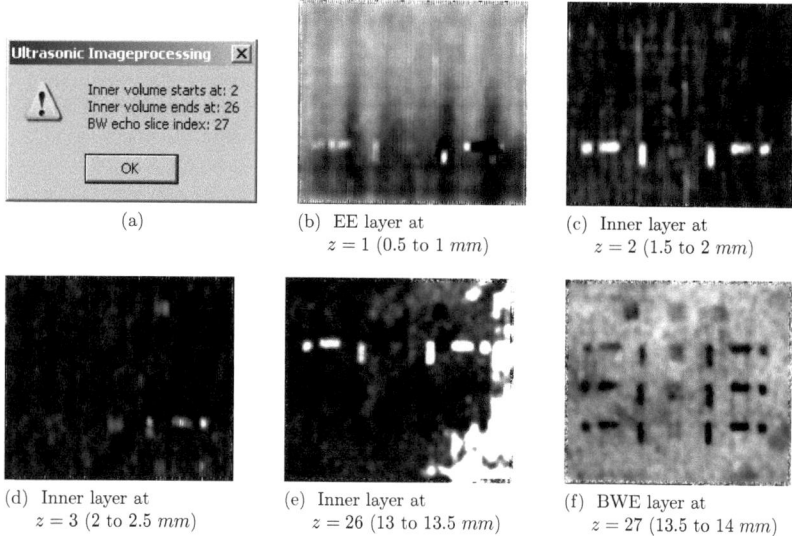

Figure C.1.: V14-70: (a) Output of the Ultrasound Image processing tool. (b) Last layer of the EE volume. (c,d) First two layers of the inner volume. (e) Last layer of the inner volume. (f) The BWE slice where the shadows of the defects are visible.

C.2. V8-21 and V8-24

The volume V8-21 was measured with the SPA 1×16 technique while the V8-24 was measured with the CPA technique. The scanning speed, spatial resolution (5 MHZ) and image resolution are the same for both volumes.

For both volumes, the resolution in z direction is $0.2 \ mm$. This means that five layers correspond to $1 \ mm$ depth. The CFRP specimen is $8 \ mm$ thick. Therefore, the BWE slice should be at $z = 39$ (first layer is at $z = 0$). The output of the EE and BWE detection algorithm is presented in figure C.2.

(a) V8-21   (b) V8-24

Figure C.2.: (a) V8-21: Output of the Ultrasound Image processing tool. (b) V8-24: Output of the Ultrasound Image processing tool.

For V8-21, the inner volume starts at $z = 2$. Thus, the EE volume has a thickness of $0.4 \ mm$. For V8-24, the inner volume starts at $z = 4$, the EE volume has a thickness $0.8 \ mm$. This result shows the interest of the SPA technique which provides a better image quality near the surface of the specimen. Thus, the possibility to detect defects near the surface is improved with the SPA technique.

The backwall volume of V8-21 starts at $z = 37$ and ends at $z = 38$ which means that it has a thickness of $0.4 \ mm$. The backwall volume of V8-24 starts earlier at $z = 35$ and ends at $z = 38$, thus it has a thickness of $0.8 \ mm$. The following remarks can be concluded:

- The inner volume of V8-21 has a thickness of $7 \ mm$ since it starts at $0.4 \ mm$ ($z = 2$) and ends at $7.2 \ mm$ ($z = 36$). While the inner volume of V8-24 starts at $0.8 \ mm$ and ends at $7 \ mm$ $z = 35$. Thus, it is has a thickness of $6.4 \ mm$. Therefore, the CPA technique gives a inner volume of a smaller size than the inner volume given by the SPA technique.

- The BWE echo obtained by the CPA technique has a strong influence on the layers close to the backwall of the specimen. It starts to appear at $7.2 \ mm$ and it could hide defects that are located near the end of the specimen. Indeed, it was noticed that one inclusion located near the end of the specimen (ca. $7.2 \ mm$) is missed from the inner volume of V8-24 and is included in the BWE volume.

- The BWE echo in the V8-21 starts at 7.4 mm, i.e. 0.2 mm are less disturbed by the strong echo reflected by the end of the specimen. Therefore, defects close to the end are better detected with SPA technique. Indeed, all defects are included in the extracted inner volume of V8-21.

- There is a 0.2 mm error in the thickness estimation of the specimen for both SPA and CPA techniques

(a) V8-21: Inner layer at $z = 3$ (0.6 to 0.8 mm)

(b) V8-24: EE layer at $z = 3$ (0.6 to 0.8 mm)

Figure C.3.: (a) Inner layer of V8-21 at $z = 3$. (b) Layer part of the EE volume of V8-24 at $z = 3$.

C.3. V8-22

The volume's resolution in depth is 0.05 mm and its size in z direction is 161 layers ($z = 0$ to $z = 160$). Since the specimen has 8 mm as thickness, the BWE slice should be at $z = 159$. The output of the proposed algorithm is given in figure C.4. The inner volume starts at $z = 12$ (0.6 mm) and ends at $z = 145$ (7.25 mm), thus, the inner volume thickness is 6.7 mm. The first defect starts to appear at $z = 12$, it will be completely included in the inner volume. As for the BWE volume, it starts at $z = 146$ (7.3 mm), defects that may appear after this depth will be lost. However, the last inclusion is at ca. 7.2 mm, therefore it is detected. The BWE slice is at $z = 160$, this corresponds to a thickness of 8.05 mm, which is a very good estimation of the real thickness of the specimen.

The resolution in V8-22 volume is much higher than in V8-21. However, the thickness of the inner volume is almost the same in both cases. The only difference is that the image quality in V8-22 is much better than in V8-21 as it can be seen from figure C.5. Thus, the SPA technique should be used with a image high resolution (small voxel size) in order to have a better quality of reconstruction.

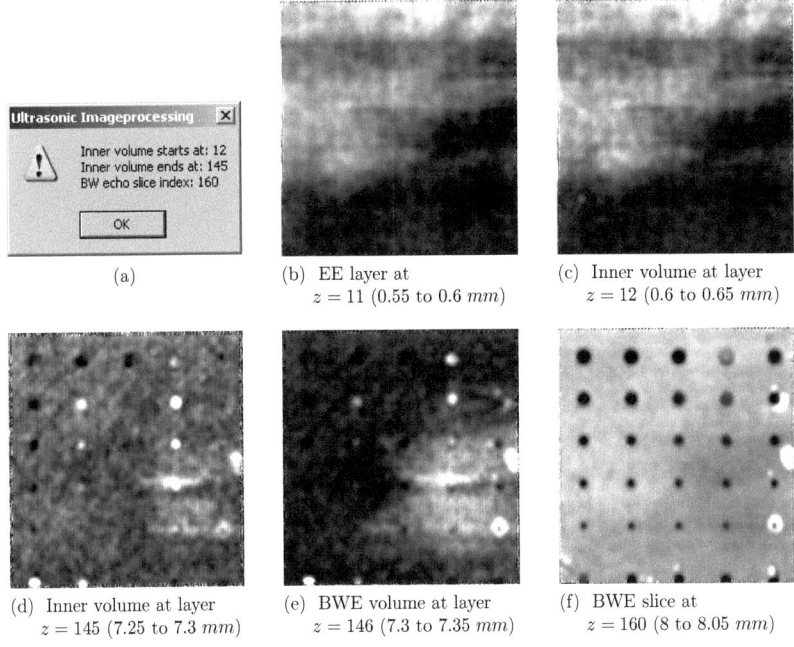

Figure C.4.: V8-22: (a) Output of the Ultrasound Image processing. (b) Last layer of the EE volume. (c) First layer of the inner volume. (d) Last layer of the inner volume. (e) A layer of the BWE volume. (f) the BWE slice where defects shadows can be seen.

(a) V8-21: Inner layer at $z = 4$ (0.8 to 1 mm)

(b) V8-22: Inner layer at $z = 16$ (0.8 to 0.85 mm)

Figure C.5.: Comparison of image quality with SPA technique using different depth resolutions (a) Inner layer of V8-21 at $z = 4$. (b) Inner layer of V8-22 at $z = 16$.

D. Experimental results: hysteresis thresholding

D.1. V14-15

The number of defects in this volume is 24. Thresholding results for this volume using a reference zone without defects are presented in table D.1. The satisfactory value of NTP was given by several selections. Still, the lowest NFP is given by two thresholds selection, one of them is: $T_L = 2 \cdot \text{mean}[Z_{ref}]$, $T_H = 3 \cdot \text{mean}[Z_{ref}]$. Same as in the case of V14-70: a) one very low contrasted defect is missed and b) a defect near the backwall is set as foreground, nevertheless it gets attached to a BWE artifact. The same procedure of manual thresholding, followed for V14-70, was followed to detect the low contrasted defect in V14-15.

Hysteresis thresholds	NTP	NFP
$T_L = \text{mean}[Z_{ref}]$, $T_H = 2 \cdot \text{mean}[Z_{ref}]$	22	35
$T_L = \text{mean}[Z_{ref}]$, $T_H = 3 \cdot \text{mean}[Z_{ref}]$	22	9
$T_L = 2 \cdot \text{mean}[Z_{ref}]$, $T_H = 2 \cdot \text{mean}[Z_{ref}]$	22	56
$T_L = 2 \cdot \text{mean}[Z_{ref}]$, $T_H = 3 \cdot \text{mean}[Z_{ref}]$	22	9
$T_L = 3 \cdot \text{mean}[Z_{ref}]$, $T_H = 3 \cdot \text{mean}[Z_{ref}]$	22	10
Manual threshold $T_L = T_H = M_{\text{def}}$	23	71

Table D.1.: Number of defects (NTP>21) and false positives (NFP) obtained by different hysteresis thresholds selections applied on the volume V14-15. Last row in the table is for the manual threshold using the low contrasted defect to compute T_L and T_H as: $T_L = T_H = $ mean of the selected low contrasted defect.

Figures D.1 and D.2 illustrate the obtained results. In total 94 suspicious regions (NTP=23, NFP=71) are detected. All defects are seen in the original volume, only one defect gets attached to a BWE artifact.

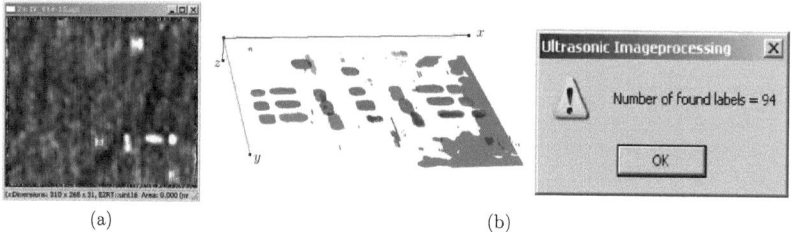

(a)   (b)

Figure D.1.: (a) V14-15: selection of the low contrasted defect to compute T_L and T_H as both equal to the mean of the selected defect. (b) 3D view of suspicious regions obtained using the low contrasted defect to select the thresholds. Total number of suspicious regions is 94.

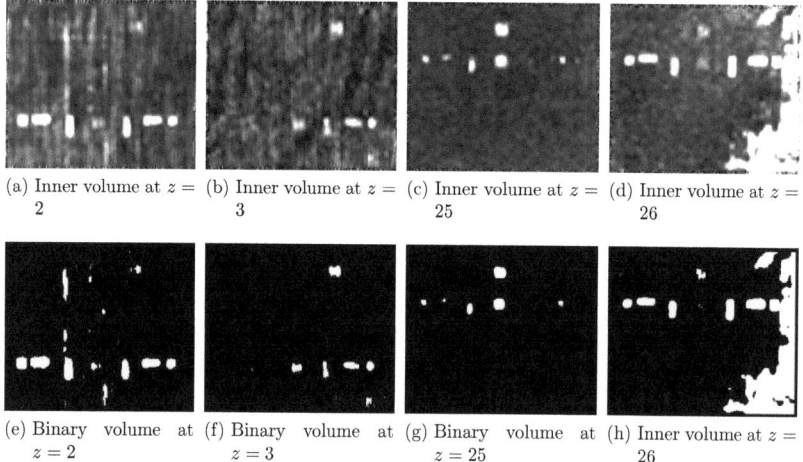

(a) Inner volume at $z = 2$ (b) Inner volume at $z = 3$ (c) Inner volume at $z = 25$ (d) Inner volume at $z = 26$

(e) Binary volume at $z = 2$ (f) Binary volume at $z = 3$ (g) Binary volume at $z = 25$ (h) Inner volume at $z = 26$

Figure D.2.: V14-15: (a,b,c) Original inner layers near the EE and the BWE layers. (d,e,f) Output binary layers. Note that one defect gets attached to a BWE artefact

D.2. V14-100

The number of defects in this volume is 24. Using a reference zone without defects, thresholding results for this volume are presented in table D.2. The maximal NTP is given by several sources. While the lowest NFP is given by the selection: $T_L = \text{mean}[Z_{ref}]$, $T_H = 3 \cdot \text{mean}[Z_{ref}]$. Note that the difference in NFP is only 1 between this selection and the thresholds selection $T_L = 2 \cdot \text{mean}[Z_{ref}]$, $T_H = 3 \cdot \text{mean}[Z_{ref}]$. Thus, the last selection is also optimal. Same as in the case of V14-70 and V14-15: a) one very low contrasted defect is missed and b) a defect near the backwall is set as foreground, nevertheless, it gets attached to a BWE artifact. The same procedure, followed for V14-70 and V14-15, was followed to detect the low contrasted defect in V14-100. Results are presented in the last row of the table D.2. All defects were set as foreground and only one defect gets attached to a BWE artifact.

Hysteresis thresholds	NTP	NFP
$T_L = \text{mean}[Z_{ref}]$, $T_H = 3 \cdot \text{mean}[Z_{ref}]$	22	33
$T_L = 2 \cdot \text{mean}[Z_{ref}]$, $T_H = 2 \cdot \text{mean}[Z_{ref}]$	22	160
$T_L = 2 \cdot \text{mean}[Z_{ref}]$, $T_H = 3 \cdot \text{mean}[Z_{ref}]$	22	34
Manual threshold $T_L = T_H = M_{\text{def}}$	23	157

Table D.2.: Number of defects (NTP>21) and false positives (NFP) obtained by different hysteresis thresholds selections applied on the volume V14-100. Last row in the table is for the manual threshold using the low contrasted defect to compute T_L and T_H as: $T_L = T_H$ = mean of the selected low contrasted defect.

Figures D.3 and D.4 illustrate the obtained results. In total 180 suspicious regions are detected.

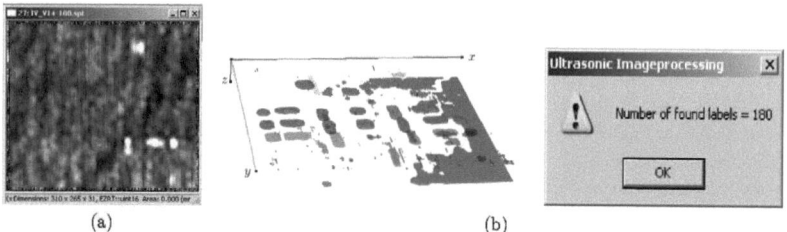

(a)   (b)

Figure D.3.: V14-100: (a) selection of the low contrasted defect to compute T_L and T_H as both equal to the mean of the selected defect. (b) 3D view of suspicious regions obtained using the low contrasted defect to select the thresholds. Total number of suspicious regions is 180.

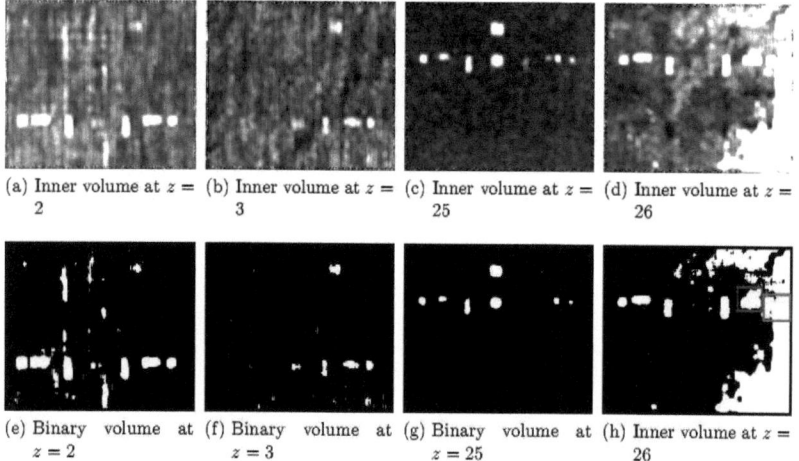

(a) Inner volume at $z = 2$ (b) Inner volume at $z = 3$ (c) Inner volume at $z = 25$ (d) Inner volume at $z = 26$

(e) Binary volume at $z = 2$ (f) Binary volume at $z = 3$ (g) Binary volume at $z = 25$ (h) Inner volume at $z = 26$

Figure D.4.: V14-100: (a,b,c) Original inner layers near the EE and the BWE layers. (d,e,f) Output binary layers. Notice in (f) that, one defect gets attached to a BWE artifact (red box) and another defect has a distorted shape (blue box).

D.3. V8-21

The number of defects in this volume is 30. Hysteresis thresholds were computed on a reference zone without defects. The obtained thresholding results are presented in table D.3. The thresholds selection $T_L = \text{mean}[Z_{ref}]$, $T_H = 3 \cdot \text{mean}[Z_{ref}]$ slightly outperforms the selection $T_L = 2 \cdot \text{mean}[Z_{ref}]$, $T_H = 3 \cdot \text{mean}[Z_{ref}]$ by giving less amount of NFP. Nevertheless, both selections could successfully detect all defects and give the lowest NFP. Figure D.5 illustrates the obtained thresholding results for

Hysteresis thresholds	NTP	NFP
$T_L = \text{mean}[Z_{ref}]$, $T_H = 3 \cdot \text{mean}[Z_{ref}]$	30	44
$T_L = 2 \cdot \text{mean}[Z_{ref}]$, $T_H = 3 \cdot \text{mean}[Z_{ref}]$	30	47
$T_L = 3 \cdot \text{mean}[Z_{ref}]$, $T_H = 3 \cdot \text{mean}[Z_{ref}]$	30	64

Table D.3.: Number of defects ((NTP $\geq$ 27)) and false positives (NFP) obtained by different hysteresis thresholds selections applied on the volume V8-21.

$T_L = 2 \cdot \text{mean}[Z_{ref}]$ and $T_H = 3 \cdot \text{mean}[Z_{ref}]$. In total 77 suspicious regions are detected including all defects seen in the original volume.

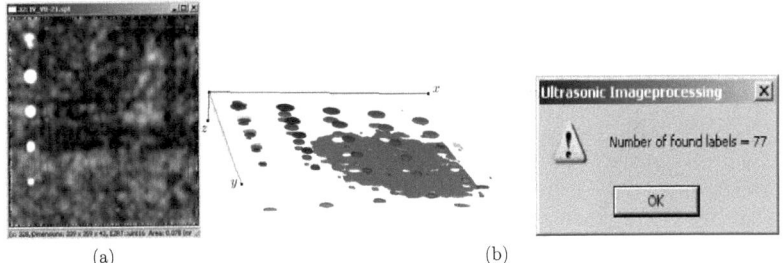

(a)   (b)

Figure D.5.: V8-21: (a) selection of the reference zone to compute T_L and T_H. (b) 3D view of suspicious regions obtained for $T_L = 2 \cdot \text{mean}[Z_{ref}]$ and $T_H = 3 \cdot \text{mean}[Z_{ref}]$. Total number of suspicious regions is 77.

D.4. V8-24

Thresholding results for this volume are presented in table D.4 and figure D.6. Two thresholds selections give the optimal values of NTP=29 and NFP=7. One of the selections is: $T_L = 2 \cdot \text{mean}[Z_{ref}]$ and $T_H = 3 \cdot \text{mean}[Z_{ref}]$. In total 36 suspicious regions are detected using this selection. However, one defect is missing. This defect is a border rectangular inclusion, very close to the BWE. It starts to appear at $z = 36$ (7.2 mm), while the end of the inner volume as given by entrance and backwall detection step was at $z = 35$ (7 mm). Thus, the defect is outside the inner volume and is therefore lost. Otherwise, all defects inside the inner volume are successfully kept after thresholding.

Hysteresis thresholds	NTP	NFP
$T_L = \text{mean}[Z_{ref}]$, $T_H = 3 \cdot \text{mean}[Z_{ref}]$	29	7
$T_L = 2 \cdot \text{mean}[Z_{ref}]$, $T_H = 3 \cdot \text{mean}[Z_{ref}]$	29	7
$T_L = 3 \cdot \text{mean}[Z_{ref}]$, $T_H = 3 \cdot \text{mean}[Z_{ref}]$	28	4

Table D.4.: Number of defects ((NTP $\geq$ 27)) and false positives (NFP) obtained by different hysteresis thresholds selections applied on the volume V8-24.

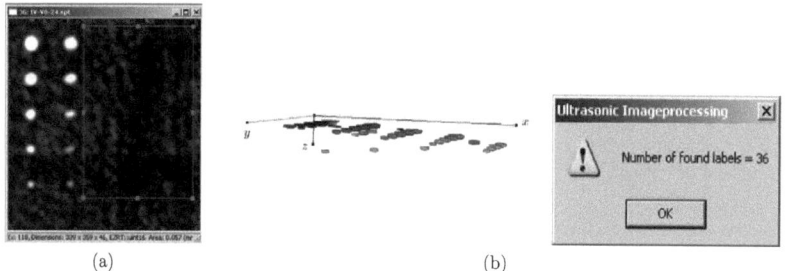

(a) (b)

Figure D.6.: V8-24: (a) selection of the reference zone to compute T_L and T_H.(b) 3D view of suspicious regions obtained for $T_L = 2 \cdot \text{mean}[Z_{ref}]$ and $T_H = 3 \cdot \text{mean}[Z_{ref}]$. Total number of suspicious regions is 36.

List of abbreviations and symbols

Ⓐ	Cautious conjunctive combination rule
Ⓒ	Conjunctive combination rule
$*$	Convolution operator
$\oplus$	Dempster combination rule
$\wedge$	Minimum operator
$1 \times N$	Operating mode of the SPA transducer, in which one element sends and all other elements receive.
2^Θ	Power set or fusion space
$[P, S, T]$	Dimensions of the volume respectively in x, y and z direction
α_i	Amplitude of the back scattered echo $\in \mathbb{R}_+$
β	Scaling parameter of the pdf $\in \mathbb{R}_+^*$
$\nabla^2 G_\sigma$	Laplacian of Gaussian (LoG)
$\Delta P_{A,B}$	Derivative of $P_{A,B} \in \mathbb{R}_+$
η	Gaussian noise of zero-mean
γ	Translation parameter of the pdf $\in \mathbb{R}$
$\Gamma(.)$	gamma function
λ	Random variable of a known distribution, $\in \mathbb{R}$
$\|\cdot\|_{2,\sigma}^2$	Gaussian weighted Euclidean distance $\in \mathbb{R}_+$
CNR	Contrast to Noise Ratio $\in \mathbb{R}_+$
DV	Derivative variation: threshold on $\Delta P_{A,B} \in \mathbb{R}_+$
fp	False positives rate $\in [0, 1]$
NFN	Number of False Negatives $\in \mathbb{N}$
NFP	Number of False Positives $\in \mathbb{N}$
NN	Number of Negatives $\in \mathbb{N}$
NP	Number of Positives $\in \mathbb{N}$
NRF	Noise Reduction Factor $\in \mathbb{R}$

NTN	Number of True Negatives $\in \mathbb{N}$
NTP	Number of True Positives $\in \mathbb{N}$
PCD	Correct decision rate $\in [0,1]$
Perc	Threshold on the percentage of points inside each region of confidence $\in \mathbb{N}$
PFD	Rate of false defects correctly classified $\in [0,1]$
PSNR	Peak Signal to Noise ratio $\in \mathbb{R}_+$
PTD	Rate of true defects correctly classified $\in [0,1]$
RMSE	Root Mean Square Error $\in \mathbb{R}_+$
R	Overall classification rate $\in [0,1]$
S_m	Decision threshold on the mass value $\in [0,1]$
tp	True positives rate $\in [0,1]$
μ	Location parameter of the pdf $\in \mathbb{R}$
μ_i	Degree of membership $\in [0,1]$
ν	Shape parameter of the pdf $\in \mathbb{R}_+^*$
$\Omega^{P,S,T}$	Set of coordinates or volume grid over which the noisy volume u is defined, $\subset \mathbb{N}^3$
$\overline{d_P}$	Mean value of Pearson distance
ϕ_i	Phase of the back scattered echo $\in [0, 2\pi[$
ψ	Factor related to ultrasound image formation $\in \mathbb{R}$
σ	Standard deviation of the Gaussian kernel $\in \mathbb{R}_+$
$\sigma_{background}^2$	Variance of intensities value of a background zone $\in \mathbb{R}_+$
σ_{def}^2	Variance of intensities value of a defect's zone $\in \mathbb{R}_+$
$\mathbf{u}(B_{x,y,z}^d)$	Vector gathering the intensities of voxels inside the block $B_{x,y,z}^d$
$\mathbf{u}^{(p)}(B_{x,y,z})$	Intensity value in vector u at index p
Θ	Frame of discernment $\subset 2^\Theta$
θ	Incidence angle $\in [-\frac{\pi}{2}, \frac{\pi}{2}]$
$\Delta\tau$	Time delay between adjacent elements (unit: second)
ε_a	Additive noise
ε_m	Multiplicative noise
Λ	Sum of all back scattered echoes interfering in the resolution cell
Λ_i	Back scattered echo from a random scatterer i, $\in \mathbb{C}$

$\varnothing$	Empty set $\subset 2^\Theta$
ϑ	Velocity of particle (unit: m/s)
$\widetilde{v}(x_i)$	Correspond to the filtered original image u
$\widetilde{v}_{in}$	Inner volume located between the end of the entrance volume and the start of the backwall volume.
ξ	Power of the pdf $\in \mathbb{R}_+^*$
a	Width of the transducer (unit: mm)
A_{ij}	detected reflection of the signal emitted by array element i and received by array element j, $\in \mathbb{R}_+$
$B_{x,y,z}^{d,0}$	2D Block centered at voxel of coordinates (x,y,z)
$B_{x,y,z}^{d}$	3D Block centered at voxel of coordinates (x,y,z)
bel	Belief function
c	Speed of sound m/s
C_r	Reflection coefficient $\in \mathbb{R}$
C_t	Transmission coefficient $\in \mathbb{R}_+$
D	K-S distance $\in \mathbb{R}_+$
D_i, D_j	Distance between elements i, j and the central axis (unit: mm)
d_P	Pearson distance $\in \mathbb{R}_+$
D_T	Distance between adjacent elements of the array (unit: mm)
DI	Damage index
EE_{blob}	Zone occupied by the blob projection on the BWE layer
EE_{blob}	Zone occupied by the blob projection on the EE layer
Exy, Exz, Eyz	Blob elongations in the respective xy, xz and yz planes
$f(x_r, z_r)$	back projected signal amplitude function at focusing point (x_r, z_r), $\in \mathbb{R}_+$
f_k	Information source $f_k(X) \in \mathbb{R}$
F_α	Feret diameter: diameter of the blob's projection on direction of angle α in the plane.
g	Filtering operator
G_σ	Gaussian kernel of zero mean
h	Smoothing factor $\in \mathbb{R}$
H_1	Hypothesis of True Defects $\subset \Theta$
H_2	Hypothesis of False Defects $\subset \Theta$

$H_3 = \Theta = \{H_1, H_2\}$	Ignorance Hypothesis
$h_A(i), h_B(i)$	Number of data points of class A (TDs) and class B (FDs) respectively inside the interval $i, \in \mathbb{N}$
I	Vector gathering the mean intensity of each layer of a volume
$I_0(\cdot)$	Modified Bessel function of the first kind of order zero
K	Measure of conflict between sources
$K_{N_s}(\cdot)$	Modified Bessel function of second kind and order N_s
Lxy, Lxz, Lyz	Maximal values of Feret diameters in the respective xy, xz and yz planes
m	Mass function
$m(H_1)$	Mass value attributed to the hypothesis $H_1 \in [0, 1]$
$M_{\text{background}}$	Mean intensity value of a background zone $\in \mathbb{R}_+$
M_{def}	Mean intensity value of a defect's zone $\in \mathbb{R}_+$
M_{T_H}	Weight of the mean value of intensities in the high threshold computation
M_{T_L}	Weight of the mean value of intensities in the low threshold computation
N	Number of elementary transducers in the array $\in \mathbb{N}$
$N \times 1$	Operating mode of the SPA transducer, in which all elements send and only one element receives.
$N \times N$	Operating mode of the SPA transducer, in which all elements send and receive.
N_s	Number of scatterers interfering in a resolution cell
N_L	Number of layers inside a volume considered for the speckle estimation $\in \mathbb{N}$
P_N	pdf of Nakagami distribution
$P_{A,B}(i)$	Proportion of points from class A in interval $i \in [0, 1]$
P_{GTD}	pdf of Four-Parameters Generalized Gamma distribution
P_{GTD}	pdf of Generalized Gamma distribution
P_K	pdf of K-distribution
P_{Rician}	pdf of the Rician distribution
P_R	pdf function of Rayleigh distribution
Pac	Acoustic pressure (unit: N/m^3 or Pa)
pl	Plausibility function

q	Commonality function
r	Focal length $\in \mathbb{R}_+$
R_j	Region of confidence
r_k	Discrete focal distance in the sampled image $\in \mathbb{N}$
s	Intensity value in the range cell of the transducer
S_{T_H}	Weight of the standard deviation of intensities in the high threshold computation
S_{T_L}	Weight of the standard deviation of intensities in the low threshold computation
t_0	Travel time from the central element of the transducers array to a focal point (unit: second)
t_i	Travel time from the element i of the transducers array to a focal point (unit: second)
t_r	Travel time in the forward and backward path from the transducer to the focusing point (x_r, z_r) (unit: second)
T_H	High threshold $\in \mathbb{R}_+$
T_L	Low threshold $\in \mathbb{R}_+$
u	Noisy ultrasound image
$u(x, y, z)$	Intensity value in volume u at voxel of coordinates (x, y, z)
v	Noise free image
$V_{x,y,z}^{M,0}$	Similarity searching 2D window centered at voxel (x, y, z)
$V_{x,y,z}^{M}$	Similarity searching 3D window centered at voxel (x, y, z)
V_{ref}	A reference volume obtained by inspecting a sample without defects.
w	Weight function
w_s	Similarity weight $\in [0, 1]$
W_c	Weight given for correct classification $\in \mathbb{R}_+$
W_{tn}	Weight given for false defects classification $\in \mathbb{R}_+$
W_{tp}	Weight given for true defects classification $\in \mathbb{R}_+$
Wxy, Wxz, Wyz	Minimal values of Feret diameters in the respective xy, xz and yz planes
X	Suspicious region
x, y, z	Cartesian coordinates
Z	Acoustic impedance (uint: $N.s.m^{-3}$)

Z_{ref}	A reference zone with no defect inside it.
$Z_{x,y,z}$	Normalization factor $\in \mathbb{R}_+$
2D	Two dimensional
3D	three dimensional
$\mathbb{I}$	The indicator function
A-scan	Amplitude modulation scan
ANN	Artificial Neural Networks
B-scan	Brightness scan
Blob	Binary large object
BWE	Backwall of the specimen
BWE slice	Last layer of the backwall of the specimen
C-scan	Computerized scan
cdf	Cumulative distribution function
CFRP	Carbon Fiber Reinforced Polymers
CPA	Conventional Phased Array
CT	Computed Tomography
DFC	Data Fusion Classification
DSF	Dempster-Shafer fusion
DWT	Discrete Wavelet Transform
E-scan	Electronic scanning
ecdf	Empirical cumulative distribution function
EE	Entrance of the specimen
FD	False defect
FRP	Fiber Reinforced Polymer
K-S	Kolmogorov-Smirnov
ML	Maximum Likelihood
NDT	Non-destructive testing
NL-means	Non Local means filter
pdf	Probability density function
ROC	Receiver Operating Characteristics
S-scan	Sector scan

SAFT .... Synthetic Aperture Focusing Technique
SAR .... Synthetic Aperture Radar
SPA .... Sampling Phased Array
SVM .... Support Vector Machine
SynFo-SPA ..... Synthetic Focusing-Sampling Phased Array
TD .... True defect
TGC .... Time Compensation Gain

Bibliography

[1] A. Fenster, D. B. Downey, and H. N. Cardinal, "Three-dimensional ultrasound imaging," *Phys. Med. Biol.*, vol. 46, R67-R99, May, 2001.

[2] A. Fenster and D. B. Downey, "3-d ultrasound imaging-a review," *IEEE Engineering in Medicine and Biology Magazine*, vol. 15, no. 6, pp. 41–51, Nov/Dec 1996.

[3] A. Bulavinov, R. Pinchuk, S. Pudovikov, and C. Boller, "Ultrasonic sampling phased array testing as a replacement for x-ray testing of weld joints in ship construction," *In Proceedings of the 9th International Navigational Symposium on Marine Navigation and Safety of Sea Transportation, Gdynia, Poland*, pp. 91–94, June, 2011.

[4] R. W. Prager, W. Z. Ijaz, A. H. Gee, and G. M. Treece, "Three-dimensional ultrasound imaging," *Proceedings of the Institution of Mechanical Engineers, Part H: Journal of Engineering in Medicine*, pp. 193–224, February, 2010.

[5] W. Liu, J. A. Zagzebski, T. J. Hall, E. L. Madsen, T. Varghese, M. A. Kliewer, S. Panda, C. Lowery, and S. Barnes, "Acoustic backscatter and effective scatterer size estimates using a 2d cmut transducer," *Phys. Med. Biol.*, vol. 53, no. 15, pp. 4169–4183, July, 2008.

[6] C. Daft, D. Brueske, P. Wagner, and D. Liu, "A matrix transducer design with improved image quality and acquisition rate," *In Proceedings of the IEEE Ultrasonics Symposium, New York, USA*, pp. 411–415, July 2007.

[7] Q. Duan, S. Homma, and A. F. Laine, "Analysis of 4d ultrasound for dynamic measures of cardiac function," *In Proceedings of the IEEE Ultrasonics Symposium, New York, USA*, pp. 1492–1495, 28-31 October, 2007.

[8] A. H. Gee, R. W. Prager, G. M. Treece, and L. H. Berman, "Engineering a freehand 3d ultrasound system," *Pattern Recognition Letters*, vol. 24, no. 4-5, pp. 757–777, February, 2003.

[9] H. Yu, M. S. Pattichis1, C. Agurto, and M. B. Goens, "A 3d freehand ultrasound system for multi-view reconstructions from sparse 2d scanning planes," *BioMedical Engineering Online*, vol. 10:7, January, 2011.

[10] A. Bulavinov, "Der getaktete gruppenstrahler," *Dissertation, Naturwissenschaftlich-Technischen Fakultät III Chemie, Pharmazie, Bio- und Werkstoffwissenschaften der Universität des Saarlandes*, Saarbrücken 2005.

[11] R. A. Smith, L. J. Nelson, M. J. Mienczakowski, and R. E. Challis, "Automated non-destructive analysis and advanced 3d defect characterisation from ultrasonic scans of composites," *In proceedings of the 17th International Com-*

mittee on *Composite Materials, ICCM, Edinburgh, Scotland*, 27-31 July, 2009.

[12] G. S. Passi, Y. Shoef, and M. V. Kritsky, "Reducing the influence of human factors on the reliability of manual ultrasonic weld inspection," *Insight - The Journal of British Institute of Non-Destructive Testing*, vol. 37, no. 10, pp. 788–791, 1995.

[13] QNET, "Sampling phased array tauchtechnik-ultraschall-prüfsystem mit wassertank," tech. rep., Q NET Engeneering GMBH.

[14] E. C. Weiss, P. Anastasiadis, G. Pilarczyk, M. R. Lemor, and P. V. Zinin, "Mechanical properties of single cells by high-frequency time-resolved acoustic microscopy," *IEEE Transactions on ultrasonics, ferroelectrics, and frequency control*, vol. 54, no. 11, pp. 2257–2271, November, 2007.

[15] M. Kröning, A. Bulavinov, K. Reddy, and V. B. L., "Verfahren zur zerstörungsfreien untersuchung eines prüfkörpers mittels ultraschall.," *Deutsche Patentanmeldung Nr. 10 2004 059 856.8-52*, 18.06.2004.

[16] J. C. Somer, "Electronic sector scanning for ultrasonic diagnosis," *Ultrasonics*, vol. 6, no. 3, pp. 153–159, July, 1968.

[17] W. Gebhardt, F. Bonitz, and H. Woll, "Defect reconstruction and classification by phased arrays," *Materials Evaluation*, vol. 4, no. 1, pp. 90–95, January, 1982.

[18] O. T. Von Ramm and S. W. Smith, "Beam steering with linear arrays," *Transactions on Biomedical Engineering*, vol. 30, no. 8, pp. 438–452, August, 1983.

[19] S. Wooh and Y. Shi, "Optimum beam steering of linear phased arrays," *Wave Motion*, vol. 29, no. 3, pp. 245–265, April, 1999.

[20] A. D. Armitage, N. R. Scales, P. P. A. Hicks, P. J., Q. X. Chen, and J. V. Hatfield, "An integrated array transducer receiver for ultrasound imaging," *Sensors and Actuators A: Physical*, vol. 47, no. 1-3, pp. 542–546, March-April, 1995.

[21] H. Wüstenberg and G. Schenk, "Entwicklungen und trends bei der anwendung von steuerba-ren schallfeldern in der zfp mit ultraschall," *DGZfP-Jahrestagung, Mainz, Germany*, 26-28 May, 2003.

[22] H. Wüstenberg, A. Erhard, and G. Schenk, "Some characteristic parameters of ultrasonic phased array probes and equipments," *NDT.net*, vol. 4, no. 4, April, 1999.

[23] E. Brunner, "Ultrasound system considerations and their impact on front-end components," *log Devices, Inc.*, 2002.

[24] T. Armitt, "Phased arrays not the answer to every application," *In Proceedings of the 9th European Congress on Non-Destructive Testing, Berlin, Germany*, November, 2006.

[25] S. R. Doctor, L. J. Busse, and H. D. Collins, "The saft-ut technology evolution," *In Proc. 6th Inter. Conf. on NDE in the Nuclear Industry, Zürich. ISBN: 0-87170-192-8*, December, 1983.

[26] C. W. Sherwin, J. P. Ruina, and R. D. Rawcliffe, "Some early developments in synthetic aperture radar systems," *IRE Transactions Military Electronics*,

vol. 6, no. 2, pp. 111–115, 1962.

[27] C. A. Wiley, "Synthetic aperture radars," *IEEE Transactions on Aerospace and Electronic Systems*, vol. 21, no. 3, pp. 440–443, May, 1985.

[28] S. R. Doctor, T. E. Hall, and L. D. Reid, "Saft – the evolution of a signal processing technology for ultrasonic testing," *NDT International*, vol. 19, no. 3, pp. 163–167, June, 1986.

[29] K. Mayer, R. Marklein, K. Langenberg, and T. Kreutter, "Three-dimensional imaging system based on fourier transform synthetic aperture focusing technique," *Ultrasonics*, vol. 28, pp. 241–255, July, 1990.

[30] A. W. Elbern and L. Guimaraes, "Synthetic aperture focusing technique for image restauration," *NDT.net*, vol. 5, no. 8, August, 2000.

[31] S. Nikolov, "Synthetic aperture tissue and flow ultrasonic imaging," *PhD thesis, Technical University of Denmark*, 2001.

[32] F. Lingvall, "Time-domain reconstruction methods for ultrasonic array imaging - a statistical approach," *PhD thesis, Uppsala University, ISBN 91-506-1772-9*, September 2004.

[33] A. Bulavinov, M. Kröning, K. Reddy, and J. Gabriel H Ribeiro, "Real-time quantitative ultrasonic inspection," *IV Conferencia Panamericana de END, Buenos Aires, Argentina*, 22-26 October, 2007.

[34] L. v. Bernus, A. Bulavinov, D. Joneit, M. Kröning, M. Dalichov, and K. M. Reddy, "Sampling phased array a new technique for signal processing and ultrasonic imaging," *In Proceedings of the 9th European Conf. Non-Destructive Testing (ECNDT), Berlin, Germany*, September 25-29, 2006.

[35] P. Fellinger, R. Marklein, K. J. Langenberg, and S. Klaholz, "Numerical modeling of elastic wave propagation and scattering with efit elastodynamic finite integration technique," *Wave Motion*, vol. 21, no. 1, pp. 47–66, February, 1995.

[36] M. Kröning, A. Bulavinov, and K. Reddy, "Verfahren zur zerstörungsfreien untersuchung eines wenigstens akustisch anisotropen werkstoffbereich aufweisenden prüfkörpers," *Deutsche Patentanmeldung Nr. 10 2006 003 978.5*, 27.01.2006.

[37] S. V. Ramanan, A. Bulavinov, S. Pudovikov, C. Boller, and T. Wenzel, "Quantitative non-destructive evaluation of cfrp components by sampling phased array," *In Proceedings of the International Symposium on NDT in Aerospace, Hamburg, Germany*, November, 2010.

[38] O. N. R. Tech, "Inspection of composite radii," Retrived: Octobre 2012. Application Notes, http://www.olympus-ims.com/en/applications/composite-inspection-radii/. Date of access: October 2012.

[39] P. Balaguru, P. N. Balaguru, A. Nanni, and J. Giancaspro, "Frp composites for reinforced and prestressed concrete structures: A guide to fundamentals and design for repair and retrofit," *Publisher: Tayler and Francis Group. ISBN 0-203-92688-9, New York, USA*, 2009.

[40] V. M. Karbhari, H. Kaiser, R. Navada, K. Ghosh, and L. Lee, "Methods for

detecting defects in composite rehabilitated concrete structures," *Oregon Department of Transportation*, vol. 336, April, 2005.

[41] M. K. Feldman, S. Katyal, and M. S. Blackwood, "Us artifacts," *Radiographics*, vol. 29, no. 4, pp. 1179–1189, July, 2009.

[42] J. Huang, J. K. Triedman, N. V. Vasilyev, Y. Suematsu, R. O. Cleveland, and P. E. Dupont, "Imaging artifacts of medical instruments in ultrasound-guided interventions," *American Institute of Ultrasound in Medicine, J. Ultrasound Med. 2007*, vol. 26, pp. 1303–1322, October, 2007.

[43] F. W. Kremkau and K. J. W. Taylor, "Artifacts in ultrasound imaging," *Journal of Ultrasound in Medicine*, vol. 5, no. 4, pp. 227–237, April, 1986.

[44] S. H. Contreras Ortiz, T. Chiu, and M. D. Fox, "Ultrasound image enhancement: A review," *Biomedical Signal Process. Control. Article in press*, February, 2012.

[45] F. Laing and A. Kurtz, "The importance of ultrasonic side-lobe artifacts," *Radiology*, vol. 145, no. 3, pp. 763–768, December, 1982.

[46] J. A. Noble, "Ultrasound image segmentation and tissue characterization," *Proc. IMechE Vol. 224 Part H: J. Engineering in Medicine*, vol. 224, no. 2, pp. 307–316, June, 2009.

[47] J. A. Noble and D. Boukerroui, "Ultrasound image segmentation: A survey," *IEEE Trans. on Medical Imaging*, vol. 25, no. 8, pp. 987–1010, August, 2006.

[48] F. Destrempes, J. Meunier, M. F. Giroux, G. Soulez, and G. Cloutier, "Segmentation in ultrasonic b-mode images of healthy carotid arteries using mixtures of nakagami distributions and stochastic optimization," *IEEE Trans. on Medical Imaging*, vol. 28, no. 2, pp. 215–229, February, 2009.

[49] Z. Tao, H. D. Tagare, and J. D. Beaty, "Evaluation of four probability distribution models for speckle in clinical cardiac ultrasound images," *IEEE Trans. Med. Imaging*, vol. 25, no. 11, pp. 1483–1492, November, 2006.

[50] C. Kotropoulos and I. Pitas, "Segmentation of ultrasonic images using support vector machines," *Pattern Recognition Letters*, vol. 24, no. 4-5, pp. 715–727, June, 2009.

[51] J. Huang and X. Yang, "A fast algorithm for global minimization of maximum likelihood based on ultrasound image segmentation," *Inverse Problems and Imaging, American Institute of mathematical sciences*, vol. 5, no. 3, pp. 645–657, August, 2011.

[52] A. Sarti, C. Corsi, E. Mazzini, and C. Lamberti, "Maximum likelihood segmentation with rayleigh distribution of ultrasound images," *IEEE Computers in Cardiology*, vol. 5, no. 3, pp. 329–332, September, 2004.

[53] M. R. Cardinal, J. Meunier, G. Soulez, R. L. Maurice, E. Therasse, and G. Cloutier, "Intravascular ultrasound image segmentation: A three-dimensional fast-marching method based on gray level distributions," *IEEE Trans. on Medical Imaging*, vol. 25, no. 5, pp. 590–601, May, 2006.

[54] W. Zhang, C. Li, J. A. Noble, and M. Brady, "Spatio-temporal segmentation of left ventricle in real-time 3d echocardiographic images using phase information,"

In *Proceedings of Medical Image Understanding and Analysis, University of Wales, Aberystwyth*, July, 2007.

[55] X. Ye, J. A. Noble, and D. Atkinson, "3d freehand echocardiography for automatic left ventricle reconstruction and analysis based on multiple acoustic windows," *IEEE Trans. on Medical Imaging*, vol. 12, no. 9, pp. 1051–1058, September, 2002.

[56] C. M. Chen, H. S. Lu, and K. C. Han, "A textural approach based on gabor functions for texture edge detection in ultrasound images," *Ultrasound Med. Biol*, vol. 27, no. 4, pp. 515–534, April, 2001.

[57] D. Shen, Y. Zhan, and C. Davatzikos, "Segmentation of prostate boundaries from ultrasound images using statistical shape model," *IEEE Trans. Med. Imag.*, vol. 22, no. 4, pp. 539–551, April, 2003.

[58] J. Shan, H. D. Cheng, and Y. Wang, "Completely automated segmentation approach for breast ultrasound images using multiple-domain features," *Ultrasound in Medicine and Biology*, vol. 38, no. 2, pp. 262–275, January, 2012.

[59] D. Shen, Z. Lao, J. Zeng, W. Zhang, I. A. Sesterhenn, L. Sun, J. W. Moul, E. H. Herskovits, G. Fichtinger, and C. Davatzikos, "Optimized prostate biopsy via a statistical atlas of cancer spatial distribution," *Med. Image Anal.*, vol. 8, pp. 139–150, June, 2004.

[60] L. X. Gong, S. D. Pathak, D. R. Haynor, P. S. Cho, and Y. Kim, "Parametric shape modeling using deformable superellipses for prostate segmentation," *IEEE Trans. on Medical Imaging*, vol. 23, no. 3, pp. 340–349, March, 2004.

[61] J. Xie, Y. Jiang, and H.-T. Tsui, "Segmentation of kidney from ultrasound images based on texture and shape priors," *IEEE Trans. on Medical Imaging*, vol. 24, no. 1, pp. 45–57, January, 2005.

[62] P. Yan, S. Xu, B. Turkbey, and J. Kruecker, "Discrete deformable model guided by partial active shape model for trus image segmentation," *IEEE Trans. Biomed. Eng.*, vol. 57, no. 5, pp. 1158–1166, May, 2010.

[63] P. Yan, S. Xu, B. Turkbey, and J. Kruecker, "Adaptively learning local shape statistics for prostate segmentation in ultrasound," *IEEE Trans. Biomed. Eng.*, vol. 58, no. 3, pp. 633–641, March, 2011.

[64] E. C. Kyriacou, C. Pattichis, M. Pattichis, C. Loizou, C. Christodoulou, S. K. Kakkos, and A. Nicolaides, "A review of noninvasive ultrasound image processing methods in the analysis of carotid plaque morphology for the assessment of stroke risk," *IEEE Trans. Inform. Technol. Biomed.*, vol. 14, no. 4, pp. 1027–1038, July, 2010.

[65] E. Brusseau, C. De Korte, F. Mastik, J. Schaar, and A. Van der Steen, "Fully automatic luminal contour segmentation in intracoronary ultrasound imaging- a statisitical approach," *IEEE Trans. on Medical Imaging*, vol. 23, no. 5, pp. 554–566, May, 2004.

[66] S. Osher and J. A. Sethian, "Fronts propagating with curvature-dependent speed: Algorithms based on hamilton-jacobi formulations," *J. Comput. Phys.*, vol. 79, pp. 12–49, November, 1988.

[67] B. Liu, H. D. Cheng, H. Huang, Jianhua, J. Tian, X. Tang, and J. Liu, "Probability density difference-based active contour for ultrasound image segmentation," *Pattern Recognition*, vol. 43, no. 6, pp. 2028–2042, June, 2010.

[68] E. Kollorz, D. Hahn, R. Linke, T. Goecke, J. Hornegger, and T. Kuwert, "Quantification of thyroid volume using 3-d ultrasound imaging," *IEEE Transactions on Medical Imaging*, vol. 27, no. 4, pp. 457–466, April, 2008.

[69] R. Y. Wu, K. V. Ling, and W. Ng, "Automatic prostate boundary recognition in sonographic images using feature model and genetic algorithm," *J. Ultrasound Med.*, vol. 19, no. 11, pp. 771–782, November, 2000.

[70] D. R. Chen, R. F. Chang, W. J. Kuo, M. C. Chen, and Y. L. Huang, "Diagnosis of breast tumors with sonographic texture analysis using wavelet transform and neural networks," *Ultrasound Med. Biol.*, vol. 28, no. 10, pp. 1301–1310, October, 2002.

[71] O. Pujol, M. Rosales, P. Radeva, and E. Nofrerias-Fernandez, "Intravascular ultrasound images vessel characterization using adaboost," *In Proc. Functional imaging and modelling of the heart, Springer, Lyon, France*, pp. 242–251, 5-6 June, 2003.

[72] M. Yaqub, P. Mahon, M. K. Javaid, C. Cooper, and J. A. Noble, "Weighted voting in 3d random forest segmentation," *In Proc. Medical Image Understanding and Analysis, Warwick, UK*, pp. 261–266, July, 2010.

[73] L. Breiman, "Random forests," *Machine Learning*, vol. 45, no. 1, pp. 5–32, October, 2001.

[74] V. Matz, M. Kreidl, and R. Smid, "Classification of ultrasonic signals," *Proceedings of the 8th International Conference of the Slovenian Society for Non Destructive Testing, Portoroz, Slovenia*, vol. 45, no. 1, pp. 27–33, September, 2005.

[75] R. Otero, C. Correia, C. Ruiz, and J. Michinaux, "Statistical characterization from ultrasonic signals using time-frequency representation," *NDT.net*, vol. 8, no. 5, May, 2003.

[76] C. Shitole, O. Zahran, and W. Nuaimy, "Combining fuzzy logic and neural networks in classification of welds defects using ultrasonic time-of-flight diffraction," *Annual British Conference on NDT, United Kingdom*, September, 2006.

[77] O. Zahran and W. Nuaimy, "Automatic classification of defects in time-of-flight diffraction data," *ndt.net*, 30 Aug - 3Sep 2004.

[78] C. Correia, R. Otero, and G. Sulbaran, "Classification of real flaws using ultrasonic signals," *ndt.net*, February, 2007.

[79] R. Polikar, S. Satish, and T. Taylor, "Frequency invariant classification of ultrasonic weld inspection signals," *IEEE Trans. Ultrasonics, Ferroelectrics, and Frequency Control*, vol. 45, no. 3, pp. 614–625, May, 1998.

[80] J. Spanner, L. Udpa, R. Polikar, and P. Ramuhalli, "Neural networks for ultrasonic detection of intergranular stress corrosion cracking," *ndt.net*, vol. 5, no. 7, July, 2000.

[81] A. Mandal, S. Samanta, and D. Datta, "Application of statistical pattern recognizing classifiers in identifying defects in frp composites," *Proc. National Seminar on Non Destructive Evaluation, Hyderabad, India*, December, 2006.

[82] H. Kieckhoefer, J. Baan, A. Mast, and W. F. A. Arno Volker, "Image processing techniques for ultrasonic inspection," *Proc. 17th World Conference on Nondestructive Testing, Shanghai, China*, October, 2008.

[83] I. Cornwell and A. McNab, "Towards automated interpretation of ultrasonic ndt data," *Elsevier Science Ltd, NDT&E International 32*, vol. 32, no. 2, pp. 101–107, March, 1999.

[84] K. Y. E. Leung, M. Stralen, G. van Burken, N. d. van Jong, and J. G. Bosch, "Automatic active appearance model segmentation of 3d echocardiograms," *Proc. IEEE Int. Symp. Biomedical Imaging: from Nano to Macro, Rotterdam, The Netherlands*, pp. 320–323, April, 2010.

[85] A. Nemes, K. Y. E. Leung, G. Burken, M. van Stralen, J. van Bosch, O. Soliman, B. J. Krenning, W. B. Vletter, F. J. Cate, and M. L. Geleijnse, "Side-by-side viewing of anatomically aligned left ventricular segments in three- dimensional stress echocardiography," *Echocardiography*, vol. 26, pp. 189–195, February, 2009.

[86] J. Hansegard, S. Urheim, K. Lunde, S. Malm, and S. Rabben, "Semi-automated quantification of left ventricular volumes and ejection fraction by real-time three dimensional echocardiography," *Cardiovascular Ultrasound*, vol. 7:18, April, 2009.

[87] T. Eltoft, "Modeling the amplitude statistics of ultrasound images," *IEEE Transactions on Medical Imaging*, vol. 25, no. 2, pp. 229–240, February, 2006.

[88] M. Duan, F. anf Xie, X. Wang, Y. Li, L. He, L. Jiang, and Q. Fu, "Preliminary clinical study of left ventricular myocardial strain in patients with non-ischemic dilated cardiomyopathy by three-dimensional speckle tracking imaging," *Cardiovascular Ultrasound*, vol. 10, no. 8, March, 2012.

[89] J. Crosby, B. H. Amundsen, T. Hergum, R. E. W., S. Langeland, and H. Torp, "3-d speckle tracking for assessment of regional left ventricular function," *Ultrasound in Medicine and Biology*, vol. 35, no. 3, pp. 458–471, March, 2009.

[90] J. A. Noble, N. Navab, and H. Becher, "Ultrasonic image analysis and image-guided interventions," *Interface Focus*, June, 2011.

[91] P. E. H. Duda, R. O. and D. G. Stork, "Pattern classification (2nd edition)," *J. C. Dainty, Ed. New York: Springer-Verlag*, 2001.

[92] T. Yamaguchi, S. Zenbutsu, Y. Igarashi, N. Kamiyama, J. Mamou, and H. Hachiya, "Echo envelope analysis method for quantifying heterogeneity of scatterer distribution for tissue characterization of liver fibrosis," *Ultrasonics Symposium (IUS), 2010 IEEE*, pp. 1412–1415, October, 2010.

[93] P. M. Shankar, "Ultrasonic tissue characterization using a generalized nakagami model," *Ultrasonics, Ferroelectrics and Frequency Control, IEEE Transactions on*, vol. 48, no. 6, pp. 1716–1720, November, 2001.

[94] S. B. Serpico, L. Bruzzone, and F. Roli, "An experimental comparison of neural

and statistical nonparametric algorithms for supervised classification of remote sensing images," *Pattern Recognition Letters, Special Issue on Non-conventional Pattern Analysis in Remote Sensing*, vol. 17, no. 13, pp. 1331–1341, November, 1996.

[95] C. Burckhardt, "Speckle in ultrasound b-mode scans," *IEEE Trans Sonics and Ultrasonics*, vol. 25, no. 1, pp. 1–6, January, 1978.

[96] P. M. Shankar, "A general statistical model for ultrasonic scattering from tissues," *IEEE Trans. Ultrason. Ferroelect. Freq. Control*, vol. 47, no. 3, pp. 727–736, May, 2000.

[97] G. Moser, J. Zerubia, and S. B. Serpico, "Sar amplitude probability density function estimation based on a generalized gaussian model," *IEEE Trans. Image Process.*, vol. 15, no. 6, pp. 1429–1442, June, 2006.

[98] B. J. Oosterveld, J. M. Thijssen, and W. A. Verhoef, "Texture of b-mode echograms: 3-d simulations and experiments of the effects of diffraction and scatterer density," *Ultrason.Imag.*, vol. 7, no. 2, pp. 142–160, April, 1985.

[99] C. J. Oliver and S. Quegan, "Understanding synthetic aperture images," *Norwood, MA: Artech House, Boston, USA*, 1998.

[100] J. W. Goodman, "Some fundamental properties of speckle," *Journal of the Optical Society of America*, vol. 66, no. 11, pp. 1145–1150, 1976.

[101] E. E. Kuruoglu and J. Zerubia, "Modeling sar images with a generalization of the rayleigh distribution," *IEEE Trans. Image Process*, vol. 13, no. 4, pp. 527–533, April, 2004.

[102] V. Dutt and J. Greenleaf, "Statistics of log-compressed envelope," *Journal of the Acoustical Society of America*, vol. 99, no. 6, pp. 3817–3825, June, 1996.

[103] A. Papoulis, "A. probability, random variables, and stochastic processed," *3rd ed.; McGraw Hill: New York, NY, USA*, 1991.

[104] P. M. Shankar, V. A. Dumane, and G. T., "Classification of breast masses in ultrasonic b scans using nakagami and k distributions," *Phys. Med. Biol.*, vol. 48, pp. 2229–2240, 1993.

[105] J. W. Goodman, "Laser speckle and related phenomenon," *J. C. Dainty, Ed. New York: Springer-Verlag*, 1975.

[106] J. M. Thijssen, "Ultrasonic speckle formation, analysis and processing applied to tissue characterization," *Pattern Recognition Letters*, vol. 24, no. 4-5, pp. 659–675, February, 2003.

[107] D. Nicholas, "Evaluation of backscattering coefficients for excised tissues: Results, interpretation and associated measurements," *Ultrasound Med. Biol.*, vol. 8, no. 1, pp. 17–28, 1982.

[108] E. Jakeman and R. J. A. Tough, "Generalized k distribution: A statistical model for weak scattering," *J. Opt. Soc. Amer.*, vol. 4, no. 9, pp. 1764–1772, September, 1987.

[109] L. Weng, J. Reid, P. M. Shankar, and K. Soetanto, "Ultrasound speckle analysis

based on k-distribution," *The Journal of the Acoustical Society of America*, vol. 89, no. 6, pp. 2992–2995, June, 1991.

[110] V. and J. Greenleaf, "Ultrasound echo envelope analysis using homodyned k distribution signal model," *Ultrason Imaging*, vol. 16, no. 4, pp. 265–87, October, 1994.

[111] T. Eltoft, "A new model for the amplitude statistics of sar imagery," *In Proc. Geoscience and Remote Sensing Symposium, IEEE International*, vol. 3, pp. 1993–1995, July, 2003.

[112] V. Anastassopoulos, G. A. Lampropoulos, A. Drosopoulos, and M. Rey, "High resolution radar clutter statistics," *IEEE Trans. on Aerospace and Electronic Systems*, vol. 35, no. 1, pp. 43–59, January, 1999.

[113] E. W. Stacy, "A generalization of the gamma distribution," *Ann. Math. Statist.*, vol. 33, no. 3, pp. 1187–1192, September, 1962.

[114] E. W. Stacy and G. A. Mihram, "Parameter estimation for a generalized gamma distribution," *Technometrics*, vol. 7, no. 3, pp. 349–358, August, 1965.

[115] R. D. Pierce, "Rcs characterization using the alpha-stable distribution," *In Proceedings of IEEE National Radar Conference, Ann Arbor, Michigan, USA*, pp. 394–419, 13-16 May, 1996.

[116] E. E. Kuruoglu, "Density parameter estimation of skewed alpha-stable distributions," *IEEE Transactions Signal Process.*, vol. 49, no. 10, pp. 2192–2201, October, 2001.

[117] E. E. Kuruoglu and J. Zerubia, "Skewed alpha-stable distributions for modeling textures," *Pattern Recognition Letters*, vol. 24, no. 1-3, pp. 339–348, January, 2003.

[118] R. Kappor, "Uwb radar detection of targets in foliage using alpha-stable clutter models," *IEEE Transactions on aerospace and electronic systems*, vol. 35, no. 3, pp. 819–833, July, 1999.

[119] A. Banerjee, P. Burlina, and R. Chellappa, "Adaptive target detection in foliage-penetrating sar images using alpha-stable models," *IEEE Trans. Image Processing*, vol. 8, no. 12, pp. 1823–1831, December, 1999.

[120] G. Vegas-Sanchez-Ferrero, D. Martín-Martinéz, S. Aja-Fernández, and C. Palencia, "On the influence of interpolation on probabilistic models for ultrasound images," *International Symposium on Biomedical Imaging: From Nano to Macro, IEEE, Rotterdam, Netherlands*, pp. 292–295, 14-17 April, 2010.

[121] I. B. Ayed, A. Mitchie, and Z. Belhadj, "Multiregion level-set partitioning of synthetic aperture radar images," *IEEE Trans. Pattern Anal. Mach. Intell.*, vol. 27, no. 5, pp. 793–800, May, 2005.

[122] C. J. Oliver, "Optimum texture estimators for sar clutter," *J. Phys. D.: Appl. Phys.*, vol. 26, no. 11, pp. 1824–1835, November, 1993.

[123] C. Tison, J. M. Nicolas, F. Tupin, and H. Maitre, "New statistical model for markovian classification of urban areas in high-resolution sar images," *IEEE Trans. Geosci. Remote Sens.*, vol. 42, no. 10, pp. 2046–2057, October, 2004.

[124] W. Szajnowski, "Estimator of log-normal distribution parameters," *IEEE Trans. Aerosp. Electron. Syst.*, vol. 13, no. 15, pp. 533–536, September, 1977.

[125] S. George, "The detection of non fluctuating targets in log-normal clutter," *NRL Report 6796; Naval Research Laboratory: Washington, DC, USA*, October, 1968.

[126] Y. Zimmer, R. Tepper, and S. Akselrod, "A lognormal approximation for the gray level statistics in ultrasound images," *Proceedings of the 22 Annual EMBS International Conference, Chicago, IL*, vol. 4, pp. 2656–2661, 23-28 July, 2000.

[127] G. Xiao, M. Brady, J. A. Noble, and Y. Zhang, "Segmentation of ultrasound b-mode images with intensity inhomogeneity correction," *IEEE Trans. Med. Imag.*, vol. 21, no. 1, pp. 48–57, January, 2002.

[128] R. B. D'Agostino and M. A. Stephens, "Goodness-of-fit techniques," *New York: Marcel Dekker*, June, 1986.

[129] O. Michailovich and D. Adam, "Robust estimation of ultrasound pulses using outlier-resistant de-noising," *IEEE Transactions on Medical Imaging*, vol. 22, no. 3, pp. 368–392, March, 2003.

[130] H. C. Li, W. Hong, Y. R. Wu, and P. Z. Fan, "On the empirical-statistical modeling of sar images with generalized gamma distribution," *IEEE Journal of selected topics in signal processing*, vol. 5, no. 3, pp. 386–397, June, 2011.

[131] C. Tison, J. Nicolas, and F. Tupin, "Accuracy of fisher distributions and log-moment estimation to describe histograms of high-resolution sar images over urban areas," *In Proceedings of IGARSS, Toulouse, France*, vol. 3, pp. 1999–2001, 21-25 July, 2003.

[132] C. J. Oliver, I. McConnell, and R. G. White, "Optimum edge detection in sar," *IEE Proceedings Radar, Sonar and Navigation*, vol. 143, no. 1, pp. 31–40, February, 1996.

[133] O. Germain and P. Réfrégier, "Edge location in sar images: Performance of the likehood ratio filter and accuracy improvement with an active contour approach," *IEEE Trans. Image Processing*, vol. 10, no. 4, pp. 72–77, January, 2001.

[134] F. Galland, N. Bertaux, and P. Réfrégier, "Minimum description length synthetic aperture radar image segmentation," *IEEE Trans. Image Processing*, vol. 12, no. 9, pp. 995–1006, September, 2003.

[135] G. Slabaugh, U. Gozde, T. Rang, and M. Wels, "Ultrasound-specific-segmentation via decorrelation and statistical region-based active contours," *In Proceedings of the 2006 IEEE Computer Society Conference on Computer Vision and Pattern Recognition.*, vol. 1, pp. 45–53, 17-22 June, 2006.

[136] K. Kokkinakis and A. K. Nandi, "Generalized gamma density-based score functions for fast and flexible ica," *Signal Processing*, vol. 87, no. 5, pp. 1156–1162, October, 2006.

[137] V. Krylov, G. Moser, S. B. Serpico, and J. Zerubia, "On the Method of Logarithmic Cumulants for Parametric Probability Density Function Estimation," *Rapport de recherche, Université de Nice Sophia Antipolis (INRIA), Depart-*

ment of Biophysical and Electronic Engineering, no. 7666, July, 2011.

[138] M. Technologies, "Easyfit 5.5," Software available at http://www.mathwave.com/help/easyfit/index.html. Date of access: September 2012.

[139] B. I. Raju and M. A. Srinivasan, "Statistics of envelope of high-frequency ultrasonic backscatter from human skin in vivo," *IEEE Trans. Ultrasonics, Ferroelectrics, and Frequency Control*, vol. 49, no. 7, pp. 871–882, July, 2002.

[140] M. M. Nillesen, R. G. P. Lopata, I. H. Gerrits, L. Kapusta, J. M. Thijssen, and C. L. de Korte, "Modeling envelope statistics of blood and myocardium for segmentation of echocardiographic images," *Ultrasound in Medicine and Biology*, vol. 34, no. 4, pp. 674–680, April, 2008.

[141] A. K. Jain, "Fundamental of digital image possessing," *Englewood Cliffs, NJ: Prentice-Hall*, 23 September 1988.

[142] X. Zong, A. F. Laine, and E. A. Geiser, "Speckle reduction and contrast enhancement of echocardiograms via multiscale nonlinear processing," *IEEE Trans. on Medical Imaging*, vol. 17, no. 4, pp. 532–540, August, 1998.

[143] C. Sheng, Y. Xin, Y. Liping, and S. Kun, "Total variation-based speckle reduction using multi-grid algorithm for ultrasound images," *Springer-Verlag Berlin Heidelberg*, November, 2005.

[144] X. Hao, S. Gao, and X. Gao, "A novel multiscale nonlinear thresholding method for ultrasonic speckle suppressing," *IEEE Trans. Med. Imag.*, vol. 18, no. 9, pp. 787–794, September, 1999.

[145] K. Krissian, K. Vosburgh, R. Kikinis, and C.-F. Westin, "Speckle-constrained filtering of ultrasound images," *EEE Computer Society Conf. Computer Vision and Pattern Recognition*, pp. 547–552, June, 2005.

[146] F. Argenti and G. Torricelli, "Speckle suppression in ultrasonic images based on undecimated wavelets," *EURASIP J. Adv. Signal Process.*, vol. 5, pp. 470–478, January, 2003.

[147] M. P. Wachowiak, A. S. Elmaghraby, R. Smolikova, and J. M. Zurada, "Classification and estimation of ultrasound speckle noise with neural networks," *In Proc. IEEE Int. Symp. Bio-Informatics and Biomedical Engineering*, pp. 245–252, January, 2000.

[148] P. Coupé, P. Hellier, C. Kervrann, and C. Barillot, "Nonlocal means-based speckle filtering for ultrasound images," *IEEE Trans. on image processing*, vol. 18, no. 10, pp. 2221–2229, October, 2009.

[149] J. S. Lee, "Digital image enhancement and noise filtering by use of local statistics," *IEEE Trans. Pattern Anal. Mach. Intell.*, vol. 2, no. 2, pp. 165–168, March, 1980.

[150] D. Kuan, A. Sawchuck, T. Strand, and P. Chavel, "A model for radar images and its application to adaptive digital filtering of multiplicative noise," *IEEE Trans. Pattern Anal. Mach. Intell.*, vol. 7, no. 2, pp. 165–177, 1985.

[151] V. Frost, J. Stiles, K. Shanmugan, and J. Holtzman, "A model for radar images and its application to adaptive digital filtering of multiplicative noise," *IEEE*

Trans. Pattern Anal. Mach. Intell., vol. 4, no. 2, pp. 157–166, March, 1982.

[152] T. Loupas, W. McDicken, and P. Allan, "An adaptive weighted median filter for speckle suppression in medical ultrasound image," *IEEE Trans. Circuits Syst.*, vol. 36, no. 1, pp. 129–135, January, 1989.

[153] M. Karaman, M. A. Kutay, and G. Bozdagi, "An adaptive speckle suppression filter for medical ultrasonic imaging," *IEEE Trans. on Medical Imaging*, vol. 14, no. 2, pp. 283–292, June, 1995.

[154] S. J. Heims, J. Von Neumann, and N. Wiener, "From mathematics to the technologies of life and death," *MIT Press*, June 1980.

[155] Y. Yu and S. Acton, "Speckle reducing anisotropic diffusion," *IEEE Trans. on Image Processing*, vol. 11, no. 11, pp. 1260–1270, November, 2002.

[156] C. Aja-Fernandez, S.and Alberola-Lopez, "On the estimation of the coefficient of variation for anisotropic diffusion speckle filtering," *IEEE Trans. on Image Processing*, vol. 15, no. 9, pp. 2694–2701, September, 2005.

[157] K. Krissian, C. F. Westin, R. Kikinis, and K. Vosburgh, "Oriented speckle reducing anisotropic diffusion," *IEEE Trans. on Medical Imaging*, May, 2007.

[158] P. C. Tay, S. T. Acton, and J. A. Hossack, "A stochastic approach to ultrasound despeckling," *In Proc. 3rd IEEE Int. Symp. Biomedical Imaging: Nano to Macro*, pp. 221–224, April, 2006.

[159] K. Thangavel, R. Manavalan, and I. Aroquiaraj, "Removal of speckle noise from ultrasound medical image based on special filters: comparative study," *ICGST International Journal on Graphics, Vision and Image Processing, GVIP, ISSN 1687-398X*, vol. 9, no. III, June, 2009.

[160] A. Buades, B. Coll, and J. M. Morel., "A review of image denoising algorithms, with a new one," *Multiscale Modeling and Simulation*, vol. 4, no. 2, pp. 490–530, 2005.

[161] C. Kervrann and J. Boulanger, "Unsupervised patch-based image regularization and representation," *In Proc. Eur. Conf. Comp. Vis. (ECCV'06, Graz, Austria*, pp. 555–567, May, 2006.

[162] M. Mahmoudi and G. Sapiro, "Fast image and video denoising via nonlocal means of similar neighborhoods," *IEEE Signal Process. Letters*, vol. 12, no. 12, pp. 839–842, December, 2005.

[163] P. Coupé, P. Yger, and C. Barillot, "Fast non-local means denoising for 3d mr images," *Med Image Comput Comput Assist Interv., Copenhagen*, pp. 33–40, September, 2006.

[164] G. Gilboa and S. Osher, "Nonlocal linear image regularization and supervised segmentation," *Multiscale Modeling and Simulation*, vol. 6, no. 2, pp. 595–630, 2007.

[165] F. Fontes, G. A. Barroso, and P. Hellier, "Real time ultrasound image denoising," *Author manuscript published in Journal of Real-Time Image Processing*, 2010.

[166] P. Coupé, P. Yger, S. Prima, P. Hellier, C. Kervrann, and C. Barillot, "An optimized blockwise non local means denoising filter for 3d magnetic resonance images," *IEEE Trans. on Medical Imaging*, vol. 27, no. 4, pp. 425–441, April, 2008.

[167] Y. Yue, M. M. Croitoru, A. Bidani, and J. B. Zwischenberger, "Nonlinear multiscale wavelet diffusion for speckle suppression and edge enhancement in ultrasound images," *IEEE Trans. on Medical Imaging*, vol. 25, no. 3, pp. 297–311, March, 2006.

[168] I. Daubechies, "Ten lectures on wavelets," *Philadelphia: SIAM*, June, 1992.

[169] S. Mallat, "A wavelet tour of signal processing," *Academic Press, London*, 1998.

[170] N. Gupta, M. N. S. Swamy, and E. Plotkin, "Despeckling of medical ultrasound images using data and rate adaptive lossy compression," *IEEE Trans. on Medical Imaging*, vol. 24, no. 6, pp. 743–754, June, 2005.

[171] C. P. Loizou, C. S. Pattichis, C. I. Christodoulou, R. S. H. Istepanian, M. Pantziaris, and A. Nicolaides, "Comparative evaluation of despeckle filtering in ultrasound imaging of the carotid artery," *IEEE Trans. Ultrasonics, Ferroelectrics, and Frequency Control*, vol. 52, no. 10, pp. 1653–1669, October, 2005.

[172] A. Campilho and M. Kamel, "Image analysis and recognition," *Proceedings of the 5th International Conference, ICIAR 2008, Póvoa de Varzim, Portugal*, pp. 171–172, 25-27 June, 2008.

[173] R. N. Czerwinski, D. L. Jones, and W. D. O'brien, "Ultrasound speckle reduction by directional median filtering," *IEEE Proceedings of International Conference on Image Processing*, vol. 1, pp. 358–361, 23-26 Octobre, 1995.

[174] N. H. Mahmood, M. R. M. Razif, and M. T. A. N. Gany, "Comparison between median, unsharp and wiener filter and its effect on ultrasound stomach tissue image segmentation for pyloric stenosis," *International Journal of Applied Science and Technology*, vol. 1, no. 5, pp. 218–226, September, 2011.

[175] N. Devillard, "Fast median search: an ansi c implementation," *http://ndevilla.free.fr/median/median.pdf*, 1998.

[176] N. Otsu, "A threshold selection method from gray-level histogram," *IEEE transactions on Systems, Man, and Cybernetics*, vol. 9, no. 1, pp. 62–66, January, 1979.

[177] L. P. Swiler, T. L. Paez, and M. R. L., "Epistemic uncertainty in the calculation of margins," *Proceedings of the 50th AIAA/ASME/ASCE/AHS/ASC Structures, Structural Dynamics, and Materials Conference, Palm Springs, California, USA*, 4-7 May, 2009.

[178] L. A. Zadeh, "Fuzzy sets as a basis for a theory of possibility," *Fuzzy Sets and Systems*, vol. 100, Supplement 1, no. 0, pp. 9–34, 1999.

[179] A. Dempster, "Upper and lower probabilities induced by multivalued mapping," *Annals of Mathematical Statistics*, vol. 38, no. 2, pp. 325–339, April, 1967.

[180] G. Shafer, "A mathematical theory of evidence," *Princeton University Press, Princeton.*, April, 1976.

[181] P. Smets, "The combination of evidence in the transferable belief model," *IEEE trans. Pattern Analysis and Machine Intelligence*, vol. 12, no. 5, pp. 447–458, 1990.

[182] P. Smets, "Belief functions: the disjunctive rule of combination and the generalized bayesian theorem," *International Journal of Approximate Reasoning*, vol. 9, pp. 1–35, August, 1993.

[183] P. Smets, "The canonical decomposition of a weighted belief," *In proceedings of the 14th international joint conference on Artificial intelligence, San Mateo, Ca, USA*, vol. 2, pp. 1896–1901, 1995.

[184] Z. L. Cherfi, L. Oukhellou, E. Côme, T. Denoeux, and P. Akinin, "Partially supervised independent factor analysis using soft labels elicited from multiple experts: Application to railway track circuit diagnosis," *Journal Soft Computing*, vol. 16, no. 5, pp. 741–754, May, 2012.

[185] T. Denoeux, "Conjunctive and disjunctive combination of belief functions induced by nondistinct bodies of evidence," *Artificial Intelligence*, vol. February, 172, no. 2-3, pp. 234–264, 2008.

[186] A. Osman, V. Kaftandjian, and U. Hassler, "Improvement of x-ray castings inspection reliability by using dempster-shafer data fusion theory," *Pattern Recognition Letters*, vol. 2, no. 32, pp. 160–180, January, 2011.

[187] K. A. Spackman, "Signal detection theory: valuable tools for evaluating inductive learning," *In Proc. Sixth Internat. Workshop on Machine Learning. Morgan Kaufmann Publishers Inc. San Francisco, CA, USA*, pp. 160–163, 1989.

[188] T. Fawcett, "An introduction to roc analysis," *Pattern Recognition Letters*, vol. 27, no. 8, pp. 861–874, June, 2006.

[189] A. Osman, V. Kaftandjian, and U. Hassler, "Automatic classification of 3d segmented ct data using data fusion and support vector machine," *Journal of Electronic Imaging of Spie*, vol. 21, (021111), May, 2012.

[190] T. Fuchs, U. Hassler, U. Huetten, and T. Wenzel, "A new system for fully automatic inspection of digital flat-panel detector radiographs of aluminium castings," *In Proceedings of the 9th European Conf. Non-Destructive Testing (ECNDT), Berlin, Germany*, September 25-29, 2006.

[191] A. Osman, "Improvement of casting defects detection and classification reliability by using the dempster-shafer data fusion theory," *Master thesis, INSA de Lyon*, July, 2008.

[192] A. Osman, V. Kaftandjian, and U. Hassler, "Application of data fusion theory and support vector machine to x-ray castings inspection," *Proceedings of 10th European Conference on Non-Destructive Testing (ECNDT), Moscow, Russia*, 7-11 June, 2010.

[193] A. Osman, V. Kaftandjian, and U. Hassler, "Interest of data fusion for improvement of classification in x-ray inspection," *Proceedings of International Symposium on Digital Industrial Radiology and Computed Tomography, Berlin Germany*, 20-22 June, 2011.

[194] A. Osman, V. Kaftandjian, U. Hassler, and J. Hornegger, "An automated data

processing method dedicated to 3d ultrasonic non destructive testing of composite pieces," *International Symposium on Ultrasound in the Control of Industrial Processes, Madrid Spain*, 18-20 April 2012.

[195] P. Smets, "Belief functions: the disjunctive rule of combination and the generalized bayesian theorem," *Classic Works of the Dempster-Shafer Theory of Belief Functions*, pp. 633–664, 2005.

[196] N. Cristianini and J. Shawe-Taylor, "An introduction to support vector machines and other kernel-based learning methods," *University Press, Cambridge, ISBN: 0-521-78019-5*, March, 2000.

[197] H. Niemann, "Klassifikation von mustern," *Springer, Heidelberg, Berlin, ISBN-10: 3540126422*, 1983.

[198] C. Burges, "A tutorial on support vector machines for pattern recognition," *Data Mining and Knowledge Discovery, Kluwer Academic Publishers, Boston*, vol. 2, pp. 121–167, 1998.

[199] C.-C. Chang and C.-J. Lin, "LIBSVM: A library for support vector machines," *ACM Transactions on Intelligent Systems and Technology*, vol. 2, no. 3, pp. 27:1–27:27, 2011. Software available at http://www.csie.ntu.edu.tw/~cjlin/libsvm.

[200] J. A. Hanley and B. J. McNeil, "The meaning and use of the area under a receiver operating characteristic (roc) curve," *Radiology*, vol. 143, pp. 29–36, 1982.

i want morebooks!

Buy your books fast and straightforward online - at one of world's fastest growing online book stores! Environmentally sound due to Print-on-Demand technologies.

Buy your books online at
www.get-morebooks.com

Kaufen Sie Ihre Bücher schnell und unkompliziert online – auf einer der am schnellsten wachsenden Buchhandelsplattformen weltweit! Dank Print-On-Demand umwelt- und ressourcenschonend produziert.

Bücher schneller online kaufen
www.morebooks.de

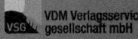 VDM Verlagsservicegesellschaft mbH
Heinrich-Böcking-Str. 6-8   Telefon: +49 681 3720 174   info@vdm-vsg.de
D - 66121 Saarbrücken   Telefax: +49 681 3720 1749   www.vdm-vsg.de

Printed by Books on Demand GmbH, Norderstedt / Germany